The Puerto Rican Woman

Perspectives on Culture, History, and Society

SECOND EDITION

Edited by

Edna Acosta-Belén

PRAEGER

New York
Westport, Connecticut
London

1979 ⊕

Library of Congress Cataloging-in-Publication Data

The Puerto Rican woman.

  Bibliography: p.
  Includes index.
    1. Women—Puerto Rico. 2. Women—Puerto Rico—
Social conditions. 3. Feminism—Puerto Rico.
I. Acosta-Belén, Edna.
HQ1522.P83   1986   305.4′2′097295   86-91521
ISBN 0-275-92133-6 (alk. paper)
ISBN 0-275-92134-4 (pbk. : alk. paper)

Library of Congress Catalog Card Number: 86-91521
ISBN: 0-275-92133-6
      0-275-92134-4 (pbk.)

First published in 1986

Praeger Publishers, 521 Fifth Avenue, New York, NY 10175
A division of Greenwood Press, Inc.

Printed in the United States of America

∞

The paper used in this book complies with the Permanent
Paper Standard issued by the National Information Standards
Organization (Z39.48-1984).

10 9 8 7 6 5 4 3 2 1

This book is dedicated to Marcolina Belén de Acosta and to the loving memory of Rita Vargas de Rodríguez (Nina) and Eloisa Cruz Seda.

Pero yo estaba hecha de presentes,
y mis pies planos sobre la tierra promisora
no resistían caminar hacia atrás,
y seguían adelante, adelante . . .

("Yo misma fui mi ruta," Julia de Burgos)

Preface

For almost two decades now, we have witnessed the resurgence of a militant feminist movement in the United States as well as in Puerto Rico, and other areas of Latin America and the world. The study of fundamental issues related to the women's experience has become a primary focus of contemporary scholarly research. This increasing awareness has produced a proliferation of materials that reevaluate and reexamine past omissions and distortions about women's place in culture, history, and society.

When the first edition of The Puerto Rican Woman was published by Praeger in 1979, the available research and information pertinent to the status of Latin American women in general and Puerto Rican women in particular, was relatively scarce. There was a pressing need at the time for a comprehensive source for the study and understanding of the many facets of Puerto Rican women's reality on the island as well as in the United States. Although the bibliography on the subject has expanded substantially since the first edition was published, the second edition of The Puerto Rican Woman still continues to be the major reference work to date.

This updated and expanded collection of essays is intended to provide primary source material for a comprehensive overview of the Puerto Rican woman within diverse cultural, historical, and socioeconomic contexts. At least half of the essays in the book were also included in the first edition; new ones are being added in an attempt to deal with other relevant areas and incorporate more recent research. Those essays that appeared in the first edition and do not appear here were omitted because of dated information. Although the majority of the studies compiled in this anthology focus on women in Puerto Rican society, close attention has also been paid to the status and experience of Puerto Rican women in the United States. The essays are interdisciplinary in nature and encompass analyses of the most relevant issues affecting Puerto Rican women from diverse academic perspectives.

My introductory chapter "Puerto Rican Women in Culture, History, and Society" is intended to provide a comprehensive general overview of the status and contributions of Puerto Rican women and present background information as well as a framework that complements the topics further developed by the contributors in the individual essays.

There are many people to thank for helping me in the preparation of both editions of this book. First of all, my appreciation to Christine E. Bose for her support, encouragement, critical opinions, patience, and confidence in my work. I would also like to express my gratitude to Susan Liberis Hill and Barbara R. Sjostrom for their invaluable assistance and friendship; to Samuel Betances and Carmen A. Pérez, who helped organize the 1976 Symposium on the Hispanic American Woman at SUNY–Albany, an activity which was of primary importance in the conception of this book; to my former colleague Elia H. Hidalgo Christensen who collaborated with me in the first edition; to Alba I. Castillo Blancovich at the University of Puerto Rico and Mariní Acín and Sylvia Aguiar of the Comisión para los Asuntos de la Mujer who assisted me at different times in locating library materials and gave me access to valuable information; and to Philippe Abraham, Victoria Horwitz, Eloisa Perez, and Blanca Ramos who helped me at different times with the clerical aspects of the book. Lastly, I thank all of the feminist women who have shared their work by contributing to this anthology. Without their academic excellence this book would not have been possible.

This book is dedicated to three exemplary women from another generation who had to face a harder path than we do. It is also an intellectual gift to all the children in my life who are the hope of the future: Carlitos David, Erin, Allison Meliza, Boris, and Yara.

Working on this project has had a special significance in my life both personally and professionally, since I view it as an extension of my commitment and dedication to the goals of the feminist movement which attempts to liberate all women from their traditional bonds of subordination and oppression. This book is intended as a small step in an arduous consciousness-raising process.

Contents

1

Puerto Rican Women in Culture, History, and Society

Edna Acosta-Belén

In order to gain a full perspective on the experience of Puerto Rican women, it is imperative to consider their presence and participation in the diverse cultural and socioeconomic processes that have taken place during Puerto Rico's historical development. Because the social and historical roles of women have generally been ignored or undermined, the task of reconstructing and reevaluating traditional inaccuracies and omissions has been and continues to be a difficult one. Fortunately, it is a task that, in recent years, has involved some of Puerto Rico's most progressive and talented scholars. The main objectives of this essay are to provide an overview of women's contributions to Puerto Rican culture, history, and society, to summarize the most relevant research on the subject, and to give a general framework for further study and research on the Puerto Rican woman.

An overview of the role and place of women in Puerto Rican culture, history, and society must begin with the examination of women's contributions to the development of pre-Hispanic Boriquén. The most complete study of women during this historical period is Jalil Sued Badillo's La mujer indigena y su sociedad (1975). In this book Sued Badillo emphasized the matrilineal tradition of Taino society, in which women had access to the highest posts of their social structure. According to him, they also had significant participation in the political life of their communities. Women such as Anacaona, Ines of the Cayacoa, Higuanama

1

of the Higüey, Luisa of the Aymanio, Guayerbas of the Otoao, and the mother and daughter, Yayo y Catalina, in the Caguas region are among several described in Spanish documents of the early sixteenth century as cacicas (chiefs) (p. 31). Sued Badillo has also pointed out that Taino women shared communal work with men and some were taught to handle weapons and often fought in battles. They participated fully in the production of goods, crafts, and in religious and other ritual ceremonies. One of the two main deities of the Tainos was Guabancex, the mother goddess. In a matrilineal horticultural society as that of the Tainos, it is not surprising that extraordinary importance was given to the female as a source of creation and that great powers were attributed to the great earth mother. This is probably the greatest contrast between the religious concepts of Antillean and Mesoamerican mythology (Fernández Mendez, 1972).

The influence and power that some women had in the island of Boriquén came to an end in the early 1500s with the Spanish conquest and colonization of what became the Isla de San Juan Bautista and later Puerto Rico. The aborigine population was subjected to systems of forced labor and other forms of exploitation which, together with the Spaniards' policy of religious and cultural genocide, tore to shreds the fabric of Taino society. During those early years in the history of Puerto Rico as a colony of Spain, the sexual exploitation of Indian women by the conquistadores and settlers was commonplace. All these developments, combined with diseases such as measles and smallpox (introduced into the island by the Europeans and against which the aborigine population had no biological immunity), brought about a catastrophic decline in the Amerindian population. By the latter part of the sixteenth century the aborigine population of the island was almost extinct. To partially replace the rapidly declining Indian labor pool, the Spaniards imported black slaves to work in the gold fields and agricultural establishments, and to provide domestic service.

In the years after the Spanish occupation of Puerto Rico, many Spaniards entered into illegitimate unions with Indian and slave women; miscegenation and concubinage were widespread realities of Puerto Rican colonial society. The offspring that resulted from most of these unions became, in most cases, the responsibility of the mothers. Thus, families headed by women were not uncommon.

Spanish women who migrated to the New World during the period of colonization and settlement played a critical role in the society that was evolving (Konetzke, 1945). Rosa Santiago-Marazzi (1974, 1984) has described how Spanish women who came to the island played significant roles in importing the institution of the family to the colonies, as transmitters of Hispanic culture and values, and in the subsequent development of a new culture and society. They actively participated in the establishment of settlements, played a reproductive role, and bore the main responsibility for child rearing and homework. During the centuries of Spanish colonial rule, women also contributed to the economy in many ways that are impossible to calculate or quantify since the large peasant population produced independently for family consumption (Rivera Quintero, 1979). It is an established fact, however, that women were engaged with men in subsistence agriculture.

Puerto Rican colonial society during the period of Spanish rule was, like societies throughout the Spanish American world, a patriarchal, paternalistic, and military-oriented society in which the subordination of women to men was almost absolute. Women of all classes were conditioned to be obedient daughters, faithful wives, and devoted mothers. Their inferior status was reinforced by juridical inequality. Laws concerning the family, the administration of community property in marriage, authority over the children, and some labor practices limited the rights of women. It was not until 1976 that both family and labor laws would be revised to make them more equitable.[1]

Throughout the first three and a half centuries of Spanish colonial rule in Puerto Rico there was an absence of a feminist consciousness or a feminist movement, in contrast to other more developed regions of the world where these movements develop in the early nineteenth century. This situation was evidently the result of the low educational and employment levels of the vast majority of the female population. Olga Jiménez Wagenheim (1981) illustrates how women in nineteenth-century Puerto Rico were shaped by the conditions and ideologies prevalent during their historical period:

> Life in the colony was extremely hard for most creoles and for women in particular. For, to the legacy of colonialism, political intolerance, educational deprivation, economic dependence and exploitation, were added racism, the division of classes, patriarchy, and the mythology of subordination implicit in the religious dogma of Catholicism (p. 197).

Isabel Pico (1979b) concurs that "under these circumstances it was not possible for a true feminist movement to
develop as it did in England, France, the U.S., and other
countries which had experienced greater economic and social
complexity" (p. 26). But the absence of a feminist movement in Puerto Rico during the nineteenth century does not
eliminate the hidden or not yet fully recognized contributions of women to Puerto Rican life during this time nor
the ideas in favor of giving women more rights and participation in society which were upheld by some intellectuals
of the period. By the second half of the nineteenth century the idea of women's emancipation and right to an
education were being discussed in some of the writings of
the liberal intellectual elite, men of the privileged creole
hacendado class, that also advocated the abolition of slavery
and independence of Puerto Rico from Spanish colonial rule.
In the writings of Salvador Brau, Gabriel Ferrer, Ignacio
Guasp, Eugenio M. de Hostos, Rafael María de Labra, José
Pablo Morales, and Alejandro Tapia y Rivera we find the
first indications of a trend to improve the general status of
women in Puerto Rican society (Picó, 1979b). For these
writers, improvements in the deprived conditions faced by
the great majority of the female population would represent
a step in the direction of social progress for the country.
Although they did not advocate or believe in total equality
among the sexes (politics, for example, was still seen as
the domain of men, and the home as the primary sanctuary
of women), they defended the right of women to an education and to not be limited to serving men.

Gabriel Ferrer in his book La mujer en Puerto Rico:
sus necesidades presentes y los medios más faciles y
adecuados para mejorar su porvenir (1881) makes it clear
that he is not an advocate of complete equality:

We are far from declaring ourselves in favor of
complete equality of rights [not legal] between a
woman and a man; neither do we want to be over
optimistic and argue that a woman represents the
symbol of perfection; but from believing that she
should not have any other role in society than
being a servant to her tyrant, there is a great
distance, a distance that we cannot dismiss unless
we forget the ideal of justice and trample over
everything without listening to the accusing voice
of our conscience (p. 4).

The essays of Salvador Brau are a good example of the
intellectual concern for improving the deprived conditions

affecting the peasant population. Aside from his traditional views, class biases, and pseudoscientific interpretations of the conditions faced by the rural proletariat, Brau's essay "La campesina" (1886; rpt. 1972) recognizes the important role played by women in socializing the new generations, and advocates their education:

> The education of women is more important than that of men. . . . Women mold the customs of all countries.
> By educating women we educate the individual; by educating women, that is the mother, we educate a whole generation. The man among our rural proletariat, does not have the extra time to dedicate himself to transmitting his intellectual knowledge to his children (1972: 104).

Among those women who did obtain an education during the 1800s, perhaps the area in which they excelled the most was in literature and the arts. Figures who stand out as some of the major contributors to cultural and intellectual life during this period include Mariana Bibiana Benítez (1783–1873), a lyric poet and initiator of a family tradition of poets; her niece Alejandrina Benítez (1819–1879), also a poet, initiator of tertulias literarias (social and intellectual writers' gatherings to read and discuss their work), one of the contributors to the literary anthology Aguinaldo Puertorriqueño (1843) which marks the birth of a Puerto Rican national literature, and the mother of José Gautier Benítez, considered the most representative poet of the Romantic period; and Lola Rodríguez de Tió (1843–1924) who not only carved herself a place in Puerto Rican letters but also in the historic separatist struggle against Spanish colonial rule.

In spite of these achievements by a handful of women, for three centuries of colonial rule, Puerto Rico remained one of Spain's most backward colonies. Education for women was practically unknown and reserved for the privileged class. Illiteracy, particularly among the peasant population, was rampant.[2] It was, however, through the efforts of women that the first schools for girls were established in Puerto Rico. The work of Celestina Cordero (circa 1790–1860), founder of one of the first schools in the 1820s, has been virtually ignored or overshadowed by the accomplishments of her brother Rafael Cordero.[3] Other women such as Bélen Zequeira (1840–1918), founder of the Ladies' Association for Women's Instruction [Asociación de Damas para la Instrucción de la Mujer] in 1886, were advocates of the right of poor women to an education (Negrón Muñoz, 1935). Zequeira also interceded in defense of the political prisoners who had fallen to the repressive measures of the Spanish colonial government under the administration of Governor Romualdo Palacio in 1887.

In the second half of the nineteenth century women also played a more viable and assertive role in Puerto Rican politics. There was a group of educated women, also members of the creole privileged class, who actively participated in the separatist movement against the Spaniards. Women such as Mariana Bracetti (1825–1903), Eduviges Beauchamp, and Lola Rodríguez de Tió are well known for their political involvement and defense of the Puerto Rican nationality. Both Bracetti, also known as "Brazo de Oro," and Beauchamp embroidered flags that were used during the abortive Lares insurrection (El Grito de Lares) of 1868, and Bracetti went to prison for her revolutionary activities.[4] Rodríguez de Tió, aside from being one of the most important literary figures of her time, was also a militant separatist. She was the author of "La Borinqueña," a poem that exorted the Puerto Rican people to join the armed struggle against Spanish colonial rule. Because of her political ideals and activities she was eventually forced into exile by the colonial authorities and died in Cuba. Her commitment to the revolutionary struggle for the independence of both Puerto Rico and Cuba has been immortalized in her verses: "Cuba y Puerto Rico son de un pájaro las dos alas" (Cuba and Puerto Rico are the two wings of one bird).

Economic changes in the second half of the nineteenth century were also having a major impact on Puerto Rican women. For slightly more than three centuries the Puerto Rican colonial economy had been characterized by independent subsistence producers. In the course of the century, however, these gave way to the expanding hacienda system of proprietors. Angel Quintero Rivera's insightful studies in Conflicto de clases y política en Puerto Rico (1974), have established that the hacienda economy on the island represented a structural step toward capitalism, since its emergence implied not only a separation of the direct producer from the means of production, but also the development of a class in need of selling its labor. As capitalism became increasingly the dominant mode of production in Puerto Rico, women were incorporated more and more into the labor force, and came to play a more visible role in society.

As a consequence of the U.S. invasion and occupation of the island of Puerto Rico in 1898, many socioeconomic changes took place that deeply affected the lives of

Puerto Rican men and women. The U.S. sugar and tobacco corporations that became established on the island gradually monopolized the Puerto Rican economy and transformed the traditional agricultural system of the semifeudal hacienda into a full-scale capitalistic plantation system. Many manufacturing industries related to the production of sugar and tobacco and other areas such as needlework were established. Some of the former and most of the latter employed primarily women. This economic transformation led to a decline of the economic base of the island's privileged class of proprietors (who ended up selling their land to the corporations), to a growing proletarianization of the masses, and to the emergence of a militant labor movement (Quintero Rivera, 1971, 1974).

The role of the Puerto Rican woman in the labor movement and the militancy of feminist groups during the first few decades of the twentieth century have been generally ignored by what are considered the country's official histories. In recent years researchers have attempted to shed light on this important period (Quintero Rivera, 1971, 1974; Silvestrini, 1975; Picó, 1979b; Rivera Quintero, 1979; Valle, 1975, 1979; Azize 1979; Burgos, 1982). They have uncovered activities and experiences of both women and men workers during the first three decades of twentieth-century Puerto Rico that have shaken the prior myths and class-biased interpretations of the passivity and uninvolvement of the Puerto Rican people in social and political struggles.

During this period the feminist movement on the island was characterized by two major trends: the petit bourgeois and the proletarian. These two trends developed in a parallel fashion, but functioned at two very distinct and separate social levels (Picó, 1979b; Valle, 1979). The suffragist leaders were educated women who were primarily concerned with obtaining the right to vote for women. Organizations such as the Puerto Rican Feminine League [Liga Femínea Puertorriqueña] and the Puerto Rican Association of Women Suffragists [Asociación Puertorriqueña de Mujeres Sufragistas] founded in 1917 and 1925 respectively, played a leading role in this effort. The work and militancy of women such as Ana Roqué de Duprey (1853–1933), Isabel Andreu de Aguilar (1887–1948), and Mercedes Solá (1879–1923), among other prominent names, were critical in bringing about the passage of the suffrage bill. Ana Roqué de Duprey, one of the founders of the suffragist organizations, was also active in journalistic, scientific, and pedagogical activities. As early as 1893 she became the publisher of the first women's magazine, La mujer, among many of her other journalistic efforts. Isabel Andreu de Aguilar was also one of the founders and leaders of the suffragist movement, and as a prominent educator she became the first female trustee of the University of Puerto Rico. Aside from her involvement in the suffragist movement Mercedes Solá's essay Feminismo (1922) stands today as a legacy and inspiration to the contemporary feminist movement:

> Feminism has not spread all over the world and in Puerto Rico because so and so has brought it. Feminism comes because during this period of evolution and world revolution the great human revindications will take place and among them the woman will have her share.
>
> Without education it is impossible for feminism to triumph, since this sustains ability and right, and the former cannot be obtained without an efficient preparation.
>
> The economic base is also indispensable since a woman cannot conquer her emancipation without first obtaining the economic independence that will relieve her from the tutelage of man (p. 17).
>
> In the new revindicated home the wife will have the same authority over the family and the right to take part in whatever interests her from public life for the benefit of the society of which her home and her children are a part (p. 23).

The efforts of the suffragists culminated in 1929 when a bill was finally approved granting literate women the right to vote. In 1932 women participated for the first time in elections. Universal suffrage was not approved by the Puerto Rican Legislature until 1936.

The proletarian trend of the feminist movement developed as an integral part of the organized labor movement. Since the beginning of the century a variety of women workers (especially tobacco strippers, seamstresses, hemstitchers, needleworkers, and domestics) had joined labor unions. It has been extensively documented that women tended to join men in the ranks of organized labor and involved themselves in the struggles for social justice and the improvement of working conditions. The vanguard of the women's emancipation movement was to be found within the ranks of the Free Federation of Labor [Federación Libre de Trabajadores, FLT] which also waged legal battles in favor of universal suffrage and against the detrimental working conditions faced by women and workers in general during this period (Manning, 1934; Quintero Rivera, 1971).

One of the most extraordinary women labor leaders of the first decades of the twentieth century was Luisa Capetillo (1880–1922), a socialist labor organizer and a writer who argued on behalf of equal rights for women, free love, and human emancipation. She was a crusader who tried to raise the consciousness of workers through her active involvement and writing, and is most remembered for her challenge to social conventions by becoming the first woman in Puerto Rico to wear slacks in public. Norma Valle's brief biography Luisa Capetillo (1975) was a significant opening into the world of this fascinating character. Capetillo's writings were well ahead of her time because of the ideas she espoused and defended. She has also been described as a precursor to the women's liberation movement in Puerto Rico (Rivera de Alvarado, 1972). In her book Mi opinión sobre las libertades, derechos y deberes de la mujer (1911) she exhorts women to fight for social equality:

Oh you woman! who is capable and willing to spread the seed of justice; do not hesitate, do not fret, do not run away, go forward! And for the benefit of the future generations place the first stone for the building of social equality in a serene but firm way, with all the right that belongs to you, without looking down, since you are no longer the ancient material or intellectual slave (p. 25).

Among other women who played leadership roles in the Puerto Rican labor movement were Concepción (Concha) Torres who in 1902 became the first woman to give a speech at a public rally; Juana Colón (1875–1971), known as the "Joan of Arc of Comerío," a leader and active organizer of the tobacco strippers who participated in strikes to improve their working conditions; Genara Pagán and Emilia Hernández, who presided over the Women's Organization Committee of the FLT; and Franca de Armiño, who led the Popular Feminine Association [Asociación Feminista Popular], founded in 1920.

Two major sources of information on the contributions of Puerto Rican women from colonial times to the 1930s have been compiled by two women who themselves played a prominent role in Puerto Rican journalism and civic life: Mujeres puertorriquenas que se han distinguido en el cultivo de las ciencias, las letras y las artes desde el siglo XVII hasta nuestros días (1908) by María Luisa de Angelis, and Mujeres de Puerto Rico: desde el periodo de la colonización hasta el primer tercio del siglo XX (1935) by Angela Negrón Muñoz. Unfortunately, the information contained herein is primarily about women of the privileged classes, and not the working-class women who played leadership roles in the labor and feminist movements during the first decades of this century.

The crisis and decline of the U.S. controlled sugar and tobacco plantation economy in Puerto Rico during the Great Depression of the 1930s and the resulting increase in unemployment, had a negative impact on the feminist movement. This decade marked a downward trend in the rate of women's participation in the labor force that lasted until recent years. It was during this decade that most feminist organizations began to dissolve. Many women were forced by circumstances to work in home-based needlework or domestic service as a way of making a living. Robert H. Weller (1968) in a historical analysis of female labor force in Puerto Rico, found that between 1935 and 1950 women were more active precisely in those sectors of the economy. There is no doubt that the decline in the labor force participation rate and the women's isolation from other workers and from the major social struggles of their time extinguished the fervor of the feminist movement that had been so militant during the earlier part of the century.

In contrast to the "desperate thirties," the 1940s was a decade of political and social optimism and reforms introduced by the newly created Partido Popular Democrático (PPD) under the charismatic leadership of Luis Muñoz Marín. Founded in 1938 as a dissenting faction of the Puerto Rican Liberal Party, the PPD committed itself to obtaining more autonomy for the island, and to a series of social and economic programs. Many party adherents including its leader Muñoz Marín, had been supporters of the independence of Puerto Rico from U.S. colonial rule. The new party was able to appeal to the discontented rural masses who had been greatly affected or displaced by the economic decline of the agrarian economy and its resulting unemployment, and who could not ideologically identify or respond to other political parties on the island. The PPD's flag was a picture of a jíbaro with a pava (a peasant with a straw hat), and its motto of "Pan, Tierra, y Libertad" (Bread, Land, and Liberty) was at that particular moment in Puerto Rican history a symbol of hope and change to the poverty-stricken masses, both in the rural and urban areas.

The success of the populist Muñocista movement has been unparalleled in Puerto Rican history. The PPD won the legislative elections of 1940 and 1944, and in 1948 its undisputed leader, Luis Muñoz Marín, became the first governor in the island's long colonial history to be elected by popular vote. By then, the party had opted against independence and for a permanent association with the United States. The reasons for this shift are complex, but it is helpful to keep in mind that the leaders of the PPD were mostly the ideological offspring of the old hacendado class. The preeminence of this class in Puerto Rican society had been preempted by the socioeconomic changes that took place when the U.S. corporations came to the island after the U.S. occupation of 1898 and established control of the economy. Through the PPD they began to at least take the reins of the island's politics. In his valuable studies about class and political struggles in Puerto Rico, Quintero Rivera (1974) contends that the new government in power needed a new economic base to establish and consolidate their hegemonic position in Puerto Rican society. According to him this group became "the technocrats of a new industrial welfare state" (p. 132). Industrialization became the main goal of the PPD government through Operation Bootstrap [Operación Manos a la Obra]. This massive industrialization scheme, however, could not be realized without a tremendous influx of U.S. capital into the country. That capital was attracted through a system of tax exemptions and assurances of cheap labor. And, as PPD advocates came to argue, that flow of capital, on which the country's economic expansion became dependent, could only be assured by the maintenance of close ties to the United States. Thus, Muñoz Marín came out clearly against independence and became instead a defender of a new status that gave greater autonomy to the island in permanent union with the United States, an effort that culminated in the establishment in 1952 of the Estado Libre Asociado or Commonwealth of Puerto Rico.

The anti-independence stand of the PPD and its subsequent persecution and repression of pro-independence factions did not, however, put an end to the activities of the latter. In 1946 disenchanted members of the PPD broke away and founded the Partido Independentista Puertorriqueño (PIP) which became the most important pro-independence party during the late 1940s and 1950s. But it was not the only one. Numerically small but far more militant than the PIP was the Nationalist Party which, since its founding in 1922, and in later years under the leadership of Pedro Albizu Campos, stood uncompromisingly against the U.S. colonial presence on the island. For many years the party was the victim of one of the most repressive government campaigns in Puerto Rican history. Women played an important role in the Nationalist Party particularly during the 1950s. The courage of nationalist women is best exemplified by the actions of Blanca Canales during the Nationalist revolt of 1950, and Lolita Lebrón (b. 1919) during the 1954 attack on the U.S. House of Representatives. Both women were imprisoned for their participation in these events and have become symbols of women's courage and patriotic sacrifice. Lolita Lebrón was, until recent years, one of Puerto Rico's most internationally prominent political prisoners.[5]

Another woman who was an active member of the Nationalist Party and joined in demonstrations and public speeches was the poet Julia de Burgos (1914–1953). She also left a literary legacy that stands today as a source of inspiration to the struggle for national liberation, social equality, and the contemporary women's movement. Her poetry is one of the best examples of a clear consciousness of the oppression faced both by women and the underprivileged class in a capitalist and patriarchal society.

The daughter of a large and poor rural family, Julia de Burgos grew near the natural beauty of the countryside and the Loíza River that so much inspired her, but also in contact with a peasant population plagued by poverty and social injustice. As a young woman she attended the University of Puerto Rico, where she developed a consciousness of the political and social struggles of her time and was trained as a teacher. In the late 1930s she published her first books of poetry and began to receive acclaim for her work. However, her political ideals and nontraditional lifestyle, her tumultous and tormented adult life of destructive relationships with men, all contributed to a self-imposed exile, alcoholism, depression, eventual isolation from Puerto Rico and its literary establishment, and to an early death in the streets of New York at the age of 39. Julia de Burgos's poetry stands today as a reflection of the many facets of her life:

> Today I want to be a man. I'd be a worker,
> cutting the sugar cane, sweating his wages,
> arms up, fists in the air,
> tearing from the world my piece of bread.
> ["Pentachromatic"]

> Río Grande de Loíza! . . . Great river. Great tear.
> The greatest of all our island tears,
> but for the tears that flow out of me
> through the eyes of my soul for my enslaved people.
> ["Río Grande de Loíza"]

The word is out that I am your enemy
that in my poetry I am giving you away.
They lie, Julia de Burgos. They lie, Julia de Burgos.
That voice that rises in my poems is not yours:
  it is my voice;
you are the covering and I the essence;
and between us lies the deepest chasm.
["To Julia de Burgos"]

I wanted to be like men wanted me to be;
an attempt at life, a hide and seek game with myself.
But I was made of todays,
and my feet planted over the promised land
could not stand to walk backwards,
and went forward, forward . . .
["I Was My Own Path"]

The rapid process of industrialization during the 1950s
and the transformation of the Puerto Rican economy from
one based on a plantation system to one characterized by an
industrial-technological mode of production was accompanied
by a process of social modernization that had a great impact
on Puerto Rican traditional values, on institutions associated
with the old agrarian society, and on the role of women.
Some intellectuals have erroneously viewed the changing
role of women and their increasing visibility in the job
market and other spheres of society as part of what they
consider to be the process of Americanization of Puerto
Rico and the acceptance of values that are detrimental to
the preservation of a Puerto Rican cultural identity. It is
common to find in the literary works of the Generation of
1950 a clash between the values and ways of life associated
with the agrarian society of the past, and those of the
modern and industrial society (Acosta-Belén, 1979). Since
industrialization and modernization are viewed as a consequence of U.S. influence, any changes in the role and
status of women are also viewed as such, and not as a
natural consequence of socioeconomic development and
consciousness-raising. [6]
Industrialization opened up new occupations for both
men and women. In most countries this process is usually
followed by the growth of service and clerical jobs which
have traditionally been filled by women and made women's
employment more visible, while men occupy the professional,
technical, and managerial positions. The posture of defensive cultural conservatism so prevalent among Puerto
Rican intellectuals partially explains why the contemporary

feminist movement has developed apart from the national liberation struggle (Zayas, 1972; Picó, 1979b). Political parties in Puerto Rico have always downplayed the issue of feminism and women's liberation since it is perceived as a threat to the institution of the family which has been so traditionally valued in Puerto Rican culture, and to the male superiority and female subordination ingrained in the patriarchal concept of machismo.

Among the many reforms and social programs introduced by the PPD government under U.S. counsel during the 1940s and 1950s were family planning and population control. Progress for a country plagued by poverty was not only linked to creating more jobs through industrialization, but also to effectively dealing with the overpopulation problem. Aside from the escape valve provided by the fostering of the immigration of workers to the United States, the sterilization of women became common practice. The uses and abuses of la operación (a surgical procedure) have been documented by researchers who have found that Puerto Rico is the country with the highest sterilization rate in the world (Vázquez Calzada, 1973; Presser, 1980). At least 35 percent of Puerto Rican women of reproductive age are sterilized, a percentage higher than in the United States where it stands at 30 percent.[7] Between 1950 and the late 1970s the total fertility rate in Puerto Rico fell by 48 percent—from 5.2 to 2.7 children per woman. An unofficial acceptance of sterilization, the failure of the government to actively promote other means of contraception, and the shift in female employment from home needlework to work outside the home and more recently, from blue-collar to white-collar employment have contributed to the high sterilization rate and the decline in fertility. A relationship can then be established between the sterilization of Puerto Rican women and market demands for their labor.

The use of abortion in Puerto Rico to terminate unwanted pregnancies is still in "legal limbo." In spite of the 1973 U.S. Supreme Court decision guaranteeing the right of women to obtain abortions, there are local laws that prohibit abortion except under exceptional circumstances. Although these laws are probably unconstitutional they have not yet been challenged (Presser, 1980). In a primarily Catholic country like Puerto Rico the issue of abortion is too sensitive for politicians to tackle. Therefore, since abortions are performed on the island as if they were illegal neither its incidence nor its complications can be documented (Presser, p. 106).

Despite the dramatic changes experienced by Puerto Rico since industrialization and the changing role of women, sexism and male chauvinism remain deeply rooted in Puerto Rican culture and society. Institutions and social and cultural patterns inherited from the past continue to deny and deprive women of real equality. Sexual discrimination in the professions and in other parts of the labor force is widespread. The Civil Rights Commission 1973 study, La igualdad de derechos y oportunidades de la mujer puertorriqueña concluded that "discrimination against women outside and inside the home exists and discriminatory practices take subtle and deceiving shadings" (p. 195). The conclusions and recommendations of this report gave impetus to the formation of militant organizations such as Mujer Intégrate Ahora [MIA, Woman Join Together Now] and the Federación de Mujeres Puertorriqueñas [FMP, Federation of Puerto Rican Women] to fight against discrimination and support women's rights. A later report, Igualdad de oportunidades de empleo para la mujer (1978) presented to the government by the Commission for the Improvement of Women's Rights, clearly established the great disadvantage faced by Puerto Rican women in government employment, and proposed guidelines for each agency to develop affirmative action plans.

The roots of sexual discrimination, job segregation, and ascribed sex roles based on male supremacy and female subordination, are ingrained in the socialization process itself. Some researchers have emphasized the role that women themselves play in this process (Guevara and Sesman, 1978). The Puerto Rican woman still continues to be the center of the home and family and her essentially domestic role still prevails. She is also primarily responsible for child rearing.

Schooling also plays a crucial role. The studies Sexism in the Classroom (1977) by the Commission for the Improvement of Women's Rights, Machismo y educación en Puerto Rico (1979a) by Isabel Picó, and La visión sobre la nina en cinco libros de lecturas escolares (1976) by Haydeé Yordán Molini have extensively analyzed basic textbooks and instructional materials used by the Department of Public Instruction throughout the Puerto Rican school system. They all concluded that ideas and models for differentiating activities according to sex and ascribing traditional roles to males and females are presented to children in these texts. While boys are shown as aggressive, strong, with mechanical ability, and engaged in a variety of activities, girls are portrayed as passive, dependent, physically and emotionally fragile, and with activities usually limited to their future role as mothers and homeworkers. In more than one-third of the cases women were portrayed as housewives.

Celia Fernández Cintrón and Marcia Rivera Quintero (1974) have also described how stereotyped concepts of women exist and are encouraged by the family and the school. They write:

Maxims such as "a woman's place is in the home," "a woman's chief functions are those of wife and mother," "the good woman is the docile one [la mansita]," are frequently heard in Puerto Rico. To these sayings is also added the notion that women, because they are nervous and emotional are not capable of solving the problems of life (p. 241).

A more modern or liberated view of the role of men and women, and any changes in sexual education in Puerto Rican society must confront the heavy weight of tradition as described by Eneida Rivero (1975):

Males have been socialized within the framework of a machismo complex that induces them to think that masculinity is contingent upon seduction. For them machismo is a quality to be constantly tested; they cannot rest on their laurels. In the sexual aspect, the male must maintain his image as a conqueror and sexually competent. The further they go in their relations with the opposite sex, the more macho they appear to themselves and to others (p. 174).

Machismo still represents a male ideal of sorts and plays an essential role in maintaining sexual restrictions and subordination for women. As a typical manifestation of patriarchal relations it emphasizes sexual freedom, virility, and aggressiveness for men in contrast to women's sexual repression, femininity, and passivity. An integral part of machismo is donjuanismo or the chronic or pathological womanizing that is often viewed as "acceptable" male behavior encouraged or tolerated by society. On the other hand women's virginity before marriage and fidelity afterward are glorified.

In Puerto Rican culture (and in Latin American culture in general), there is a tendency to classify or judge women according to their sexual behavior. The double standard is still prevalent and expressions such as la mujer buena o de su casa (literally, the good woman or the woman of her home) and la mujer mala o de la calle (the bad woman or the woman of the streets) are common. Men have the privilege and freedom to echar una canita al aire (literally, blow a gray hair to the wind; meaning to have an affair once in a while) while the mujer sacrificada (sacrificing woman) tolerates it. If by any reason a wife is unfaithful to her husband this is considered as an afront to the man's dignity and honor since she dared to ponerle los cuernos (literally, put horns on him, a symbol of infidelity and ridicule). A woman in this situation is considered una cualquiera (a nobody).

When men do not exhibit the traditional behavior norms of el que lleva los pantalones en la casa (the one who wears the pants in the family), he is said to be sentado en el baúl (literally, seated on a trunk; meaning dominated by his wife), and the wife is considered to be guilty of ponerle el delantal (literally, place an apron on him).

As part of promoting change in the socialization and educational processes and combating the traditional sexist and stereotyped male and female roles that are transmitted to children, the government's Commission for the Improvement of Women's Rights (former Comisión para el Mejoramiento de los Derechos de la Mujer; now Comisión para los Asuntos de la Mujer), established in 1974, has sponsored a series of publications intended to provide teachers and students with information, new images, and alternatives. The series of modules for elementary school teachers to combat sexism in the classroom prepared by Carmen Eneida Molina and Magali García Ramis (1977), and the Commission's Social Studies and History Project Presencia de la Mujer (1979–80) represent the kind of effort that must become an integral part of the curriculum of Puerto Rico's centralized public school system if any significant changes are to be accomplished.

The mass media have also played a powerful but detrimental role in perpetuating stereotyped or frivolous images of women. As one of the most important factors in shaping public opinion and in determining cultural patterns, media such as television, radio, cinema, newspapers, and the infamous but popular novelas (soap operas) and fotonovelas (a soap opera depicted in printed comic-booklike form using photographs and printed dialogue) have been found to reinforce the attitudes and prejudices that exploit female sentimentality and maintain women in her subordination. The books La imagen de la mujer en los medios de comunicación (Comisión para el Mejoramiento de los Derechos de la Mujer, 1978) and La mujer en los medios de comunicación social (Picó and Alegría, 1982), compile a collection of valuable studies that analyze the influence of the various media in propagandizing an image of women that responds to the dominant ideology of capitalist patriarchy.

Ironically in the realm of education, Puerto Rican women have always played a central role. Since the expansion of the school system on the island after the U.S. takeover, teaching was to become one of the few professions that drew on the pool of educated female labor in substantial numbers. The result of this segregation of the teaching profession is that approximately 75 percent of all public school teachers in Puerto Rico are women. (Teaching, however, is still a low-paying profession in Puerto Rico with an average salary of $800 a month).

The expansion of the educational system at the beginning of the twentieth century, and the gearing of Puerto Rican men and women into certain kinds of professions and occupations was a necessary step for their eventual incorporation into the work force to serve the needs of the U.S. regime and the new enterprises that came to the island. Rivera Quintero (1980) has pointed out that "the purpose of primary school expansion was to fulfill the aims of the [the American's] educational policy" (p. 350). She emphasizes that aside from the basic instruction in reading and writing, females were required to take home economics and learn the needle crafts while males took agriculture and other vocational arts. All of this was aimed at developing a work force with the skills to join the growing needle trades (which paid the lowest wages and in which women were grossly exploited), and the new agricultural enterprises (Manning, 1934; Rivera Quintero, 1980). In addition, there was a need for lawyers, engineers, scientists, doctors, managers, and other kinds of specialized or high-level professions to support the new order and develop future leaders. Men became the primary beneficiaries of these positions. This kind of job segregation also occurred at a later period during the process of industrialization when new occupations opened up for both men and women, but men dominated the higher paying manufacturing jobs, and the more technical and managerial positions.

One of the most outstanding aspects of education in Puerto Rico today is the substantial enrollment of women in the school system and in institutions of higher education. Available statistics confirm that education has been the area in which Puerto Rican women have participated in the largest numbers throughout this century (Acosta-Belén and Sjostrom, 1979).

In spite of what appears to be one of the most positive aspects of the general status of women in Puerto Rico, an analysis of the available information concerning women's involvement in education and the professions will demonstrate that although Puerto Rican women enjoy equal educational opportunities in quantitative terms, this does not hold true in qualitative terms.

Statistics describing the enrollment of women in the public school system at the elementary and secondary levels demonstrate that not only are women well represented but proportionately the percentage of women who reach the upper levels of public schooling is higher than that of men. Puerto Rican women receive approximately 56 percent of all high school diplomas. The employed population's educational mean is 12.6 years for women compared to 12.1 for men.

Although the public school system offers, in principle, equal access to education for both Puerto Rican males and females, and women take advantage of these opportunities, a careful analysis demonstrates that these opportunities are not as equal as they seem at first glance. The curriculum, as it was mentioned, is still geared toward the maintenance of male and female traditional roles. In addition, existing discrimination has been found in vocational and technical programs of the Department of Public Instruction in Puerto Rico (Hernández Alicea, 1977). Even though the majority of the total enrollment in these programs were women (55 percent), they were primarily in programs classified as "nonoccupational," which included home economics and other special programs oriented toward domestic tasks. The enrollment in vocational and technical areas was overwhelmingly dominated by males.

One of the most disturbing realities of the public school system is that although 75 percent of the teachers in Puerto Rico are women, they constitute only 55 percent of the principals and 45 percent of the superintendents.

The enrollment figures for women in higher education, as well as the number of women receiving degrees from the University of Puerto Rico, the largest educational institution in the country, reflect a pattern found in other institutions throughout the country: women outnumber men in total enrollment which evidently reflects an existing high educational motivation among Puerto Rican women (Acosta-Belén and Sjostrom, 1979). Women constitute 51 percent of the population with a higher education and occupy almost half of the professional jobs in this area.

The study Women in Higher Education in Puerto Rico (1982) by Loreina Santos and José Berríos concluded, however, that "there is definite discrimination at all levels, in higher education, whether in administrative or teaching positions," and that "women have a long way to go in their fight against discrimination in the field of higher education" (p. 20). This study also found that there were no women occupying the position of president or chancellor of a higher education institution, and that only one woman, Ana G. Méndez (b. 1908), founder of the Puerto Rico Junior College, and the University College of Turabo has ever occupied such a position.

It is also important to note that the enrollment of women in the professional schools (for example, law, medicine, architecture), that is, in programs leading to potentially influential and upper-income professions, is significantly lower than that of men (Acosta-Belén and Sjostrom, 1979). It is an obvious conclusion then that women are still guided into traditional "feminine" fields and careers. Even when they overcome the many obstacles they face and obtain degrees in professions that traditionally have been con- sidered "masculine" professions, their professional practice and employment opportunities are minimized. There is often a wide gap between the education received by women and their actual employment. And it is important to keep in mind that, although in the past four decades the level of involvement and participation by Puerto Rican women in the professions has increased dramatically and women are in- creasingly more active and visible in public life, profession- al jobs are only a small part of the economy. The propor- tion of women in the Puerto Rican labor force was for many decades lower than it was in the 1930s. It was not until the 1980s that the percentage of women in the labor force showed an upward trend rising to 27.8, a decade ago the percentage was as low as 22.9. In 1930 the figure was 26.1, the second highest recorded in history. The current rate is still well below that of all women in the United States where it stands at 53 percent. For Puerto Rican men the labor force participation rate has been declining from 70.8 percent in 1970 to 60.7 percent in 1980.

Alice Colón (1985) has pointed to the significant in- crease in Puerto Rican women's employment in financial and commercial areas as well as in public administration between the 1970s and 1980s, positions that require more leadership and offer more possibilities for advancement. She indi- cates, however, that the increase in the labor force par- ticipation experienced by Puerto Rican women during this decade has been accompanied by an increase in "unemploy- ment as well as other forms of underutilization and poverty" (p. 29). Women's unemployment has increased from 10.2 percent in 1970 to 12.3 percent in 1980 (Departamento del Trabajo y Recursos Humanos, 1981).

An overview of women in the work force will quickly reveal the disadvantageous position in which women find themselves. Extreme salary differentials between men and women in parallel positions and the generalized subuti-

lization of women still characterize the Puerto Rican labor
force (Picó, 1975; Acín, 1980; Colón, 1985). Women who
are employed have a higher educational level than men. Of
all employed women at least 38 percent have completed some
kind of university degree. However, they only make 58
cents for each dollar made by a man. It is an obvious
conclusion that Puerto Rican women represent an educated
cheap labor force.

Job segregation is another reality of the Puerto Rican
labor market. Women occupy 57 percent of all public administration jobs; however they are clustered in the following occupations: secretaries/stenographers, kitchen/food
employees, social workers, maintenance staff, and hospital
aides/nurses (Picó, 1975). Women have less participation
than men in management and other executive administrative
positions.

The present status of Puerto Rican women in the labor
market is the result of a long and complex process of
interaction between patriarchy and capitalism. Both the
sexual division of labor and male domination are inextricably
intertwined and very basic transformations at all levels of
society and culture are needed in order to eliminate these
basic inequalities.

In the political arena a lot has been said to emphasize
the contributions and "exceptional" presence of Puerto
Rican women in public life (Fonfrías, 1984). It is true that
there have been several female legislators and politicians.
Since the 1940s women have served in important government
posts as secretaries of social services and of education, in
the Supreme Court, in the Senate and House of Representatives, and in the city halls of numerous towns, including
San Juan itself. Felisa (Doña Fela) Rincón de Gautier (b.
1897), a militant of Muñoz Marín's PPD from its inception,
was mayor of the capital city of San Juan for more than two
decades, and a popular and influential figure in island
politics. Nevertheless, these are exceptions and in proportion to men women are still underrepresented in politics.
When women do make it in politics they are placed in the
role of the supermadre where their participation is largely
an extension of their mothering roles in areas such as
education, health, and welfare (Chaney, 1979).[8] The high-
level policy-making positions in politics and government
continue to be reserved for men who still have a tight rein
on the leadership of all the political parties on the island.

The contradictions between the more visible role of
Puerto Rican women, her participation in the labor force,
her sharing of the financial responsibility for supporting
the household, and the imposition of a traditional role of

subordination at home and in society has created conflicts in the institution of marriage and the nuclear family. Since the 1940s the divorce rate on the island has increased significantly; at least one in three marriages ends in divorce (Vázquez Calzada, Cunningham, and Morales del Valle, 1981). Since the 1970s the marriage rate has been declining and new types of families and relationships have been emerging. The rate of female heads of households was over 18 percent in 1980 and more than two-thirds of these families have poverty-level incomes. Consensual unions or "living together" arrangements have also increased as well as the number of fathers claiming for custody of children in divorce cases (Rivera Quintero, 1978).

In the book La mujer puertorriqueña: investigaciones psico-sociales, Alba Nydia Rivera Ramos (1985) presents a picture of the attitudes and perceptions of Puerto Rican women today trying to capture the effects of the transformations that have taken place in Puerto Rican society since the 1950s in areas such as self-perception, productivity, and job stress. Other problems faced by working women such as discrimination, harassment, and stereotyping are also explored.

In sum, in spite of the changes brought by industrialization and urbanization, and the influence of the contemporary women's liberation movement, Puerto Rican women still need the support from the socioeconomic, cultural, and juridical structures to better utilize the educational opportunities that are available to them and achieve full equality in society.

Of course, not all Puerto Rican women are in Puerto Rico and the plight of Puerto Rican women in the United States must not be overlooked. There are both parallels and differences between Puerto Rican women in Puerto Rico and those who have immigrated to the United States.

Puerto Rican women played a major role in the development of the early colonia hispana (Hispanic settlements) in New York City during the first few decades of this century (Sánchez Korrol, 1983). They often provided links between the island and U.S. enclaves. Although immigration and work did not produce major changes in their traditional roles of subordination, they were "pivotal in retaining ethnicity through the transmission of language, customs, and cultural traditions within familial settings . . . [and] functioned as part of an informal information network" (Sánchez Korrol, p. 85). Their labor has sustained the garment and other manufacturing industries of the city and they played an active role in the workers' struggles that were so characteristic of the early decades of the century

(Colón, 1961; Andreu Iglesias, 1977; Ortiz, 1984; Ríos, 1984). The contemporary conditions affecting Puerto Rican women in the United States have been characterized by declining labor force participation (37 percent in 1980, the lowest among minority women), and by an increasing rate in female heads of households (Santana Cooney, 1979; Santana Cooney and Colón 1979, 1980; Bose, 1986). At least 44 percent of Puerto Rican families in the United States are headed by women.

For the Puerto Rican woman in the United States as for the Puerto Rican community in general, the environment is one plagued by poverty and discrimination. In the areas of education and employment Puerto Ricans have the lowest rates among minority groups in U.S. society (see Bose, 1986). Aside from socioeconomic deprivation, Puerto Rican women are confronted with both racial and sex discrimination (Jorge, 1979; Miranda King, 1979).

With the resurgence of a militant feminist movement in the United States and other parts of the world during the late 1960s and 1970s, the study of fundamental subjects related to the experience of Puerto Rican women as the forgotten or hidden participants of history and productive members of society has become a primary focus of open debate and of contemporary research. The influence of women's organizations such as the now defunct Federación de Mujeres Puertorriqueñas (FMP) and Mujer Intégrate Ahora (MIA), the government's Commission for Women's Affairs (Comisión para los Asuntos de la Mujer) in Puerto Rico, and the National Conference of Puerto Rican Women (NACOPRW) in the United States has been of crucial importance. The creation of other research, resource, and service centers and projects such as Centro de la Mujer at the Colegio Regional de Aguadilla (CORA), the Centro Coordinador de Estudios, Recursos y Servicios a la Mujer (CERES) at the University of Puerto Rico, the Centro de Investigación y Documentación de la Mujer (CIDOM) at the Inter American University Metropolitan Campus, the Proyecto Sobre los Derechos de la Mujer of the Puerto Rican Civil Rights Institute, the establishment of grassroots shelters to offer assistance and guidance to battered women or rape victims, and the emergence of new organizations such as Feministas en Marcha [FEM, Feminists Marching Ahead], and Organización Puertorriqueña de la Mujer Trabajadora [OPMT, Puerto Rican Organization for the Woman Worker] are the best examples of a generalized commitment to the improvement of the status of women (Pensamiento Crítico, 1985). They have all contributed in some way to generating an atmosphere of discussion and debate of issues affecting women, and provided important services and developed valuable materials as part of the necessary but arduous consciousness-raising process.

Because sexism and male chauvinism remain so deeply rooted in Puerto Rican culture and society, there is often the tendency to dismiss the issue of women's liberation as merely a manifestation of the increasing American influence on Puerto Rico and as a divisive issue in the more important struggle for independence. This type of argument is often simply a manifestation of disguised machismo and a subtle way of attempting to perpetuate the inferior status of women. The goal of egalitarian relations between men and women is not by any means an imported value. Women have been subjugated for centuries by patriarchy and capitalism all over the world. Just as many countries (including Puerto Rico) have struggled against colonialism and imperialism, women continue to confront the sources of their own oppression. Therefore, there is no contradiction between the Puerto Rican woman's struggle for equality and national liberation. The two are complementary, not mutually exclusive or antagonistic. Puerto Rican women will thus continue to struggle through individual and collective efforts to achieve full equality in society and to foster and promote the difficult but necessary cultural and social change that is so long overdue.

NOTES

1. See Evelyn Narváez Ochoa, "Nuevas herramientas para nuestra liberación," Palabra de Mujer (1977):14–15.
2. Just before the U.S. takeover of the island the illiteracy rate in Puerto Rico was 85 percent. See Marcia Rivera Quintero, "Educational Policy and Female Labor, 1898–1930," in The Intellectual Roots of Independence, ed. I. Zavala and R. Rodríguez (New York: Monthly Review Press, 1980), pp. 349–53.
3. Rafael Cordero ("el maestro Rafael") is usually presented as an example of the black man who became "a credit to his race" for his role as a teacher and educator of Puerto Rican youth. However, the comparable work of his sister Celestina is hardly ever mentioned.
4. The figure of Mariana Bracetti has inspired many literary works, among them, El Grito de Lares (1913 rpt. Río Piedras, P.R.: Editorial Cordillera, 1967) by Luis Lloréns Torres, and Mariana o el alba (Río Piedras, P.R.: Editorial Antillana, 1968) by René Marqués.
5. Lolita Lebrón was pardoned by President Jimmy

Carter in 1977 after 25 years in prison. See Federico Ribes Tovar Lolita Lebrón: la prisionera (New York: Plus Ultra, 1974).

6. In his El país de cuatro pisos (Río Piedras, P.R.: Ediciones Huracán, 1981), the writer José Luis González argues that "Northamericanization has served the popular masses to challenge and displace the cultural values of the propertied class." He adds: "Would it occur to anybody to deny that the present women's liberation movement—essentially progressive, aside from its possible limitations—is to a great extent a result of the 'norteamericanización' of Puerto Rican society?" (p. 36). René Marqués, a member of the same generation of writers, also espoused the same idea in his Ensayos (Río Piedras, P.R., Editorial Antillana, 1966). See Edna Acosta-Belén, "Ideology and Images of Women in Contemporary Puerto Rican Literature," in The Puerto Rican Woman, ed. E. Acosta-Belén (New York: Praeger, 1979), pp. 85–109. Also in this volume.

7. It has also been argued that Puerto Rican women were used as guinea pigs for the testing of the pill before it was introduced in the U.S. market.

8. In her biography Felisa Rincón de Gautier: The Mayor of San Juan (New York: Dell, 1972), Ruth Gruber tells of Doña Fela's traditional Christmas and Three Kings Day's parties for the children of San Juan, and how one year she had snow flown from the United States so that Puerto Rican children could have their first white Christmas.

REFERENCES

Acín, María N. 1980. Información estadística sobre la mujer puertorriqueña. San Juan, P.R.: mimeograph.
Acosta-Belén, Edna, and Barbara R. Sjostrom. 1979. "The Educational and Professional Status of Puerto Rican Women." In The Puerto Rican Woman, edited by Edna Acosta-Belén, pp. 64–74. New York: Praeger.
Aguinaldo Puertorriqueño. 1971. San Juan: Ediciones Porta Coelli. (First edition 1843).
Andreu Iglesias, César, ed. 1977. Memorias de Bernardo Vega. Río Piedras, P.R.: Ediciones Huracán. Memories of Bernardo Vega, trans. by Juan Flores. 1984. New York: Monthly Review Press.
Angelis, María Luisa de. 1908. Mujeres puertorriqueñas que se han distinguido en el cultivo de las ciencias, las letras y las artes desde el siglo XVII hasta nuestros días. San Juan: Tipografía del Boletín Mercantil.

Azize, Yamila. 1979. Luchas de la mujer en Puerto Rico: 1898–1919. San Juan: Graficor.

Bose, Christine E. 1986. "Puerto Rican Women in the United States: An Overview. In this volume.

Brau, Salvador. 1972. Ensayos: Disquisiciones Sociológicas. Río Piedras, P.R.: Editorial Edil. (First edition, 1886.)

Burgos, Nilsa M. 1982. "A Preliminary Historical Analysis of Women and Work in Puerto Rico." In Work, Family and Health: Latina Women in Transition, edited by Ruth E. Zambrana, pp. 75–86. New York: Hispanic Research Center.

Capetillo, Luisa. 1911. Mi opinión sobre las libertades, derechos y deberes de la mujer. San Juan, P.R.: The Times Publishing Co.

Chaney, Elsa. 1979. Supermadre: Women in Politics in Latin America. Austin, TX: University of Texas Press.

Colón, Alice. 1985. "La participación laboral de las mujeres en Puerto Rico: empleo o sub-utilización." Pensamiento Crítico, 8, no. 44 (mayo/junio): 25–30.

Colón, Jésus. 1982. A Puerto Rican in New York and Other Sketches. New York: International Publishers. (First edition, 1961).

Comisión de Derechos Civiles. 1973. La igualdad de derechos y oportunidades de la mujer puertorriqueña. San Juan: Estado Libre Asociado de Puerto Rico.

Comisión para el Mejoramiento de los Derechos de la Mujer. 1978a. Igualdad de oportunidades de empleo para la mujer. San Juan: La Comisión.

————. 1978b. La imagen de la mujer en los medios de comunicación. San Juan: La Comisión.

————. 1977. Sexism in the Classroom. San Juan: La Comisión.

Departamento del Trabajo y Recursos Humanos. 1981. Negociado de Estadísticas del Trabajo. La participación de la mujer en la fuerza laboral. San Juan: ELA.

Fernández Méndez, Eugenio. 1972. Art and Mythology of the Taino Indians of the Greater West Indies. San Juan: Ediciones El Cemí.

Ferrer, Gabriel. 1881. La mujer en Puerto Rico: Sus necesidades presentes y los medios más fáciles y adecuados para mejorar su porvenir. San Juan: Imprenta El Agente.

Fonfrías, Ernesto Juan. 1984. La mujer en la política de Puerto Rico. Hato Rey, P.R.: Master Typesetting and Word Processing.

Guevara, Carlos and Myrna J. Sesman. 1978. La madre y el aprendizaje del nino: La experiencia urbana puertorriqueña. Río Piedras, P.R.: Editorial Universitaria.

Hernández Alicea, Carmen. 1979. "El discrimen contra la mujer en el Programa de Instrucción Vocacional y Técnica del Departamento de Instrucción Pública de Puerto Rico." Master's thesis, University of Puerto Rico.

Jiménez Wagenheim, Olga. 1981. "The Puerto Rican Women in the 19th Century: An Agenda for Research." Revista/Review Interamericana 11, no. 2 (Summer): 196–203.

Jorge, Angela. 1979. "The Black Puerto Rican Woman in Contemporary American Society." In The Puerto Rican Woman, edited by Edna Acosta-Belén, pp. 134–41. New York: Praeger.

Konetzke, Richard. 1945. "Emigración de mujeres españolas a la América durante la época colonial." Revista Internacional de Sociología 3:123–50.

Manning, Caroline. 1934. The Employment of Women in Puerto Rico. Washington D.C.: Government Printing Office.

Miranda King, Lourdes. 1979. "Puertorriqueñas in the United States: The Impact of Double Discrimination." In The Puerto Rican Woman, edited by Edna Acosta-Belén, pp. 124–33. New York: Praeger.

Molina, Carmen E., and Magali García Ramos. 1977. Módulos de una serie para maestros de escuela elemental. San Juan: Comision para el Mejoramiento de los Derechos de la Mujer.

Negrón Muñoz, Angela. 1935. Mujeres de Puerto Rico: desde el primer siglo de la colonización hasta el primer tercio del siglo XX. San Juan: Imprenta Venezuela.

"Organizaciones y proyectos sobre la mujer puertorriqueña." 1985. Pensamiento Crítico 8, no. 44 (mayo/junio): 21–24.

Ortiz, Altagracia. "Puerto Rican Women in the ILGWU, 1940–1950." 1984. Paper presented at the Women's Studies Conference, Brooklyn College, April.

Picó, Isabel. 1975. "Estudio sobre el empleo de la mujer en Puerto Rico." Revista de Ciencias Sociales 19, no. 2 (June): 141–65.

——————. 1979b. "The History of Women's Struggle for Equality in Puerto Rico." In The Puerto Rican Woman, edited by Edna Acosta-Belén. New York: Praeger.

——————. 1979a. Machismo y educación en Puerto Rico. San Juan: Comisión para el Mejoramiento de los Derechos de la Mujer.

Picó, Isabel, and Idsa Alegría. 1982. La mujer en los

medios de comunicación social. Río Piedras, P.R.: University of Puerto Rico.

Presser, H. B. 1980. "Puerto Rico: Recent Trends in Fertility and Sterilization." Family Planning Perspectives 12, no. 2: 102–6.

Quintero Rivera, Angel. 1974. Conflicto de clases y política en Puerto Rico. Río Piedras, P.R.: Ediciones Huracán.

——————. 1971. Lucha obrera en Puerto Rico. Río Piedras, P.R.: CEREP.

Ríos, Palmira. 1984. "Puerto Rican Women in the United States Labor Markets." Paper presented at a conference on "The Changing Hispanic Community in the United States," State University of New York at Albany, March.

Rivera de Alvarado, Carmen. 1972. "La contribución de la mujer al desarrollo de la nacionalidad puertorriqueña." In La mujer en la lucha hoy, edited by Nancy Zayas and Juan A. Silén, pp. 37–47. Río Piedras, P.R.: Ediciones KIKIRIKI.

Rivera Quintero, Marcia. 1980. "Educational Policy and Female Labor, 1898–1930." In The Intellectual Roots of Independence, edited by I. Zavala and R. Rodríguez, pp. 349–53. New York: Monthly Review Press.

——————. 1979. "The Development of Capitalism and the Incorporation of Women into the Labor Force." In The Puerto Rican Woman, edited by Edna Acosta-Belén, pp. 8–24. New York: Praeger. Also in this volume.

——————. 1978. "Las adjudicaciones de custodia y patria potestad en los tribunales de Puerto Rico." Revista del Colegio de Abogados de Puerto Rico 39, no. 2 (mayo): 177–200.

Rivera Ramos, Alba Nydia. 1985. La mujer puertorriqueña: investigaciones psico-sociales. Río Piedras, P.R.: CEDEPP.

Rivero, Eneida. 1975. "Educación sexual en Puerto Rico." Revista de Ciencias Sociales 19, no. 2 (junio):161–91.

Sánchez Korrol, Virginia. 1983. From Colonia to Community: The History of Puerto Ricans in New York City. Westport, CT: Greenwood Press.

Santana Cooney, Rosemary. 1979. "Intercity Variations in Puerto Rican Female Participation." Journal of Human Resources 14, no. 2: 222–35.

Santana Cooney, Rosemary, and Alice Colón. 1980. "Work and Family: The Recent Struggle of Puerto Rican Women." In The Puerto Rican Struggle: Essays on Survival in the U.S., edited by C. Rodríguez, V. Sánchez Korrol, and José O. Alers, pp. 58–73. New

York: Puerto Rican Research Migration Consortium.
————. 1979. "Declining Female Participation among Puerto Rican New Yorkers." Ethnicity 6, no. 3 (September): 281–97.

Santiago-Marazzi, Rosa. 1984. "La inmigración de mujeres españolas a Puerto Rico en el periodo colonial español." Homines 7, no. 1 (enero-junio): 291–302. Also in mimeograph. 1974 San Juan: Comisión para el Mejoramiento de los Derechos de la Mujer.

Santos, Loreina, and José Berríos. 1982. Women in Higher Education in Puerto Rico. Mayaguez, P.R.: University of Puerto Rico.

Silvestrini, Blanca. 1975. "Women as Workers: The Experience of the Puerto Rican Woman in the 1930s." In Women Cross-Culturally: Change and Challenge, edited by Ruby Rohrlich-Leavitt, pp. 247–60. The Hague: Mouton.

Solá, Mercedes. 1922. Feminismo. San Juan: Cantero Fernández y Cia.

Sued Badillo, Jalil. 1979. La mujer indígena y su sociedad. San Juan: Editorial Antillana. (First edition 1975).

Valle, Norma. 1979. "Feminism and its Influence on Women's Organizations in Puerto Rico." In The Puerto Rican Woman, edited by Edna Acosta-Belén, pp. 38–50. New York: Praeger.

————. 1975. Luisa Capetillo. San Juan: n.p.

Vázquez Calzada, José. 1973. "La esterilización femenina en Puerto Rico." Revista de Ciencias Sociales 17, no. 3 (September): 281–308.

Vázquez Calzada, José, Ineke Cunningham, and Zoraida Morales del Valle. 1981. "Patrones de nupcialidad de la mujer puertorriqueña." Revista/Review Interamericana 9, no. 3 (Fall): 418–37.

Weller, Robert H. 1968. "A Historical Analysis of Female Labour Force Participation in Puerto Rico." Social and Economic Studies 17, no. 1 (March): 60–72.

Yordán Molini, Haydeé. 1976. La visión de la niña en cinco libros de lecturas escolares. San Juan: Comisión para el Mejoramiento de los Derechos de la Mujer.

Zayas, Nancy. 1972. "La mujer en la lucha de hoy." In La mujer en la lucha hoy, edited by Nancy Zayas and Juan A. Silen, pp. 67–72. Río Piedras, P.R.: Ediciones KIKIRIKI.

2

The Development of Capitalism in Puerto Rico and the Incorporation of Women into the Labor Force

Marcia Rivera

The development of capitalism as a dominant mode of production in Puerto Rico accelerated the incorporation of
women into the labor market on an unequal and sexist
basis. With few exceptions, historical works on Puerto Rico
ignore the impact of the transition from servile to capitalist
relations of production upon women.[1] Though research on
this problem is still largely in an embryonic stage, the
analysis of a number of key processes will help to understand the role played by women in the development of
capitalism in a dependent colonial society, such as Puerto
Rico.

Reconstructing the history of Puerto Rican women is not
an easy task. Our official history of Puerto Rico is one
virtually without women; and in the few instances where
women appear, they are presented in exceptional or unique
situations where a woman is given recognition for a particular act, or for being the mother, wife, or daughter of a
male leader or patriot. Therefore, those of us who have
undertaken the study of the historical processes of our
society in order to understand the factors that contribute
to the continuing subordination of women have been led to a
painstaking but fascinating task. We have had to begin by
studying the most basic facts of our economy and by
searching statistical sources that are often incomplete or
inadequate since women's work has, for the most part, not
been accounted for.

WOMEN AND SOCIAL PRODUCTION
IN PRE-CAPITALIST PUERTO RICO

Prior to the late nineteenth century, when the island was still a Spanish colony, Puerto Rican women had a very scant participation in the production of goods and services for the market. But this does not mean that women did not play an important role in the overall production system. Production involves not only the productive process per se, but also what is produced by individuals in a society and the reproduction of the labor force. The reproduction of the labor force is as important as the reproduction of the conditions sustaining a social system. The reproductive capacity of women acquired a tremendous economic and political importance throughout the Spanish conquest and colonization of the island. Spanish control over the new possessions was achieved not only through armed struggle and religious conversion, but also through directly populating and settling the new territories (Konetzke, 1945). The conquerors undertook the task of forming towns and villages that could re-create the Spanish way of life and would abide by Spanish civil law.

Throughout the colonization period, the Spanish Crown set forth a number of regulations and executive orders aiming at this objective, and provided special incentives in the assignment of lands, Indians, and public posts to those who were married (Santiago-Marazzi, 1974). Historical evidence points to the Spanish concern for having the colonists send for their wives once they were established in Puerto Rico. And the question was clearly not a moral one; it was a political and economic concern. Since women were capable of reproducing labor power, the "possession" of a wife was both politically convenient and economically important.

Until the end of the eighteenth century and beginning of the nineteenth, the Puerto Rican economy was organized on the basis of independent peasants producing for family consumption. Women had some participation in this subsistence agriculture; but since the work involved in the production for family consumption is not defined in monetary terms, it is almost impossible to calculate or quantify women's contribution to subsistence agriculture. The eighteenth-century Puerto Rican family was a production unit that consumed whatever it produced, and within the family the members shared the agricultural work.

During the nineteenth century, commercial cultivation of sugar and coffee was expanded under a hacienda social structure with servile relations of production. Subsistence agriculture, however, coexisted with the hacienda structure throughout the century (García, 1974). At the time, land was the most abundant economic element and was frequently given in usufruct to landless peasants (agregados), who in return would work on the hacienda, become sharecroppers, or, less frequently, pay some sort of cash rent, thus providing for the appropriation of surplus labor by the hacendado.

Historical evidence indicates that women from agregado families had some participation in agricultural production on the haciendas (mostly in harvesting and animal care), but sexual division of labor seems to have been very strict. Women were rarely recruited to work on the land even when there was a desperate need for agricultural laborers throughout the century. The scarcity of labor was such that the Spanish government, in the interests of the proprietors, enacted several measures designed to force the landless peasants to work as jornaleros (laborers) on the haciendas. One such measure, enforced by the Spanish Governor Miguel López de Baños in 1838, stated that "all inhabitants are to be in possession of a property that will provide the means for subsistence or else be engaged at the services of someone that can take care of his needs" (Gómez, 1970: 485).

These regulations, besides imposing the obligation to work, established penalties for its violations and determined procedures for its implementation. Every individual had to carry a signed form on which the details of his or her employment were stated. The regulations enforced by Governor Juan de la Pezuela in 1849 were even more far-reaching, and explicitly included women. The first article of the Reglamento de Jornaleros began by defining jornalero:

> Any person lacking capital or industry will be obliged to occupy himself at the service of another, be that in agriculture, mechanics, transportation, or domestic service through an agreed wage salary [emphasis added] (Ramos, 1966).

Women, then, were also required to work as jornaleras; but they seem to have been induced to take up employment as domestic servants, cooks, seamstresses, or laundresses on the haciendas. According to the 1899 Census of Puerto Rico, the 43,189 women engaged in such jobs accounted for 91 percent of all women employed in the country. There were only 1,868 women engaged in agricultural work (less than 1.0 percent of all agricultural workers), even when laborers were in great demand. Why were women excluded from paid agricultural work? The ruling class, instead of hiring them as jornaleras, induced women of the bondless classes to work in occupations that served to strengthen the social hegemony of one class over another, and that maintained women in a subordinate position, subject to constant economic, social, and sexual exploitation.

THE EARLY YEARS OF CAPITALIST DEVELOPMENT

The incorporation of women into the labor force increased drastically after the U.S. takeover of Puerto Rico in 1898. The expansion of North American imperialist capitalism required the development of a new socioeconomic structure to replace the hacienda social structure which prevailed until then. An export-oriented sugar economy was envisaged and toward that end a number of economic policies were devised to weaken or eliminate many haciendas and small farms. Through tax laws, limitations imposed upon credit facilities, and other such measures, the development of a sugar plantation-based economy was to be achieved (Herrero, 1971). During the first three decades of the twentieth century, Puerto Rico's economic structure completed the process of transformation initiated at the end of the nineteenth century, and capitalist relations of production became predominant within a sugar cane plantation system. With the change of political power to an imperialist colonial system in 1898 and the subsequent development of a capitalist mode of production, the importance of the traditional rural world diminished and other sectors of the economy began to expand (Quintero Rivera, 1974: 174).

The expansion of sugar cane plantations with capitalist relations of production split the hacienda social organization and forced the agregados and small peasants to opt for one of two feasible alternatives: to become wage earners on the plantations (rural proletarians) or migrate to the urban centers in search of a job (and become urban proletarians). These economic processes encompassed changes in the class structure of the society. The traditional classes of nineteenth-century Puerto Rico, immersed in a culture of deference generated by the hacienda social structure, were broken up and aggressive struggle replaced deference and paternalism. The proletarization of the rural plantation workers and urban artisans led to the development of a clear class consciousness among workers, and to the formation of workers' unions and a workers' political party during the early years of the twentieth century (Quintero

Rivera, 1974: 174–83).

The prevalence of an export-oriented sugar economy during the first decades of the twentieth century led to higher imports of foodstuffs and machinery, and generated a number of jobs in the commercial and service sectors of the economy. There was also an increase in different manufacturing activities: processing of agricultural products, needlework, and others.

The expansion of the manufacturing and commercial sectors of the economy brought radical changes in the structure of the labor market, and the impact of these changes upon women was considerable. The immediate recruitment of women as salaried workers was evident within a sexually-segregated labor market (see Table 2.1). According to the population census between 1899 and 1910 the total female employment increased by 61.2 percent, whereas male employment increased by only 17.7 percent. Besides domestic servants, women were recruited in large numbers for tobacco stripping, home needlework, and elaboration of straw hats, holding the lowest-paid jobs and working under sordid conditions.

A similar situation was observed toward the end of the nineteenth century in those countries where capitalism became the dominant mode of production after the Industrial Revolution. In England, for example, male employment increased by 7.9 percent between 1871 and 1891, whereas female employment increased by 21 percent in the same period; in Germany male employment increased by 6.4 percent between 1875 and 1882, while women's employment increased by 35 percent (Bebel, 1904). Further, the occupational distribution of workers and the position of women in the labor market also followed very similar lines. Initially almost all of the female employment was concentrated in domestic service, with other job opportunities appearing gradually. But a sexually-segregated market was evident: women were found in the lower-paying jobs, and the wages of women were, in almost all occupations, considerably lower than the wages of men for the same hours. This was the case in all the industries that employed women in Puerto Rico.

In cigar manufacturing, an industry where women came to represent 53 percent of all workers, production was organized along a strict sexual division of labor: tobacco stripping and classification of leaves was done mostly by women, while the cigars were made by men. Tobacco stripping paid the lowest wages in the industry.

Because of the nature of the jobs done by Puerto Rican women during the first decades of the twentieth century, the effective length of the working day was indeed increased. Since women's work has historically been seen as merely a supplementary income for the family (and thus has been devalued), the incorporation of women into the labor force had the effect of reducing the value of labor power and increasing the rate of exploitation during the first decades of the twentieth century.

TABLE 2.1 Major Female Occupations in Puerto Rico, 1899-1930

	1899	1910	1920	1930	% Change 1899-1930
Servant	18,453	18,781	15,382	20,300	10.0
Laundresses (private homes)	16,855	25,884	16,317	14,952	11.3
Seamstresses	5,785	11,200	12,650	34,345	493.7
Teacher	563	1,172	2,636	4,254	655.6
Nurse	64	189	362	921	1,399.0
Straw hatmaker	387	2,862	3,633	691	78.5
Sales	25	108	376	828	3,212.0
Office worker	NA	189	937	2,500	1,222.7*
Needleworker	NA	NA	384	3,635	846.6*
Garment worker	NA	NA	3,568	6,383	78.9
Operator, tobacco factories	60	3,204	8,573	9,290	15,383.4
Public Service	NA	--	63	49	

*Change in percentage from 1920 to 1930
NA = not available; -- = too few cases to be significant
Source: U.S. Department of Labor, The Employment of Women in Puerto Rico by Caroline Manning. Washington, D.C.: Government Printing Office, 1934.

The U.S. Department of Labor report The Employment of Women in Puerto Rico prepared by Caroline Manning (1934) reveals the extent of exploitation of female workers in a number of trades, particularly in home needlework. The report reveals that

women worked extremely long hours, days and evenings. . . .
Hourly earnings in needlework were extremely low: for 31.4% of the women they were less than 1 cent, for 31.1% they were 1 and under 2 cents, and for 31.4% they were 2 and under 4 cents.

Unfair practices in home needlework included payment in groceries; payment in keep; delays in supplying work and payment; retention by agent of wage increases (pp. 1–2).

The question arises then, as to why women were recruited as salaried workers and why they accepted conditions in which such inequality of treatment prevailed between the sexes. Again, if one goes back to the emergence of capitalism in European societies one finds exactly the same phenomenon. As Bebel (1904) points out:

The endeavor, on the part of employers, to extend the hours of work, with the end in view of pumping more surplus values out of their employees, is made easier to them thanks to the slighter power of resistance possessed by women. Hence the phenomenon that, in the textile industries, for instance, in which women frequently constitute far more than one-half of the total labor employed, the hours of work are everywhere longest. Accustomed from home to the idea that her work is "never done," the woman allows the increased demands to be placed upon her without resistance (p. 168).

The question leads us to consider the interrelationship between the productive and the reproductive activities of women. Women's participation in productive activities seems to be conditioned by their role in physical reproduction and the control exercised over their reproductive activities (Benería, 1978). The biological reproduction of women, as well as other aspects of reproduction of the labor force, and the reproduction of use values, are within the domestic sphere of women's activities. Since the production of use values within the household is not considered by society to be as important as the production of commodities within a market value, women's productive activities have historically been devalued. Thus, when a woman enters the labor market and seeks a paid job, both her and her employer have internalized the belief that any wage is better than no wage at all—since at home the woman was not paid a wage for the use values she produced or for the reproduction of the labor force in which she engaged. Women's participation in production has, then, been viewed as secondary to their reproductive activities; hence their subordination and marginality in the labor market.

The early stages of development of capitalism in Puerto Rico had many contradictory effects upon women. Capital-

ism opened the labor market to women and offered a somewhat wider spectrum of employment possibilities, but at the
same time it increased their exploitation as wage earners.
On the other hand, the proletarianization of women through
their massive incorporation into the ranks of salaried
workers (particularly in the tobacco industry) impelled their
participation in labor struggles. In many instances women
even became symbols of militant labor struggle. Hand in
hand with their male counterparts, women workers rejected
views of feminine fragility, moral superiority, and passivity
that were attributed to women by other social classes.
Relative equality between the sexes was thus achieved in
the process of proletarianization (Quintero Rivera, 1978).

The achievement of an independent economic life by
women meant the development of different conceptions of
relationships between the sexes. Women were perceived as
comrades (compañeras) by the male workers with whom they
shared their daily lives. Labor leader Juan S. Marcano
expressed this conception in 1919:

> Women have always been the proprietary victims of
> the tyranny, despotism, and authority of men and
> society over them. But, it is time to put an end to
> these practices. Working class women are our
> comrades, they share our misery and privations.
> The Socialist Party, through its struggles, rec-
> ognizes and supports the right of women to a full
> participation in all social affairs; the party exists
> for the defense of women and humanity in general.

This new conception of women represented a negation of the
male-centered ideology of hierarchical paternalism of the
hacienda culture (Quintero Rivera, 1978).

TRANSFORMATIONS IN THE PUERTO RICAN
ECONOMY SINCE 1930

The capitalist agricultural economy of Puerto Rico went
through a severe crisis during the 1930s, a crisis that was
a product of the development of capitalism. While sugar
production dominated the economy, the dependency on
external trade increased. And from 1925 on Puerto Rico
experienced a continuing and mounting determination of
trade-exchange terms that had a serious impact on the
national income. Furthermore, the directly productive
sectors of the economy suffered a great contraction during
those years. Between 1920 and 1930 the income generated

by tobacco exports decreased 51.9 percent, and by 1939 tobacco exports were practically nil (Quintero Rivera, 1978). (See Figure 2.1.)

In addition, the sugar industry, the most important in the agricultural sector, began to show signs of a crisis

Figure 2.1   Puerto Rican Manufactured Tobacco Exports, 1901–40

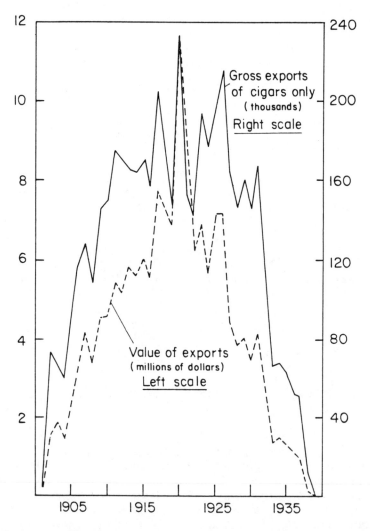

Source: This graph has been traced with data from Sol L. Descartes, Basic Statistics on Puerto Rico, Washington, D.C., 1946, pp. 50–55.

which was to bring about its downfall in the following decades (see Figure 2.2). This situation led to an outbreak of structural unemployment, and the resultant decrease in the rate of participation in the labor force and

Figure 2.2   Puerto Rican Agricultural Exports, 1894–1940 (millions of dollars)

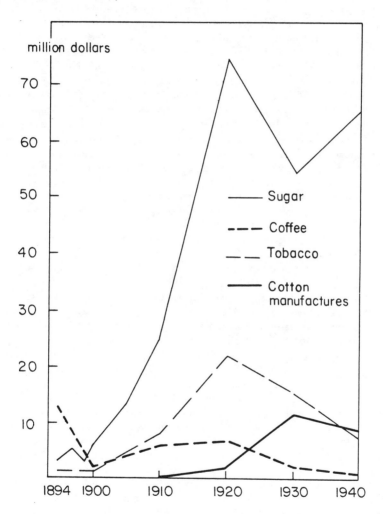

Source: This graph has been traced with data from U.S. Congress, Production and Commercial Movement of Sugar 1895–1905, Washington, D.C.: Government Printing Office, 1906; Sol L. Descartes, Basic Statistics on Puerto Rico, Washington, D.C., 1946, pp. 50–55.

the growth of unstable, part-time, or miscellaneous jobs (chiripeo). While population increased 22 percent between 1930 and 1940, employment only increased 1.7 percent.

During this period many families turned again to badly paid female work, such as home-based needlework. For them this was the only means of subsistence, and it was precisely in this industry where the worst working conditions and lowest salaries were found (see Table 2.2). The militancy and class solidarity achieved by women in the tobacco factories were destroyed, since needlework was mostly done in the individual home, where women could not share their feelings of oppression and exploitation.

The increase of marginal and unemployed workers presented a difficult juncture for the working class. Not having shared the life experiences of the proletariat and thus not being able to develop a sense of collective struggle, the marginalized workers developed an attitude of individual hustling for survival. This, alongside internal contradictions of the working-class organizations, led to the fragmentation of the working class as a class, and to the deterioration of many of its institutions. In the 1940 elections the working class was fragmented at the political level, and its organizations, having lost the ideological-cultural appeal of their former defiance and mystique, were demoralized (Quintero Rivera, 1978). This served as the basis for the emergence of a new political alternative, the Popular Democratic Party, which sought to develop a manufacturing economy with U.S. support and backing.

Toward the end of the 1940s the establishment of U.S. subsidiary manufacturing plants was brought about by direct investment in production. Lower wage levels than in the United States, the advanced stage of capital accumulation in North America, the availability of trained workers, and the basic infrastructure in Puerto Rico joined to attract light manufacturing industries (basically textiles and garments) to the island.[2] The manual dexterity of thousands of women who had been engaged in home needlework served as an added incentive to the establishment of a garment industry, which was transferred from the home to the factory.

The Popular Democratic Party, which assumed power amidst chaos and economic crisis, requested the full cooperation of workers with the new program for economic reconstruction (cooperation clearly meant not interfering with government's or industry's plans). In many instances the subsidiary firms that came to Puerto Rico brought with them their own labor organizers who would "organize" workers in the Puerto Rican factories and would affiliate

TABLE 2.2 Average Hours and Days Worked Weekly, and Hourly, Daily, and
Weekly Incomes, Selected Working-Class Families, Puerto Rico, 1941-42

	Number of Workers	Weekly Average			Income	
		Hours	Days	Income	Per Hour	Per Day
All workers	6,111	36.4	4.8	$ 5.78	15.9¢	$1.21
Cane (agriculture)	1,641	32.1	4.1	4.88	15.2	1.18
Construction (nondefense)	501	38.5	4.9	9.45	24.5	1.94
Construction (defense)	493	43.3	5.4	11.91	27.5	2.21
Needlework in home (for export)[a]	367	31.8	5.0	2.15	6.8	.43
Personal, domestic service	200	30.5	4.6	1.72	5.6	.37
Minor products	367	35.9	4.6	2.91	8.1	.63
Coffee (agriculture)	342	35.1	4.6	2.48	7.1	.54
Tobacco (agriculture)	266	34.0	4.4	2.32	6.8	.53
Tobacco (factory)	217	40.8	5.3	4.35	10.7	.82
Sugar (factory)	157	39.0	5.4	10.61	27.2	1.97
Needlework in factory (for export)	152	36.3	5.0	4.18	11.5	.83
Docks	105	26.6	3.3	11.43	42.9	3.46
Federal government	96	37.1	5.2	7.01	18.9	1.35
Self-employed	91	26.9	4.6	2.74	10.2	.59
Buses, taxis	88	44.1	5.7	8.75	19.8	1.54
Dairies, dairy outlets	76	57.4	6.7	5.39	9.4	.81
Retail business	74	48.4	6.0	5.26	10.9	.87
Road construction	70	36.0	4.6	6.34	17.6	1.37
Other[b]	736	41.5	5.3	6.92	16.7	1.30

[a] The low average income of 6.8 cents per hour is possibly due to violations of the federal law governing reasonable working norms and to workers' giving erroneous information to the researchers, since many of them
were not in a position to know if their work was for the local market or
for export.

[b] All other industries represented by less than 70 workers.

Note: Survey covered 6,111 workers in 4,999 families.

Source: Compiled by the author.

them to their U.S. labor unions. Immediately upon recruitment, factory workers found themselves paying dues to an
unknown union with a questionable commitment to labor.
Women who were recruited in large numbers for the industries in the 1950s, joined by the thousands the International
Ladies Garment Workers Union, which had extremely good
relations with entrepreneurs in the United States. The

application of the Taft-Hartley Act to Puerto Rico in 1947, which forbade solidarity strikes (strong ammunition in the labor struggles until then), represented a big blow to the labor movement. The fragmentation of working-class solidarity found in the first decade of the century was almost complete by 1950.

In conjunction with the expansion of manufacturing industries after the 1940s, there was an increase in Puerto Rico's dependency on the imports of foodstuffs and other consumer goods from the United States. This resulted in the expansion of commerce and service sectors of the economy. By 1950 it was already evident that a tendency to concentrate female employment in office and sales occupations was on course and the labor market was clearly sexually segregated. Up to 1940 only 6.2 percent of all women employed in Puerto Rico were engaged in those occupations; by 1950 the proportion had doubled to 12.1; and by 1977 it stood at 31 percent. The service sector has shown a similar increase: it held only 3.4 percent of all women employed in 1940, whereas it had 18 percent in 1977. Practically all the employment of women since the 1940s has been in service, sales, and office occupations. Recent figures show that 50 percent of all women employed in Puerto Rico are in these occupations. Even though the proportion of women in the professions has grown, the increase has been practically absorbed by teaching and nursing, which have traditionally been seen as "female" occupations.

The economic situation of Puerto Rico in the 1960s presents important considerations in the analysis of the participation of women in the labor force. The value of labor (expressed in wage terms) began to increase as a result of the higher cost of living, thus reducing the rates of profit for the entrepreneur, and reducing Puerto Rico's competitiveness in light manufacturing within the world market. This and other factors, such as increased transportation costs and new tariff agreements, resulted in a decrease in the relative importance of light manufacturing in Puerto Rico. Those traditional industries disappeared through the dynamics of capitalist accumulation, which seeks to generate the maximum surplus of labor power. Since the late 1960s manufacturing growth in Puerto Rico has been geared to industries that are more capital intensive; and the expansion in this sector has been due not to recruitment of additional workers, but, rather, to increased worker productivity, which is responsible for dramatic increases in the gross national product. This has been accompanied by ever increasing unemployment rates and stagnant or decreasing participation rates in the labor force for both males and females.

The consolidation of a manufacturing economy where industries with a high organic composition of capital prevail, has increased unemployment rates to a current official level of around 20 percent. This poses a phenomenal problem for trade union organization, particularly for the organization of women workers. Generalized unemployment implies a large reservoir of labor power for the entrepreneur, who is, therefore, able to use all sorts of devices to dissuade workers from organizing a labor union. Threatening workers with losing their jobs if they unionize, offering incentives for increased individual productivity and seemingly better fringe benefits, hiring "undercover" workers to keep them informed of possible labor unrest, and laying-off potential union organizers are common practices among entrepreneurs in Puerto Rico. In industries where a large proportion of women work, these tactics are reinforced by cultural conventions of the dominant classes, which still perceive women as docile, submissive, and timorous. The realities of the labor market intermingle with psychological and cultural factors to dissuade workers in general, and women in particular, from becoming involved in labor struggles. Since 1970 the level of trade union organization in Puerto Rico has steadily decreased to a low 13 percent of all workers, even though the rates of exploitation have increased.

Besides a low rate of participation by women in the labor force and the tendency to segregate the work force by sex, the present day situation of female workers in Puerto Rico is clear evidence of other forms of sex discrimination. Women are underutilized in relation to their educational qualifications (19 percent of women with a college degree are currently employed as operators, sales persons, and office and service workers), and are paid less than their male counterparts. In addition, they constantly face a labor market where sex segregation is prevalent.

NOTES

1. The works of Angel Quintero Rivera are a remarkable exception. See "La clase obrera y el proceso político en Puerto Rico," Revista de Ciencias Sociales 8, nos. 1–2 (marzo–junio 1974): 145–61; 8, no. 3–4 (sep.-dic. 1974): 61–107; 9, no. 3 (sept. 1975): 261–300; 10, no. 1 (marzo 1976): 3–48. See also "Background to the Emergence of Imperialist Capitalism in Puerto Rico," in Puerto Rico and

Puerto Ricans: Studies in History and Society, ed.
Adalberto López and James Petras (New York: John Wiley
and Sons, 1974), pp. 87–117.
  2. The average wage in Puerto Rico at the onset of
industrialization was barely 27 percent of the average wage
in manufacturing in the United States. See Lloyd Reynolds
and Peter Gregory, Wages, Productivity and Industrialization in Puerto Rico (New Haven: Yale University Press,
1965), p. 20.

REFERENCES

Bebel, Augusto. [1904] 1975. Women Under Socialism.
    New York: Labor News. Reprint New York: Schocken.
Benería, Lourdes. 1978. Reproduction, Production, and
    the Sexual Division of Labour. Geneva: International
    Labour Organization.
García, Gervasio. 1974. "La economía natural colonial del
    siglo XIX." Río Piedras, P.R.: CEREP. Mimeograph.
Gómez, Labor. 1970. Organización y reglamentación del
    trabajo en Puerto Rico del siglo XIX. San Juan: Ins-
    tituto de Cultura Puertorriqueña.
Herrero, José A. 1971. La mitología del azúcar. San
    Juan: CEREP.
Konetzke, Richard. 1945. "Emigración de mujeres españo-
    las a la América durante la época colonial." Revista
    Internacional de Sociología 3: 123–50.
Manning, Caroline. 1934. The Employment of Women in
    Puerto Rico. Washington, D.C.: Government Printing
    Office.
Marcano, Juan S. 1919. Páginas Rojas. Humacao, P.R.:
    n.p.
Quintero Rivera, Angel. 1978. "De artesano a proletario."
    Sin Nombre 8 (enero-marzo): 100–37.
————. 1976. "The Working Class and Puerto Rican
    Politics in an Agricultural Economy." Ph.D. diss.
    University of London.
————. 1974. "Background to the Emergence of Imper-
    ialist Capitalism in Puerto Rico." In Puerto Rico and
    Puerto Ricans: Studies in History and Society, edited
    by Adalberto López and James Petras, pp. 87–117. New
    York: John Wiley and Sons.
Ramos, Francisco, ed. 1966. "Reglamento de jornaleros."
    In Prontuario de disposiciones oficiales de Puerto Rico.
    San Juan: Imprenta J. González Font.
Santiago Marazzi, Rosa. 1974. "La inmigración de mujeres
    españolas a Puerto Rico durante el periodo colonial

español." San Juan: Comisión para el Mejoramiento de los Derechos de la Mujer. Mimeograph.

U.S. Bureau of the Census. 1970, 1950, 1940, 1930, 1910. Census of Population: Puerto Rico. Washington, D.C.: Government Printing Office.

U.S. War Department. 1899. Report of the Census of Porto Rico. Washington, D.C.: Government Printing Office.

Valle, Norma. 1975. Luisa Capetillo. San Juan: n.p.

3

The History of Women's Struggle for Equality in Puerto Rico

Isabel Picó

In Puerto Rico the concern for women's history has been directly related to the intensity of organized women's movements. Not since 1930, when the suffrage movement ended, has there been the interest found today. Women are again asking historical questions in search of their collective identity and for an analysis of their condition. However, Puerto Rican women trying to understand themselves in a historical perspective have few facts to rely on. We still know very little about how women lived at different times, how they interacted with their children, husbands, and parents, and how they began to develop a consciousness of their distinct role in society.

In my academic research on Puerto Rican women, I have studied the social and economic forces that shaped and changed women's lives in the twentieth century and the nature of, and factors involved in the development of feminist consciousness in Puerto Rico. I would like to present in this essay some preliminary notes for the study of Puerto Rican women and their participation in social conflicts of the early twentieth century.

Published in Sex and Class in Latin America, ed. June Nash and Helen I. Safa. New York, Praeger Publishers, 1976, pp. 202–13. Reprinted with permission of the author and publisher.

Most of the nineteenth century has been marked by the lack of both a feminist movement and a strong feminist consciousness. This is understandable due to the precarious educational and employment situation of women on the island. According to the U.S. Census of Population conducted in Puerto Rico in 1899, out of a total population of 953,243 inhabitants, there were only 5,045 Puerto Ricans with more than primary education, 72 percent of whom were men. Of the 1,387 women with some education beyond primary schooling, 82 percent remained at home, outside of the labor force. Under these circumstances it was not possible for a true feminist movement to develop in the nineteenth century as it did in England, France, the United States, and other countries which had experienced greater economic and social complexity.[1]

The development of capitalism at the turn of the century started a slow transformation in the economic function of women from unpaid production for home consumption to gainful employment in the manufacture of articles for sale. In the late nineteenth century only a limited number of women (47,701) were employed outside the home in gainful occupations and, according to the 1899 census, the great majority were employed as domestic servants (18,453), laundresses (16,855), and seamstresses and embroiderers (5,785). Only 3,910 were classified by the census as laborers. Women's rate of participation in the labor force would increase substantially during the first three decades of the twentieth century. From a rather low rate of participation in the labor force of 9.9 percent in 1899, it had reached 26.1 percent by 1930, the highest we have experienced in our history until the 1980s (see Table 3.1).

This dramatic increase in labor force participation in a predominantly agrarian economy was due primarily to the growth of manufacturing industries such as the elaboration of tobacco and home needlework.[2] The development of new commercial enterprises in Puerto Rico and the influx of foreign capital searching for cheap labor accelerated women's participation in the labor force. In 1930, 52.3 percent of all women in paying jobs were working in the manufacturing sector of the economy, 29.7 percent in domestic and personal services, and only 9.4 percent in agriculture. While the percentage of women in domestic and personal services declined from 78.4 percent to 29.7 percent, this sector remained the second most important area for women's work (see Table 3.2).

It may be noted that before 1930, the largest number of women were employed in the manufacture of tobacco, while the sugar and molasses industry gave employment to the

TABLE 3.1   Participation in Puerto Rican Labor Force, by Sex, 1899-1970

	Females		Males	
Year	Number	Percent of Female Population	Number	Percent of Male Population
1899	47,701	9.9	268,664	59.9
1910	73,596	21.7	303,993	93.1
1920	84,094	21.6	319,201	84.1
1930	122,488	26.1	374,958	81.0
1940	144,360	25.0	457,630	79.4
1950	138,517	21.3	458,950	70.7
1960	144,260	20.0	449,840	65.7
1970	212,421	22.9	471,369	54.7

Source: U.S. Department of Commerce, Census of Population. Washington, D.C.: Government Printing Office, 1899, 1910, 1920, 1930, 1940, 1950, 1970.

largest number of children. In 1909, of the 1,654 female wage earners in all industries combined, 1,342 or 81.1 percent were employed in the manufacture of tobacco; and of the 758 wage earners under 16 years of age in all industries, 601 or 79.3 percent were in the sugar and molasses industries.[3] By 1920 the number of women working as operatives in cigar and tobacco factories increased to 8,573 and by 1930, to 9,290. In both years women outnumbered men working in these jobs.[4] Almost all hand stemming in the tobacco leaf industry was done by females.[5]

Needlework attained the status of an industry of commercial importance in the late 1920s.[6] While some fine needlework was made before that date, production was small. It was not until World War I interfered with the supply of embroidery work from Europe that needlework extended throughout rural communities, small towns, and cities in Puerto Rico. With this gain in production, there was an increase in employment. The census of 1920 showed roughly 16,000 persons in the cotton garment industry; the census of 1930 showed 40,000. Over a fourth of these were employed in factory work, the great majority being home workers. The needlework industry in Puerto Rico was predominantly a women's industry. In the 1935 Census of Population, 99 percent of the persons who gave their gainful occupation as "home needlework and embroidery worker" were female. During the 1930s, home work in the needle

TABLE 3.2 Female Participation in Puerto Rican Labor Force, by Economic Sector, 1899-1930

	1899		1910		1920		1930	
	Number	Percent	Number	Percent	Number	Percent	Number	Percent
All sectors	47,701	100.0	76,892	100.0	86,462	100.0	125,777	100.0
Agriculture, fishing, mining	1,868	3.9	10,779	14.0	17,719	20.3	11,948	9.4
Commerce, transportation	1,729	3.6	1,037	1.0	1,199	1.3	2,349	1.8
Manufacturing, mechanical industries	6,389	13.3	18,194	20.3	30,809	22.8	65,846	52.3
Professional services	311	.6	1,487	1.8	3,253	3.6	5,661	4.5
Domestic, personal services	37,407	78.4	45,149	58.0	32,482	27.1	37,424	29.7
Clerical occupations	--	--	139	.2	937	.9	2,500	1.9
Public services, other	--	--	47	.06	63	.07	49	.03

Sources: U.S. War Department, Census of Population, Washington, D.C.: Government Printing Office, 1899; U.S. Department of Commerce, Census of Population, Washington, D.C.: Government Printing Office, 1910, 1920, 1930.

trades overshadowed most other lines of women's employment both in abuses and numbers involved.[7]

Women's participation in professional services and clerical occupations also increased substantially during the first three decades of the twentieth century. With the expansion of the public school system under U.S. domination, teaching became one of the main occupations of upper- and middle-class women. Gradually teaching became, for all practical purposes, a "female" occupation. In 1899 there were 246 female teachers in Puerto Rico and they constituted 30 percent of all persons engaged in the teaching profession. By 1930, 74.5 percent of all teachers were women (see Table 3.3).

TABLE 3.3 Women in the Teaching Profession (1899-1930)

Year	Total	Women	Percent	Men	Percent
1899	809	246	30.0	563	69.9
1910	2,239	1,172	52.3	1,067	47.6
1920	3,742	2,636	70.4	1,106	29.5
1930	5,730	4,254	74.5	1,456	25.4

Sources: U.S. War Department, Census of Population. Washington, D.C.: Government Printing Office, 1899; U.S. Department of Commerce, Census of Population. Washington, D.C.: Government Printing Office, 1910, 1920, 1930.

A similar situation was found in the fields of nursing and clerical occupations. Women constituted 50 percent of all persons engaged in these two fields in 1910. By 1930, 66 percent of all clerical workers and 94 percent of the nurses were women (see Tables 3.4 and 3.5).

This fundamental change in the economic function of women had profound repercussions on the social order of the Puerto Rican community. The new relationship of women to production brought about changes in social and sexual patterns expressed by different classes. For the first time in our history, women recognized a collective experience as a position of subjugation. This new consciousness was based on the new roles of women as producers, introduced by the process of industrialization.

For those women who entered the labor force at the beginning of the twentieth century, oppression was part of their new collective experience. But oppression meant different things to different groups and classes of women.

The growing working force of women had developed an internal hierarchy. While the unskilled, industrial workers showed life styles and attitudes characteristic of the proletariat, women in the growing professions, such as teaching and nursing, set themselves apart from their sisters. Moreover, the dichotomy between women who worked and those who remained at home was further accentuated by the culturally defined "proper-sphere" of women.

TABLE 3.4 Women Employed as Typists and Secretaries in Puerto Rico, 1910-1930.

Year	Total	Males	Females	Percent of Women
1910	225	112	113	50.0
1920	839	333	506	60.0
1930	2,309	776	1,533	66.0

Sources: U.S. War Department, Census of Population. Washington, D.C.: Government Printing Office, 1899; U.S. Department of Commerce, Census of Population. Washington, D.C.: Government Printing Office, 1910, 1920, 1930. Compiled by the author.

TABLE 3.5 Women Employed as Nurses in Puerto Rico, 1899-1930.

Year	Total	Males	Females	Percent of Women
1899	127	63	64	50.0
1910	252	63	189	75.0
1920	393	31	362	92.0
1930	976	55	921	94.0

Sources: U.S. War Department, Census of Population. Washington, D.C.: Government Printing Office, 1899; U.S. Department of Commerce, Census of Population. Washington, D.C.: Government Printing Office, 1910, 1920, 1930. Compiled by the author.

Working-class women at the beginning of the century felt their oppression in class terms and organized around their work. In studies about the development of the Puerto Rican working-class movement, Angel Quintero Rivera describes how women's participation in the growing tobacco industry gradually broke the traditional patterns of women's employment as mere collaborators of men in agricultural tasks.[8] It raised women to a relatively equal position with men in the productive process within similar conditions of exploitation. Economic exploitation by employers under the new system of production was definitely inhumane. A report on The Employment of Women in Puerto Rico, conducted in 1933 under the joint auspices of the federal and insular departments of labor, showed that substandard wages in factory sweatshops, long hours, and poor sanitary conditions prevailed in canneries, tobacco stemmeries, cigar factories, and home needlework.[9] Gradually these conditions generated a spirit of solidarity and a common struggle among workers against employers that to a great extent blurred the traditional differentiation between the sexes.

By and large, women tended to join men in the ranks of organized labor and experienced their own sense of strength and power in trade unions. As early as 1904, working-class women had organized female associations within trade unions. Some of them were La Unión de Damas de Puerta de Tierra, La Unión Federada de Patillas, La Unión de Escogedoras de Café de Arecibo, La Unión de Damas Obreras de Guayama, La Unión Protectora de Damas de Mayagüez, and La Unión de Obreras Domesticas de Ponce. Later on, numerous women participated in the creation of the Free Federation of Labor (Federación Libre de Trabajadores). Josefa Perez, a female worker from Puerta de Tierra, wrote, in 1904, a letter to Romero Rosa, a member of the propaganda Commission of the Federation, demanding that women workers be organized within the union:

> If you volunteer to organize the working men, why not do the same for working women? Here in Puerta de Tierra where thousands of women work like busy bees, it is your support which is necessary to help so many deprived women to unite and defend themselves from the exploitation to which they have been subjected.[10]

During the period of 1910–20, some outstanding working-class women became symbols of militant trade unionism. Among them can be mentioned Concha Torres, another leader from Puerta de Tierra who was the first woman in Puerto Rico to speak in a political rally; Paca Escabí de Peña, a union leader from Mayagüez; Francisca Andújar; and Juana Colón from Comerío, who was very active in organizing tobacco strippers (despalilladoras de tabaco) at the big factory of La Colectiva and became one of the most militant women in the Socialist party founded by Santiago Iglesias Pantín in 1916.[11]

Naturally, most women workers directed their attention to the subjects of wages and hours. They realized their wages were three to four times lower than those of men working in comparable jobs due to the inferiority ascribed to their position as workers. As working women, they pronounced a total rejection of the ideal woman that prevented their full participation and remuneration in industry. They rejected notions of feminine frailty, weakness, social purity, moral superiority, and passivity.

The best exponent of the new ideology was Luisa Capetillo in her writings Ensayos Libertarios (1904–1907), Mi opinión sobre las libertades, derechos, de la mujer como compañera, madre y ser independiente (1911), and Influencias Modernas (1916).[12] This last book is a collection of essays which could well be considered the first "women's lib" manifesto in Puerto Rico. Luisa Capetillo was a highly exceptional woman who participated in the formation of the first artisan groups that the Free Federation of Labor organized in urban centers. Later on, she participated in a crusade in sugar plantations, raising the class consciousness among workers. She was also a reporter for the newspaper Unión Obrera and established the journal La Mujer, devoted to women's issues. In her writings, Luisa Capetillo defended libertarian socialism, rationalism, internationalism, and women's liberation. She condemned religious fanaticism, the double standard, women's slavery in marriage, and economic exploitation in the factory. A brief quote from one of the plays she wrote provides ample proof of her defense of free love. At the end of the last scene, Angelina, the heroine, addresses the public with these words:

> Beautiful girls who have heard this, if you wish to be the mothers of future and conscious generations who are free, do not engage in civil or religious contracts because they are sales and sales are a way of prostitution. Love should be free like the air one breathes, like the flowers that open up to receive the pollen that fertilizes them and carries their scent into the air. You should give love in the same way and prepare to have children out of love.[13]

Luisa Capetillo also challenged social conventionalisms of her time. She was the first woman to wear slacks in public in

Puerto Rico, and she had children outside of the marriage institution.

Women's active participation in the working-class struggles engendered a different conception of the woman as "comrade" (compañera). This new conception of which Luisa Capetillo was the most radical expression, was a denial of the patriarchal ideology so typical of the hacienda social system. To a certain extent, the struggle for woman's equality had its origins in the artisan's tradition of dissent from the Puerto Rican landowners and employers.[14]

Long before women were granted the right to vote, the Socialist party had a requirement in its party bylaws that no committee could be organized unless one-third of the members were females. In its 1919 political platform, the Socialist party defended universal suffrage for men and women.[15] But in general, the ballot, legal rights, and other social reform issues seemed irrelevant or secondary compared to the more pressing problems of daily life. Trade unionism absorbed their attention and energy. At the same time, working-class women viewed the women's suffrage movement as designed for those of the privileged class. They feared what actually happened in 1929, that the right to vote be granted only to literate women, thus increasing the power of those political parties that represented the propertied class. Naturally, the Socialist party opposed those legislative bills that granted the ballot exclusively to women who could read and write.

The seed bed of the suffrage movement that developed in Puerto Rico was the increase in respectable jobs open to women of the upper and middle classes. With the transformation of the social system of haciendas to a new economic system of sugar plantations controlled by U.S. corporations, Puerto Rican upper classes suffered structural changes that directly affected the women's condition. Many small and middle-sized landowners lost their lands, moved into town, and gave their children an education in the traditional professions. Within this process of déclassement emerged a growing number of women for whom work meant not only a form of self-fulfillment and personal independence, but also an economic necessity. This social phenomenon occurred at a time when the new colonial administrators had decided to expand the educational system, to make it coed and available to females on a relatively equal basis.[16] These reforms were well received by women from the petite bourgeoisie and the traditional land-owning class. They probably explain why women from these classes were more tolerant with the colonial power than their male counterparts. To a great extent, the first generation of professional women were rather insecure about their individual fate, wanted to be accepted, and frequently assimilated the values of the prevailing political system to achieve their individual aims. This defensive cultural conservatism was part of a reaction against the imposition of a foreign culture and way of life that characterized the anticolonial struggle in Puerto Rico. As a result, the feminist movement emerged and developed apart from the movements of anticolonial protest. On some occasions, it was to be in conflict with them.[17]

However, the goal of the electoral franchise acquired a special meaning for the growing sector of professional women who were deprived of the most fundamental civil and political rights. The new study and work experiences raised women's consciousness in relation to their position of inequality vis-à-vis their male counterparts. In 1909, female school teachers demanded eligibility to be appointed to local school boards. In 1917, the first feminist organization, The Puerto Rican Feminine League (La Liga Femínea Puertorriqueña) was established and later, in 1925, the Puerto Rican Association of Suffragist Women (La Asociación Puertorriqueña de Mujeres Sufragistas) demanded from the U.S. Congress, and from our local legislature, the ballot for women. After more than ten years of continuous struggle, literate Puerto Rican women acquired the right to vote in general elections. The bill was approved in 1929, but they were not able to vote until 1932. It was not until 1936 that the literacy requirement was finally abolished.[18]

Even though the suffrage movement eliminated the most obvious forms of deprivation for women in the juridical superstructure and promoted reforms in the fields of education and labor, it did not alter fundamentally the patriarchal society. Unfortunately, the revolutionary promise of changing radically the quality of life for women never materialized for the great majority of Puerto Rican women.

The feminist movement's single-minded emphasis on obtaining the vote helps to explain not only the movement's failure to reach working-class women, but also its increasing inability to move beyond its immediate goal of the franchise. By the time the bill was passed, the vote was no longer a means to an end. It was the only end most suffragists envisioned. In the 1930s feminism as a movement and a consciousness would become increasingly isolated.

NOTES

1. Only a small sector of women from the upper classes fought in their own sweet way for the right to education. At the same time they enriched our cultural heritage, particularly in the arts and sciences. Among them can be mentioned Alejandrina Benítez de Gautier, Lola Rodríguez de Tío, María Bibiana Benítez, and many others who devoted themselves to women's education in the few schools available at the time. As it usually happens at the beginning of social movements, the struggle for equal educational opportunities received a tremendous boost from an important group of men associated with the liberal reform movement. Ignacio Guasp and Alejandro Tapia y Rivera founded La Guirnalda Puertorriqueña in 1856 and La Azucena in 1870; both reviews promoted women's right to education. Gabriel Ferrer, José María de Labra, and Eugenio María de Hostos followed in the tradition of John Stuart Mill and also defended women's rights. For biographical sketches of prominent women of the seventeenth through nineteenth centuries, see María Luisa de Angelis, Mujeres puertorriqueñas (San Juan: Tipografía Real Hnos., 1910). See also Lola Rodríguez de Tío, Obras completas (San Juan: Instituto de Cultura Puertorriqueña, 1971). For a defense of women's right to an education, see Alejandrina Benítez de Gautier, "Sobre la educación de las mujeres," Guirnalda Puertorriqueña 1 (junio 20, 1856): 1–3; Alejandro Tapia y Rivera, "El aprecio de la mujer," La Azucena 1 (noviembre 30, 1870): 9–10; Gabriel Ferrer, La mujer en Puerto Rico (San Juan: Imprenta El Agente, 1881); and Rafael María Labra, Conferencias dominicales sobre la educación de la mujer (Madrid: Imprenta Rivadeneyra, 1869).

2. See Robert H. Weller, "A Historical Analysis of Female Labor Participation in Puerto Rico," Socio-Economic Studies 17 (March 1968): 62. See also N. L. McBride, "Women Workers of Porto Rico," International Socialist Review 18 (June 1917): 717.

3. See U.S. Department of Commerce and Labor, Bureau of the Census, Thirteenth Census of the United States, Manufacturers, 1909 (Washington, D.C.: Government Printing Office, 1912).

4. There were 7,602 men working in the cigar and tobacco industries in 1920 and 4,090 in 1930. Apparently men were gradually displaced from their jobs or promoted to skilled jobs within the industry. See U.S. Department of Labor, Bureau of the Census, Census of the United States (Washington, D.C.: Government Printing Office, 1920, 1930).

5. See U.S. Department of Labor, Puerto Rico: The Leaf Tobacco Industry (Washington, D.C.: Government Printing Office, 1941).

6. See U.S. Department of Labor, Wages and Hours Division, Report on Puerto Rico: The Needlework Industry (Washington, D.C.: Government Printing Office, 1950).

7. See U.S. Department of Labor, The Employment of Women in Puerto Rico by Caroline Manning (Washington, D.C.: Government Printing Office, 1934).

8. See Angel Quintero Rivera, "De artesano a proletario: Los tabaqueros y la tradición radical," in Gervasio García, Ricardo Campos, and Angel Quintero Rivera, Socialista y tabaquero: Orígenes de la lucha obrera en Puerto Rico (Río Piedras, P.R.: CEREP, n.d.)

9. See U.S. Department of Labor, The Employment of Women in Puerto Rico. Over 50,000 women who did home needlework received a wage of one, two, or three cents an hour. Most of the abuses, such as late payments, payment in merchandise instead of cash, and the withholding of pay increases by unscrupulous middlemen were perpetrated against women working at home. Nonetheless, salaries below subsistence level and long working hours were common in all factories and workshops. According to this study, in canning factories, working women were not even provided with seats; from early in the morning they were standing in front of their work tables peeling grapefruit and pineapples so close to each other that their elbows touched. Those who worked six or seven days a week received an average salary of $7.57 a week.

10. See Igualdad Iglesias Pagán, El obrerismo en Puerto Rico (Madrid: Ediciones Juan Ponce de León, 1973), p. 324. This book contains a short but well-documented description of female workers' interest and participation in the Free Federation of Labor during the first five years of this century. It reports of meetings, rallies, and other activities of women workers within the organized working-class movement.

11. See Yamila Azize, Luchas de la mujer en Puerto Rico: 1898–1919 (San Juan: Graficor, 1979).

12. Norma Valle has published a brief biography of Luisa Capetillo. See Luisa Capetillo (San Juan: n.p., 1975). See also "La primera en liberarse," La Hora, 25 de abril–1 de mayo, 1974, pp. 12–13, and Chap. 4 of this volume.

13. As cited by Carmen Rivera de Alvarado in her article "La contribución de la mujer al desarrollo de la nacionalidad puertorriqueña," in La mujer en la lucha hoy, ed. Nancy Zayas and Juan A. Silén (Río Piedras, P.R.: Ediciones KIKIRIKI, 1972), p. 43.

14. See Angel Quintero Rivera, ed., Lucha obrera en Puerto Rico (Río Piedras, P.R.: CEREP, 1973).

15. See the Socialist party program included in Quintero Rivera's Lucha obrera en Puerto Rico, pp. 89–94. Another important document that contains the Socialist party defense of women's suffrage is a memorandum of the Territorial Executive Committee dated December 29, 1923. Also see Bolívar Pagán, El sufragio femenino (San Juan: n.p., 1924).

16. The University of Puerto Rico (UPR), established in 1903 following the guidelines of North American teachers' colleges became a predominantly female institution in terms of the student body. During the 1903–23 period approximately 2,791 students graduated from the UPR. Women constituted 74 percent of all graduates. See Isabel Picó de Hernández, "Los estudiantes universitarios y el proceso político puertorriqueño," (Ph.D. diss., Harvard University, 1974), pp. 90–93.

17. In 1909, when a bill for the legal emancipation of women was presented by Nemesio Canales to the House of Delegates, José de Diego, the most important leader of the independence movement at that time, opposed it, arguing that women needed no additional rights. See Nemesio R. Canales Paliques (San Juan: Ediciones Isla, 1967), pp. 175–77. During the 1930s, Pedro Albizu Campos, president of the Nationalist party, confronted the suffragists on several occasions and urged them to give priority to the fight against colonialism. He addressed them on one occasion in these terms: "Why do you want to vote? Is it to become definitely annexed to the United States, thus giving up our national identity, or is it to make Puerto Rico a free nation, independent and sovereign . . . ? The only transcendental duty of those who are born in a colony is to redeem the country from its colonial bond." (El Mundo, May 20, 1930.)

18. For a brief but good summary of the development of the suffragist movement in Puerto Rico, see Isabel Andreu de Aguilar, "Reseña histórica del movimiento sufragista en Puerto Rico," in Revista Puerto Rico 1, no. 3 (junio 1935): 255–61. See also Mercedes Solá Feminismo (San Juan: Cantero Fernández y Cía., 1922).

4

Women as Workers: The Experience of the Puerto Rican Woman in the 1930s

Blanca Silvestrini

In recent years, there has been a surge of interest in the application of the social history approach to Caribbean historiography. However, the study of Puerto Rican history from the social history point of view has been virtually non-existent. Social scientists have directed their attention primarily to the study of institutions and organizations, and the central role of their leaders, rather than to the people who belonged to those organizations and their relationships within the group (García, 1970; Quintero Rivera, 1971). One of the most neglected areas of research has been the study of the roles that women have played in Puerto Rican society. There is a paucity of titles from a historical, anthropological, or even psychological perspective which focus on women as their major concern. Only a few studies, manily in anthropology, mention indirectly the status of women; however, the scope of these studies has been restricted to portraying the women predominantly within the family setting and usually only as enacting the mother/housewife role.

The present study was begun within the context of the limitations of the available studies, which generalize about

Published in Women Cross-Culturally: Change and Challenge. Ruby Rohrlich-Leavitt, ed. The Hague: Mouton Publishers, 1975, pp. 247–60. Reprinted with permission of the author and publisher.

women without studying their actual status in society or the particular cultural understandings within which they have to act. The purpose of this chapter is to analyze the role that women played in the socioeconomic transformation undergone by Puerto Rican society as reflected particularly in the events of the decade of the 1930s. The emphasis of the study is on the participation of women as workers, including women's role in politics since by then politics was one of the main concerns of the workers.

The decade of the 1930s in Latin America and in the United States has been described as a time of distress and of constant unrest for labor, which saw the emergence of new groups and labor alignments (Rama, 1962; Ginzberg and Berman, 1963; Bernstein, 1960, 1970). Puerto Rico was not an exception. During those years Puerto Rican workers suffered from prolonged unemployment, extremely low wages, and deteriorating working conditions (Governor of Puerto Rico, 1933:6). These problems were not simply a product of the world economic depression; they had existed in Puerto Rico from the beginning of the century, although certainly they were aggravated by the grim economic conditions of the decade. In this panorama of economic distress, what was the status of the Puerto Rican woman?

The 1935 Census of Puerto Rico showed that 16.1 percent of all women in Puerto Rico were "gainfully occupied" and that 26.3 percent (134,371) of all women fifteen years old and over were employed (Puerto Rico Reconstruction Administration [PRRA], 1938:57,60). The gradual increase in the number of women who entered the labor force was a significant factor in altering the position of women in Puerto Rican society, since it also gave women access to other fields of social action, such as party politics and social protest movements in which they later made significant contributions. However, the above-mentioned figures were not equally divided among the various occupations and industries in Puerto Rico, but were clustered in three fields: (1) the needlework industry; (2) the tobacco industry; and (3) domestic services.[1] In view of the economic importance of the needlework and tobacco industries in the economy of Puerto Rico during the 1930s, women's participation in these two occupations is given particular consideration in this chapter.

A broad spectrum of problems converged on the island at the onset of 1930, creating unemployment and a sense of hopelessness for Puerto Rican workers. Many of these problems had their roots in the socioeconomic structures established during the Spanish regime. More difficulties ensued with changes introduced into the island's living patterns by the U.S. occupation in 1898. With the U.S. occupation the island's economy veered toward intensive commercial agriculture, thus weakening the prevailing subsistence agricultural structure and making the people more dependent upon imported foods and goods. Four major economic changes took place in Puerto Rico during this period: unprecedented growth of the sugar industry, development of the tobacco-growing industry, rise of needlework as an industry of economic value, and the decline of the coffee industry from its previously privileged position (Steward, 1956:63).

Two of these changes—the development of the tobacco-growing industry and the rise of the needlework industry—had a considerable effect on the status of women in the island, because they helped to incorporate large numbers of women as workers. Previously women had participated indirectly in agricultural activities, such as sugar and coffee production, but since they did not participate directly in the actual production or elaboration of the products, their role was less important than that of the male workers. For example, women in the sugar cane fields kept small stores, took care of animals, and were responsible for the preparation of foodstuffs for sale on payday (Mintz, 1956:371), but usually they did not work in the sugar fields as cane cutters or directly in the sugar factories.[2]

In coffee cultivation women had to help in the management of the operation or sometimes complemented the family income with their work elsewhere; however, the major responsibility for the farm often laid on the husband's shoulders. By contrast, in both the tobacco-processing and the needlework industries women constituted a significant portion of the labor force and were directly responsible for the elaboration of the end products. Thus they had the opportunity to participate actively, together with male workers, in the labor struggles of the time.

The transformation of the Puerto Rican economy during the first decades of the twentieth century generally altered the living and working patterns of the workers and encouraged the organization of a labor movement. A major change in the Puerto Rican labor scene during the twentieth century was the emergence and development of a strong trade union movement. Groups of workers throughout the island, organized either in formal unions or in sociedades de estudio (study groups), had emerged in the second half of the nineteenth century and eventually joined to establish a national federation in 1899, Federación Libre de Trabajadores de Puerto Rico (FLT). Since its beginning the Puerto Rican labor movement demanded government's recognition of labor organizations and of the collective bargaining principle, the adoption of a shorter workday, higher wages, and universal suffrage (Pagán, 1959:59–60). In addition, convinced of the need for swift political action to redress the prevailing social inequalities, this same group of workers founded the Socialist party. Although the FLT and the Socialist party were separate organizations, their local and national leaderships often coincided, and the ideals of one group complemented those of the other. Both organizations supported the woman worker's right to work and at least on paper advocated equality. In a book published by the FLT for the purpose of instructing the workers in trade unionism, Santiago Iglesias, the organization's president, summarized its policies regarding women workers when he wrote that

> the labor leaders should make every possible effort to organize all the workers of both sexes, of all trades and professions, and especially farm workers.
> We should organize the women in all the areas of industry in which they are employed. We should organize the office employees as well as the women working in the telegraph, the typists, the clerks, the seamstresses as well as the cooks and maids (Iglesias, 1914:6).

Even more interesting than the official views on women's participation in the labor movement were the ideas expressed by a rank-and-file member of that movement. Juan S. Marcano, a zapatero (shoemaker) succinctly expressed the Socialist party's cry in its initial days for better conditions for the woman worker:

> Women in Puerto Rico and in the rest of the world have yet to occupy the place they deserve as equal human beings. It is sad to see women walking to the workshops and factories—to those traps of exploitation and misery—in which they leave the best of their lives, their youth, . . . in which they suffer from being constantly at the working tables until gradually tuberculosis takes a hold of their lives. The conditions at the workshops are intolerable . . . places without ventilation in which our fellow women workers have to spend from 8 to 9 hours in daily imprisonment . . . and all of this for the wealth of a few rich owners.

> But this has to be stopped. The woman worker
> is our fellow companion in misery and depriva-
> tion—it is impossible that she continues to be
> shamefully exploited. . . . The Socialist Party will
> end this situation (Marcano, 1919, rpt. Quintero
> Rivera, 1971:66–67).

Regardless of this support for women's rights, few women
ever occupied top leadership positions in either the FLT or
the Socialist party. Nevertheless, given the precarious
state of affairs, the Socialist party and the labor federation
became useful channels through which women, as rank and
file, fought for their causes. Consequently, although
women workers did not have the same access as men to the
high policy-making positions of the labor federation, they
participated actively in its initial stages of organization.
Tomasa Yupart, for example, a representative of the Union
of Tobacco Strippers of Juncos, was among the delegates to
the Sixth Congress of the FLT in 1910 which drafted the
federation's constitution. Juana Colón, a planchadora y
lavandera (a woman who washed and pressed clothes for a
small fee) who later became a tobacco worker, organized
protests and strikes against the U.S. tobacco corporations
in Comerío, a town in the tobacco-producing area of Puerto
Rico.

At the beginning of the twentieth century Luisa
Capetillo also became a national figure among Puerto Rican
workers. She participated prominently in the labor campaigns of the FLT throughout the island, demanding both
improvement of the worker's living conditions and recognition of women's rights. In her book Mi opinión sobre las
libertades, derechos y deberes de la mujer (1911), she
described a campaign trip around the island in which she
exhorted the workers to join efforts against capitalism:

> Fellow workers you are in a state of slavery worse
> than the one of ancient times. Aren't you eager to
> abandon it? Don't forget that in your hands you
> have the redemption you need so badly. Peasants
> . . . your slavery is far from gone. Before, your
> master owned you and deprived you of your
> will—today he frees you but leaves you without
> means to exercise your will (Capetillo, 1911:23).

With impassioned oratory she described the abuses against
the workers in general, and demanded a new role for the
woman worker.

Luisa Capetillo developed the idea that a woman who

had to work outside the home and at the same time take care of the house chores could continue to develop fully as a human being. In her writings she deplored the inequalities of an economic system that favored the rich people. "The home of the rich woman is never touched by these problems," explained Luisa Capetillo (1911:24), because the rich woman either did not have to work outside her home or if she used some of her spare time in work or social activities she had another woman to take care of the house, to such an extent that even the children were reared by others. Perhaps Capetillo's most important contribution is that she went beyond the feminist point of view of defending women's rights; she also criticized some of the abuses that other women, frequently because of their social class, committed against women workers. During those years the woman worker had to deal not only with a multitude of inequalities, but also with the day-to-day confrontation with employers, at times female, who exploited her.

The living and working conditions described by Luisa Capetillo in 1911 did not improve very much during the following decades. Unemployment and underemployment, seasonal work, and low wages increased during the 1920s, and by 1930 the workers were rapidly losing their faith in the Socialist party and the FLT. A series of alliances with the conservative and bourgeois political parties gradually made both the Socialist party and FLT leadership an instrument of the large industrial and economic interests, leaving the workers without genuine representation.

By 1933 Puerto Rico was in the midst of economic chaos. Sixty-five percent of the population was reported unemployed. The Socialist party, which gained access to the government of Puerto Rico through its participation in a coalition that won the 1932 elections, tried to keep a balance between the demands of the workers and the wishes of its conservative partner in the coalition, the Union Republican party. Paradoxically, the Union Republican was a party directed by rich people who owned much of the industrial and business capital of the island. The workers had hoped that with the Socialist party and FLT leadership now in government, as well as with the implementation of the U.S. New Deal measures, rapid changes would come. But neither the Socialist party's performance in government nor the application of the New Deal programs and controls brought changes on the life of the workers. On the contrary, unemployment increased from 20 percent in 1932 to 29 percent in 1934, wages decreased, and the cost of living almost doubled. Thus strikes proliferated and tensions mounted. In August 1933 the situation in Puerto Rico

became explosive. Strikes began in various tobacco factories and in the needlework industry, and, in both, women
played a major role.

Until the mid-1920s the tobacco workers, especially in
the cigar factories, constituted the core of the Puerto Rican
labor movement.[3] In the late 1920s, with the decreasing
importance of the tobacco industry, workers from other
economic segments partially replaced the tabaqueros (tobacco workers) as the leaders of the organized labor movement
in Puerto Rico. Nevertheless, the tobacco-processing
workers continued to constitute a militant labor group.
During 1932 the workers of La Colectiva, the factory of the
Puerto Rican American Tobacco company, constantly strove
for improvements in their working conditions. They pro-
tested against the tobacco company that brought American
workers who did not speak Spanish and required the Puerto
Rican workers to use that language. By 1933 unrest in the
tobacco industry had intensified. Tobacco production was
declining rapidly. Several factories had closed, and unemployment in the tobacco industry mounted as the manufacturers forced the remaining workers to work longer hours
to compensate for the losses. Then came the strikes of
August 1933. The tobacco strippers led the strike movement in the tobacco-producing area located in the center of
the island.

In Caguas 4,000 workers, mostly women, went on strike
to protest against malpractices in the weighing of tobacco
for stripping. Irregularities in weighing methods became an
extremely important issue for the tobacco workers, since
even when the employers argued that they paid the workers
by the hour, wages really depended on daily workloads.
These women had to work in "factories" that were small
rooms without ventilation or any sanitary conditions, which
frequently bred tuberculosis and other diseases. Prudencio
Rivera Martínez, the labor commissioner, who was also a
leader of the Socialist party and the FLT, explained that
the strike had not come as a surprise to the government,
because working conditions in the tobacco industry had
been steadily deteriorating. Rivera Martínez particularly
deplored the working conditions of the women employed in
this industry.

> The exploitation of these poor women has become
> inconceivable. They have to strip more tobacco for
> twenty-five cents than what they stripped before
> for the same amount of money. During these weeks
> we have seen long caravans of these women who
> walk daily long distances . . . from other towns

. . . to come to earn a quarter. . . . For sometime
now we have been suggesting to the employers that
some temporary measure must be adopted to improve
these conditions, while a final agreement is negoti-
ated regarding the codes of the Industrial Recovery
Act (Unión Obrera, August 3, 1933).

Seasonal work was another problem for the working woman.
Different from the plants in San Juan, in which the machines were operated throughout most of the year, the
factories in the center of the island employed women as
tobacco stemmers for only three or four months at most.
While for an average week of 36.9 hours in a cigar factory
the average earnings were $7.57, in the tobacco stemmeries
the earnings averaged $2.29 for a 44-hour week (Manning,
1934:26). Despite the intensity of the tobacco workers'
protest, the strike ended without much gained for the
workers. They were forced to settle the strike for a
nominal increase in wages, which ironically they did not
receive because the employers violated the collective agreements.

Strikes also erupted during 1933 in the needlework
industry, which had gained importance after World War I.
Contractors and operators in the New York area began
sending material to the island to be embroidered by Puerto
Rican women, the finished pieces being then returned to
the United States to be sold in retail stores. Puerto Rican
women working in this industry were grievously exploited.
During the 1930s the industry operated in Puerto Rico
through a series of agents and subagents who contracted
workers, mainly women. The principal corporation remained
in the United States and very seldom had direct contact
with the workers. Instead it developed a series of talleres
(factories) that received the materials and acted as intermediaries between the corporation and the workers. Many
times the talleristas (factory owners) were Puerto Ricans,
some of whom were women with enough money to establish
and manage a factory. A limited number of persons worked
in these factories since most of the work was done at home.

In order to distribute the loads to the homeworkers,
the talleristas contracted agents and subagents who had
direct contact with the workers at their homes and who
checked that the work was done. The agents and subagents not only earned a commission from the contractors,
but they also kept a part of the already low wages of the
workers. Caroline Manning, in her report on The Employment of Women in Puerto Rico said that sometimes the agent
kept "very little of the amount paid per dozen for the

outside work, sometimes as little as 10 percent, but on the other hand a few retained as much as 40 or 50 percent" (1934:8). Manning found that the average amount that the agents retained was approximately 22 percent. If the profits of the subagents are added to the profits of the agents the conclusion is that the homeworkers ended up earning just a few cents a day.

Wages in the needlework trades varied considerably. Workers were not paid by the hour but by bundles of work, and these bundles differed greatly in the number of pieces, types of work, and total amount of work required on the various garments. In 1933 an investigation conducted by the Department of Labor found that 19 percent of the women earned less than 25 cents per bundle, 23 percent earned between 25 cents and 50 cents per bundle, and 27 percent earned between 50 cents and a dollar. Two other factors have to be considered regarding wages. Frequently it took from two to five days, and sometimes a week, to complete the work in these bundles, thus making the abovementioned wages the entire week's pay. The critical economic situation of the needleworkers was also based on the fact that although more than one member of the family usually worked to complete the load, employers paid only to the workers whom they had contracted directly; therefore, they actually paid only one worker when in fact the work was done by two or three persons. These working conditions were aggravated by unfair practices that included payment in groceries instead of cash, delays in supplying work, delays in payment, and retention by the agent of wage increases.

Confronted with low wages and soaring costs of living, the workers' position became untenable. Only one avenue was left: the strike. In Mayagüez, the largest city in the western part of the island and the center of the needlework industry, the strikes turned into violent riots at the end of August 1933, as the strikers, mostly women, clashed with strikebreakers and police. On August 30, 1933, the needleworkers declared a strike in Mayagüez to demand higher wages for the woman worker: "[the workers] . . . have not accepted the wages paid by those that have become rich at the expense of the unfortunate proletariat who spent his life working day and night . . . to earn two dollars a week" (Unión Obrera, August 31, 1933). The employers' response was to summon the police to protect their property. The toll from the confrontation was 2 dead (a woman and a three-year-old girl) and at least 70 wounded, mostly women. The chief of the police argued that the use of guns was necessary due to the "violent and disorderly attitude of the strikers, who stoned both property and the police and also stoned Representative Arcelay's workshop. . . . We have had to use rifles and with great efforts have somewhat controlled the situation" (El Mundo, August 30, 1933).

The labor newspaper Unión Obrera reported the strike as Masacre a Indefensas Mujeres (massacre of defenseless women). The newspaper explained that the only crime the workers committed was to demand higher wages to avoid starvation, since by their work they enriched others. Based on the August 31 events, Unión Obrera predicted even more violent labor struggles in which men and women would join efforts in an attempt to improve their day-to-day living conditions: "Mayagüez's proletariat struggles have been baptized with blood and this is a sign of future actions. . . . Comrades of Mayagüez, fight on within the laws . . . but if those in charge of executing the law are the first to act unlawfully then each of you should take your own guarantees" (Unión Obrera, August 31, 1933).

Mobilization for the strike provided a favorable climate for the organization of the workers in the needlework trade centers. The FLT reported that in 1933 more than 75 percent of the factory and shop workers had been organized and that a campaign to organize homeworkers was in progress. By 1934 the FLT had already organized nine unions comprised exclusively of homeworkers, with approximately 3,000 members. In its annual report to the American Federation of Labor (1934) the Puerto Rican federation stated that the strikes stirred great unrest among Puerto Rican workers and that the courage of the striking women facilitated the unionization of many others.

> The workers in Mayagüez, mostly women . . . made a most courageous protest against unbearable conditions through a general strike. This gradually affected the entire industry. Through the cooperation and mediation of the Commissioner of Labor, who took charge of the situation at the request of Governor Gore, an agreement was secured by which the workers received an increase in wages ranging from 15 to 25 cents. . . . As a result of the strike, unions have been organized in the greater number of the needle trade centers (1934:170–71).

Women's participation in the needlework strikes of 1933 raised their level of awareness and increased their collaboration with other social movements. The strikes provided an opportunity for organization. After these initial days

women realized that they needed labor unions responsive to
their social problems and thus began organizing their own
labor groups. They also participated actively in consumer
protests and those of unemployed workers. Unemployment
had been one of the major problems in Puerto Rico from the
beginning of the century; however, during the 1930s it
grew in geometric proportions. Tired of unfulfilled promises from the Puerto Rican government, from the U.S.
government, and even from the organized labor movement,
the unemployed workers around the island began a campaign
to demand more job opportunities; and in these movements
women again played an active role. Women's participation in
the unemployed workers' movements is significant because in
part it contradicts the commonly held notion that Puerto
Ricans, and especially Puerto Rican women, like to live on
welfare and to depend on state assistance. In these protests the workers' cry was unequivocal: "we don't want
relief, we want work" (El Mundo, November 24, 1934).
Ironically, for the government it was easier to provide
relief than a decent way to earn a living. The workers'
protests fell once again on deaf ears.

One of the most important outbursts of discontent from
the unemployed workers took place in Mayagüez in November 1934. Approximately 6,000 persons participated in the
protests, one-third of whom were women who had lost their
jobs in the needlework industry after the NIRA codes were
approved. Protesting against the government's failure to
keep its promises, the workers rejected the state's relief
aid and demanded work (El Mundo, July 17, 1934). In a
letter to the mayor of Mayagüez the workers described the
city's state of poverty and pointed to the thousands of
workers who needed work in order to escape starvation.
The president of the Unemployed Women Workers Association
also explained to the island's governor, Blanton Winship,
the conditions of the needleworkers who were being evicted
from their houses because they could not pay the rents.
Again the government chose to disregard the women
workers' pleas.

Women's militancy kept growing at a steady pace, in
spite of the fact that many of their protests ended in
defeat. One of the controversies in which women participated most actively during the 1930s was the debate over
the Fair Labor Standards Act (FLSA). The act, passed by
the U.S. Congress on June 25, 1938, primarily affected the
needlework industry in Puerto Rico. Puerto Rican industrialists and commercial interests vigorously opposed the
inclusion of Puerto Rico in the act, particularly objecting to
its minimum wage provisions. The Puerto Rican government

readily supported them and soon Governor Winship went to Washington in an attempt to persuade federal public officials of the disadvantages of a strict application of the law in Puerto Rico. In contrast to the government's position, the workers demanded immediate enforcement of the FLSA on the island. On October 23, 1938, the Unión de Trabaja-dores de la Aguja (Needleworkers Union) held a meeting in San Juan in which delegations of needleworkers from all over the island supported the application of the minimum wage to the industry. By January 1939 there was a rapid increase in worker protests, mostly women, against the industrialists' maneuvers which were backed by Puerto Rican government officials.

The needleworkers were alone in their struggle. Neither the FLT nor the Socialist party backed their demands. Although seemingly paradoxical, the position of the official labor organization was to be expected in view of their desire to please their partner, the Union Republican party, in the government coalition. The Union Republicans, representing the big economic interests, supported the industrialists' position. The Socialist party, out of its concern to retain political control of government, failed to challenge its partner's policy and sided with the industrialists. For example, instead of presenting a strong case for the enforcement of the law in Puerto Rico, Labor Commissioner Prudencio Rivera Martínez, an active leader of both the FLT and the Socialist party, went on record expressing his reservations about the act. His position was closer to that of the industrialists than to the workers when he claimed that "industry has a right to operate normally without delays . . . and organized labor has the duty to respond to the industrialists on the same basis" (El Mundo, June 18, 1938). At a conference with United Press, Rivera Martínez explained that the needlework employers could not pay the minimum wages mainly for three reasons: (1) the unfair competition of Chinese and Belgian cheap labor; (2) the excessive earnings of the intermediaries who contracted with the operators and the workers; and (3) the high costs of packing and transportation. However, Rivera Martínez ironically failed to describe the oppressive living conditions of the needleworkers, such as their average wage of 2 to 5 cents an hour.

Tired of depending on Governor Winship's and the FLT's "defense" of the workers, various labor groups sought help from U.S. Congressman Vito Marcantonio, who had been defending in the U.S. House of Representatives a viewpoint contrary to that supported by Puerto Rican officials. Consequently, when Representative Mary T.

Norton presented a bill to amend the FLSA, thus making special provisions for Puerto Rico and the Virgin Islands, Congressman Marcantonio was the only one who supported the workers' point of view in Congress. Even Puerto Rico's official representative to Congress, Santiago Iglesias, himself a labor leader and founder of the Socialist party, remained silent and did not oppose the conspiracy against Puerto Rican workers.

Congressman Marcantonio began his defense of the Puerto Rican workers by disclosing Governor Winship's personal involvement with industry. Subsequently he exposed the abuses to which homeworkers were subjected:

> These chisellers from New York . . . brought their work to Puerto Rico. Then they gave the work to a contractor. Then the contractor gave it to a subcontractor, . . . and it goes all the way down the line . . . each of them receiving a profit from the toil of poor women and children. The poor woman at home receives the following pay: She gets as low as 3 to 5 cents a dozen for hand-rolled handkerchiefs of the best types. They retail for $3 a dozen in Macy's in New York. This means they are paid from 8 to 15 cents a day, and no more (Congressional Record, 1939:5,466).

As in the case of previous strikes and protests, the workers were the losers. An amendment was passed in the U.S. Congress excluding Puerto Rico from the minimum wage provision of the FLSA. The women workers of Puerto Rico would remain in misery, earning a few cents for a day's work. Meanwhile the industrialists, government, and the "party of the workers" had their day. By this time the workers had learned a bitter lesson: they could not rely on labor leaders and government officials to help them in their struggles. The road was paved for increased rank-and-file militancy and for the indictment of those leaders who had betrayed the workers by joining in a conspiracy of silence.

During the 1930s the participation of Puerto Rican women workers in labor struggles was instrumental in exposing the weaknesses of the leaders of organized labor. By their efforts the Puerto Rican workers had begun a new chapter in the social history of Puerto Rico. They succeeded in showing that the workers could challenge the leaders of their own movements, hence disproving the myth that the workers were only what their leaders were. In spite of defeats, they repeatedly fought the alliance of industry and government, and struggled to teach government a lesson—they wanted work, not welfare. These years were a time of growing awareness for Puerto Rican women; their participation in the labor force was a major stride in the road toward their conscientizaçao para la libertad.

Women's work and their participation in the economy of Puerto Rico certainly facilitated their engagement in political and social struggles on the island. Gradually, women also became active in the pro-independence movement and in other political activities. Nevertheless, in few cases did they become the actual major leaders of either the political movements or the labor organizations. Unfortunately, in the late 1940s and 1950s, with the takeover of the Puerto Rican unions by U.S. labor organizations, women had a smaller chance to become the leaders and organizers of the workers in Puerto Rico; by then even Puerto Rican men had to yield to the power of international labor organizations. Discrimination against women in the new industrial structure established in Puerto Rico after the 1940s has continued to increase; recently, however, a new awareness of the inferior position of women in today's industries is slowly developing. Women's struggles in the 1930s are being rediscovered and increasingly seen as the ideological backbone for today's action movements.

NOTES

1. In the 1935 Census (PRRA 1938) the following percentages of women per occupation are given: agriculture 7.3 percent (10,451 persons); cigar and tobacco factories 7.8 percent (10,770); clothing and embroidering shops 13.8 percent (17,986); home needlework and embroidering 35.8 percent (49,714); domestic and personal services 22.7 percent (31,462).
2. The Annual Report of the Puerto Rico Department of Labor in 1940–41 shows that in 36 sugar factories inspected, the labor force was 12,687 males and 22 women.
3. During the first decades of the U.S. regime in Puerto Rico, the production of tobacco experienced a noticeable boost. Free entrance into the U.S. market, in addition to large investments of U.S. capital, especially in the purchase of the processed product, and the development of new techniques of cultivation and manufacturing, increased the production of tobacco. Until 1927 the rate of increase in the production of tobacco was greater than that of sugar. Increases in the U.S. tariff, the mechanization and increased popularity of cigarettes, and the deleterious

effects of hurricanes made the tobacco industry decline rapidly after 1927.

REFERENCES

American Federation of Labor. 1934. Report of the Proceedings of the Fifty-Fourth Annual Convention.

Bernstein, Irving. 1970. Turbulent Years: a History of the American Worker, 1933–1941. Cambridge, MA: Houghton Mifflin.

——————. The Lean Years: a History of the American Worker, 1920–1933. Cambridge, MA: Houghton Mifflin.

Capetillo, Luisa. 1911. Mi opinión sobre las libertades, derechos y deberes de la mujer. San Juan, P.R.: The Times.

Congressional Record. 1939. Seventy-sixth Congress, First Session, 84.

El Mundo. June 18, 1938; November 24, 1934; July 17, 1934; August 30, 1933.

García, Gervasio. 1970. "Apuntes sobre una interpretación de la realidad puertorriqueña," La Escalera 4: 23–31.

Ginzberg, E., and H. Berman. 1963. The American Worker in the Twentieth Century: New York: Free Press.

Governor of Puerto Rico. 1933. Thirty-Third Annual Report of the Governor of Puerto Rico. Washington, D.C.: Government Printing Office.

Iglesias, Santiago. 1914. ¿Quiénes somos? (Organizaciones Obreras). San Juan, P.R.: Tipografía de N. Burillo.

Manning, Caroline. 1934. The Employment of Women in Puerto Rico. Washington, D.C.: U.S. Department of Labor.

Marcano, Juan. 1971. "Páginas Rojas. La mujer obrera." In Lucha obrera en Puerto Rico, ed. A. G. Quintero Rivera, pp. 66–67. Río Piedras, P.R.: CEREP.

Mintz, Sidney. 1956. "Cañamelar: the Subculture of a Rural Sugar Plantation Proletariat." In The People of Puerto Rico, ed. J. H. Steward, pp. 314–417. Urbana, IL: University of Illinois Press.

Pagán, Bolívar. 1959. Historia de los partidos políticos puertorriqueños, 1898–1956. San Juan, P.R.: Librería Campos.

Puerto Rico Department of Labor. Annual Report 1940–1941.

Puerto Rico Reconstruction Administration. 1938. Census of Puerto Rico: 1935, Population and Agriculture. Washington, D.C.: Government Printing Office.

Quintero Rivera, Angel, ed. 1971. Lucha obrera en

Puerto Rico. Río Piedras, P.R.: CEREP.
Rama, Carlos M. 1962. Revolución social y facismo en el siglo XX. Buenos Aires: Palestra.
Steward, Julian H. 1956. The People of Puerto Rico. Urbana, IL: University of Illinois Press.
Unión Obrera, August 31, 1933; August 3, 1933.

5

Feminism and Its Influence on Women's Organizations in Puerto Rico

Norma Valle Ferrer

Puerto Rico has had a considerable number of women's organizations, among which we still find the traditional civic and social clubs, service and charity groups, as well as those which can be considered truly feminist. The feminist movement in our country emerged at a specific period of socioeconomic development, the same as other feminist movements in the world, even though chronologically they may have developed at different times. In studying the emergence of feminism in different countries, we have found that feminism becomes an organized movement as a consequence of the Industrial Revolution, when women began to leave the sheltered domesticity of the home in order to earn a livelihood in "public" as salaried workers. Thus, in Puerto Rico, just as in England and the United States, the feminist movement dawns in unison with the birth of industrialization. Within the feminist movement in Puerto Rico we find two clearly defined currents: the petit bourgeois of almost exclusively suffragist trend, and the proletarian current, which believes in the total emancipation of woman as worker in the productive system of society, as homemaker and mother, and as a responsible citizen.

This paper was originally presented at the Symposium on the Hispanic-American Woman held at the State University of New York at Albany in 1976. Translated from Spanish by Susan P. Liberis-Hill.

BEGINNINGS OF THE FEMINIST MOVEMENT

By the middle of the nineteenth century, the idea of women's emancipation, as well as the idea of the emancipation of slaves and workers, permeated the educated and liberal sector of Puerto Rican society. Ignacio Guasp has the distinction of being recognized as the first defender of feminist ideals in an article published in 1842, which advocated that women be provided the means to broaden and improve their education. He is joined by José Pablo Morales Miranda, who advocated that Puerto Rican women fight to emancipate themselves from an unjust social tradition and to prepare themselves adequately to participate in productive society. The prolific and multifaceted writer, Alejandro Tapia y Rivera, also allied himself with the feminist cause when he condemned the attitude of those who disapproved of or considered the education of women to be useless. He repudiated the conduct of parents who refused to let their daughters learn to read so that they could not correspond with their boyfriends, and rejected the opinion of those who maintained that, in order for a woman to receive attention, be courted, and find a husband, all she needed was beauty and natural arts. He declared, along with Concepción Arenal, that women were neither intellectually nor morally inferior to men, and that women, in addition to learning all they could in order to be good housewives and mothers, should begin to study and practice the professions (Cruz Monclova, 1974). Salvador Brau in his essays, "Las clases jornaleras de Puerto Rico" (1882, rpt. 1972) and "La Campesina" (1886, rpt. 1972), became one of our most illustrious feminists by valiantly and honestly defending the education of the peasant woman and the female laborer, the creation of women's schools, and the general improvement of the status of women. Gabriel Ferrer, in his book La mujer en Puerto Rico (1881), although departing from a traditional point of view on women, also defended the moral and intellectual capacity of women, a position that, up to that time, seemed indefensible.

It is from this intellectual-liberal line that the first Puerto Rican suffragettes-feminists descended. Outstanding among which are Ana Roqué de Duprey, Isabel Andreu de Aguilar, and Mercedes Solá (Negrón Muñoz, 1935). All three of these women completed secondary education and one of them, Isabel Andreu, was a member of the first graduating class of the University of Puerto Rico. Ana Roqué, who distinguished herself as a teacher, writer, and journalist, founded various publications and organizations whose express purpose was to enable women to fight for their rights. In 1917, the Puerto Rican Feminine League (Liga Femínea Puertorriqueña) was founded and, that same year, in the name of this organization, Isabel Andreu presented the colonial legislature of Puerto Rico with the first summation in defense of women's suffrage. In 1925, a new organization—The Puerto Rican Association of Women Suffragists—also founded by Ana Roqué, took up the baton in defense of suffrage and claimed from both the U.S. Congress and the island's legislature the vote for the literate women of Puerto Rico.

Considered to be one of the principal figures of the Puerto Rican feminist movement of her day, Inés María Mendoza, described the achievements of feminism:

> The feminist movement has obtained for women, rights reserved until now for men. This was, by right, inevitable. It is not necessary to think of feminism in terms of the women alone, but as man and woman, both forming a social and spiritual unit. Feminism is not antagonism between men and women, but rather an intermingling to the fullest extent. There are differences between men and women. There is no superiority or inferiority" (Negrón Muñoz, 1931:14).

This is how the young woman, who at the time was a member of the Nationalist party and a feminist, expressed herself in 1931. In turn, Isabel Andreu defined feminism in her summation to the legislature in the follow way: "Feminist doctrine establishes equality between the sexes as a fundamental principle, equality in duties and rights in order to build a more perfect society within its ideology of liberty. Let there be no mistake, this means liberty, not licentiousness."

In the same country, at the same time, but as if belonging to another planet, the other current of the feminist movement developed in a parallel fashion, arising as a necessary accessory to the fledgling labor movement. Proletarian women, forced by their extreme poverty, inhuman working conditions, and injustices suffered by them as salaried workers, became aware of the common cause they shared with their male coworkers. Female laborers saw in trade unionism the device for waging their own struggle for the rights of women, thus they began joining the unions, especially in the areas where there was a considerable concentration of women workers, such as domestics, seamstresses, embroiderers, hemstitchers, and tobacco strippers. From within the unions they fought the battle in favor of the emancipation of women. The Free Federation of Labor (FLT) in Puerto Rico, a union which at the beginning of the twentieth century represented nearly the entire organized labor movement, was from its inception at the vanguard of the women's emancipation movement. Prudencio Rivera Martínez, labor leader and prominent member of the Federation, commenting during an interview on the results of its Fifth Congress, held in Arecibo in 1908, stated that "women's suffrage was formally discussed and, at the Congress, the first real suffragist Puerto Rico has ever had, Luisa Capetillo, became a prominent figure, but she never received any credit for this" (Combas Guerra, 1963:2). In 1919, under the auspices of the Federation, the First Congress of Women Workers of Puerto Rico was held on the island. Important resolutions were agreed upon, such as the creation of a national entity that would group all the existing local feminist chapters; the waging of legal battles in favor of universal suffrage; and demands for better working conditions for women. Within the Federation, the Women's Organization Committee was formed and presided over by the female tobacco workers' Genara Pagán and Emilia Hernández (Tobacco Union No. 453 from Puerta de Tierra), who presented to the Tenth Congress of the Federation a proposal to "establish a minimum salary for women among other measures" (Justicia, June 14, 1920). The Popular Feminine Association of Puerto Rico (Asociación Feminista Popular de Puerto Rico) was founded in January 1920 for the purpose of training female workers in feminist ideals and struggles. In explaining why they organized they said, "it is not only to obtain concessions regarding women's suffrage, but also the acceptance of all civil and public rights for women." Franca de Armiño, also a tobacco worker, headed the organization and continuously urged the workers to organize themselves into unions and fight for their rights against exploitation by the bosses (Justicia, January 3, 1920). In September of that year, Genara Pagán, leader of the Federation and the Popular Feminist Association, initiated legal action against the Joint Board of Elections of San Juan, demanding the right to vote (Justicia, September 6, 1920). This action could be considered as a precedent of the modern day "class action" suits that questioned the constitutionality of denying the vote to women.

Proletarian and petit bourgeois feminists in Puerto Rico were never to unite in their respective struggle for suffrage, which was won for literate women in 1929 and universally in 1936. However, female workers proved in reality the visionary words of Mercedes Sola to the members of the Ateneo Puertorriqueño in 1922: "What we have here, then, is the fact that work did not come as the result of feminism, but is, rather, one of its causes." The suffragist added that "Undoubtedly, it is means by which women enjoy the utmost happiness in life" openly alluding to the petit bourgeois women who could enjoy their salaried jobs, ignoring the fact that for the great majority of the female population work constituted just another means of exploitation.

Toward the close of the 1930s, feminist organizations representing both currents began dissolving. Women suffragists were named to official posts in the government. Others, like Ana Roqué, died disillusioned, since they felt that obtaining the vote was not the panacea they had anticipated it would be, the magic formula that would free women from oppression (Rivera de Alvarado, 1972). On the other hand, the rate of participation of women in the labor force was reduced, and militant tobacco labor unions disappeared with the destruction of the tobacco industry in favor of one-crop farming (monoproduction) of sugar cane. The framework of Puerto Rican unions also suffered a transformation which affected the organized struggle by female workers. During the following decades, Puerto Rico was immersed, and so were the women, in the formulation of "Operation Bootstrap," a program of social and economic reforms sold to the people with demagoguery by the leaders of the incipient Popular Democratic party. Many women were attracted to militancy by the "feminine mystique" that evolved from this party. One of those women ideologues was none other than Inés María Mendoza, then married to the party's main leader, Luis Muñoz Marín. Other women, however, turned their efforts to working with the Puerto Rican Nationalist party, which had women's groups within the organization.

A NEW STAGE IN THE FEMINIST MOVEMENT

The second half of the 1960s was one of analysis and revitalization of the women's struggle. The world was then just a universal small town, as the Canadian communications expert Marshall McLuhan put it, and Puerto Rico felt the impact of new groups of women who struggled all over the world for the emancipation of half of the human population with new short-term goals. The status of Puerto Rican women had by then changed considerably. By the second half of the 1960s, a large percentage had completed secondary studies and represented a third of the labor force and

46 percent of all government employees. In spite of this, and as exposed in the 1973 report of the Commission of Civil Rights, Equality of Rights and Opportunities of the Puerto Rican Woman (La igualdad de derechos y oportuni- dades de la mujer puertorriqueña) (1973), the Puerto Rican woman lives in a position of inferiority that limits and curtails her fulfillment as a human being and the develop- ment of talents to be offered for the benefit of society. She receives lower salaries, and does not enjoy the same opportunities for promotion and pay increases. Her educa- tional opportunities to prepare her for better paying occu- pations and professions are limited in the face of this disadvantaged position, which is the result of centuries of discrimination.

The Puerto Rican woman—now with new duties and responsibilities—is clamoring again for her rights. Strong efforts often disorganized, have become frequent in terms of divulging the problems surrounding the woman's issue. The traditional women's organizations still have some weight; and these organizations, as well as influential individuals at different levels of society, try to popularize the myth—some do it unconsciously, others very intention- ally—that feminism in Puerto Rico is only one more import from the United States. The commercial press in Puerto Rico, as well as in the United States and in almost all capitalist countries, discredits the movement toward equality of all human beings in society, describing it as a charac- teristic of sexual licentiousness and superficiality; and most of all, alienates the women's struggle from other social, political, and economic problems of the country. As is characteristic of Puerto Rican history, which has been minimized and ignored by colonialist propaganda, the histo- ry of women is little known. Therefore, the people are often easy prey to fallacies and myths concerning the women's struggle.

In speaking about women's groups in Puerto Rico, we find that some definitely exemplify these myths, in that they are superficial and lack the real values of humanity. However, other women's organizations are honestly commit- ted to the defense of the rights of women.

Women's organizations can be grouped under various classifications: service, civic, social, professional, and political. Under political organizations we include those identified with political parties, as well as those which perceive their role as political in terms of producing social change.[1]

Among the service organizations we include the damas auxiliares of the public health centers, the damas

voluntarias to different hospitals, and the U.S. organization, Hospital Helping Hands. These organizations
prepare layettes for low-income women and they visit the
ailing, senior citizens, and handicapped.

Among the civil and social organizations we include the
Club Cívico de Damas, Club Porcia, Club Sonta, Club de
Expresidentas, sororities, groups such as the wives of the
Lions (Domadoras) and Rotary Club members, and the wives
of doctors, lawyers, engineers, architects, and others.
The number of organizations of this nature is astronomical.
These groups once in a while hold a civic activity, such as
planting ornamental trees, delivering layettes, or collecting
toys for disadvantaged children. Most of the time, how-
ever, they gather to have a snack, lunch, or cocktail.
They chat and give free rein to the useless pastime of men,
as much as of women—gossiping.

Among the professional organizations we should mention
the Federación de Clubes de Mujeres en las Profesiones y
los Negocios, the Sociedad de Mujeres Periodistas, and
others that offer clear and painful evidence of the anachro-
nism constituted by the "wives" clubs, since at least these
women belong to the groups because of their own merit,
and gather to discuss matters pertaining to their professions.

On the other hand, organizations such as the Unión de
Mujeres Americanas (UMA), the League of Women Voters,
and the Puerto Rican Chapter of the Unión de Mujeres
Cubanas en el Exilio aspire to influence the country's
politics, and their effectiveness greatly depends on the
historical moment in which they lived (such as an election
year) and the individual personality of the president they
have, since their bylaws are often ambiguous.

Let us consider further these organizations. In a
personal interview former President Rina Biaggi told me that
the objectives of the UMA were: "the unity of American
women and to work for peace and friendship among women
in addition to developing the welfare of women in their
community." In spite of its postulates the UMA is characterized as one more of those superficial organizations.
Nevertheless, in the election year of 1976, its president,
who was an intelligent and enterprising woman, urged
women to "consciously" vote for the parties representing
the Establishment and repudiate labor disputes, student
militancy, and all radical change.

The members of the UMA frequently lobbied in favor of
bills presented by the government's body, the former
Commission for the Improvement of Women's Rights (Comisión Para el Mejoramiento de los Derechos de la Mujer, now

Comisión para los Asuntos de la Mujer). These bills were kept in the drawers of the legislators of the same parties that the UMA supported and often these bills were not even considered.

The Unión de Mujeres Cubanas en el Exilio once in a while gather to relive their memories of the alleged horrors of the Cuban revolutionary government as they enjoy a snack at the Casino de Puerto Rico, which is a substitute for the social clubs of the former Havana. During an election year they gain some importance since they serve as a warning to Puerto Rican women to fear the advent of socialism.

The League of Women Voters, composed primarily of U.S. women who are residents of Puerto Rico, is involved in legislative lobbying and in the orientation of voters through the different means of communication. They also support those bills proposed by the administration of the Estado Libre Asociado de Puerto Rico.[2] It is interesting to note how the traditional political parties of Puerto Rico—the Popular Democratic party (PPD) and New Progressive party (PNP)—use those women's organizations to gain their support in an election year or when an important issue is raised in the country.

Although it is not considered a women's organization as such, it is important to mention the Commission for Women's Affairs (formerly the Commission for the Improvement of Women's Rights), an effort of the PPD to comply with the campaign promises made to Puerto Rican women in 1972. In early 1973 a bill was presented to the legislature to create a commission that would contribute to improving the status of women and protecting them from the discrimination that they had been subjected to in the past. Several persons (including this writer) participated in the public hearings sponsored by the House of Representatives and lobbied in favor of the bill so that it would have some impact. The ambitious Law 57 was approved in May 1973. The governor of Puerto Rico did not appoint the members of the commission until 1974 and when he finally did so, he paid political favors to the "wives of," "widows of," "mothers of," and to elderly women who had given their best years to the PPD. It is painful to read the approved Law 57 of 1973 and comprehend the power that it would carry if fully implemented. It provides for the initiation of legal cases for women who have been discriminated against by private agencies and even the government. The commission has completed several studies and has released several publications since its creation. However, it has primarily become, in the practice of everyday life, another bureaucratic agency with little power and/or impact on the community.

Let us examine those organizations that we consider truly feminist: Mujer Intégrate Ahora (MIA) and the now defunct Federación de Mujeres Puertorriqueñas (FMP). The former had as its main objective "to help achieve a complete realization of the woman as a self-directed individual, capable of making decisions and incorporating herself into the changing forces of society with full equality of rights in all spheres of life." Among MIA's other objectives, the organization advocated admendments to laws and greater female representation in the political structures in order to combat sexist education and help raise women's awareness toward the problems that affect them (MIA, n.d.). This organization, founded in 1972 as a result of public hearings held by the Civil Rights Commission dealing with discrimination against women, gathers a limited number of women, especially students and young professionals, around what is called "grupos de concientización." Its membership and goals changed frequently making it difficult to follow the organization's course of action.

The FMP, founded in February of 1975, defined itself in the preamble to its bylaws as "a feminist organization, in solidarity with the struggle of women all over the world who fight for social revindication; an organization that will keep on par with all of those who struggle for a just and equal society" (FMP, 1975). The organization had as its top priorities the raising of women's consciousness and the struggle for women's rights, all of this within the framework of the problems faced by the Puerto Rican people. The FMP had within its membership workers, students, professionals, and housewives, who were considered nonpaid workers. It organized women from all social, political, and religious sectors of the population. From its beginnings the FMP held close ties with the progressive labor movement and clearly manifested itself as a left-wing organization. It participated in numerous international events through which it exposed the status of Puerto Rican women. The organization had considerable success in disseminating among the people its message of militancy for women's liberation. The FMP conceived feminism as a struggle between men and women to completely eradicate the prejudice that for social, political, and economic reasons, still oppresses women.

Some of the official political parties have women "helping" groups that are active during an election year. Among them, the Female Front of the Puerto Rican Independence Party (PIP); the Comité de Damas Populares of the PPD, who are generally disorganized and whose only expressed purpose back in 1980 was, according to Marta

Balzac, a leader of the party, "to bring Hernández Colón to the governor's seat"; and El Directorio Central de Mujeres of the PNP. The latter deserves separate discussion. It emerged in 1973 when a group of women declared during internal public hearings of the PNP that one of the reasons for the party's defeat in 1972 was that the women's talent had not been effectively utilized during the campaign. Since then, the PNP has emphasized the women's organized group. According to the secretary general of the PNP, Rafael Rodríguez Aguayo, the purpose of this female organization is "to work within the structure of the party, provide orientation and training to women for encouraging them into active participation in politics and into expressing their opinions publicly, as well as internally within the party." Rodríguez Aguayo also described the organization as "definitely feminist, since it has been crucial to the development of the PNP, it has worked in a special way without selfishness or personalism in support of a particular ideology." Hilda del Toro, a militant of El Directorio stated that its goal is "to orient the female citizen about the philosophy and goals of the PNP and the government of the Estado Libre Asociado." In her opinion, El Directorio is not feminist "because to properly fight for the rights of women would be discriminatory; instead, we emphasize how important it is for the Puerto Rican women to belong to the PNP (1976:8–A).

We have specifically chosen to examine this organization because it exemplifies clearly how women are or have been used by right-wing parties to perpetuate a political establishment that is clearly based upon prejudice, social injustice, economic servitude, and political subordination. During the 1976 election campaign the executive secretary of the PNP praised the participation of women in politics "without personalism" at the same time that the party was planning the elimination from the political scenario of the only woman candidate to an important elective post, Senator Sila Nazario de Ferrer.[3] Moreover, some of the women of El Directorio in their unconditional defense of the party, took positions that were clearly antifeminist, such as was the case of Hilda del Toro, who did not consider Sila Nazario as "qualified" to be mayor of San Juan and stated in an article published in the newspaper El Mundo:

There are those who sustain that in Puerto Rican politics the woman has always been marginalized. It would be unfair to blame our political parties or our institutions for this situation. . . . In recent times the need for political parties to support the

candidacies of women has been expressed. Personally, I consider it a mistake. . . . We are not
distributing consolation prizes or straightening
twisted paths. We are integrating the government
that will lead us during the next four years and
which will reestablish the prosperity that we once
had and have lost. This is such an important and
great mission that it does not need aggregates
(Toro, 1976:8–A).

These words express a desire for women to be militant
within the ranks of the PNP with the sole purpose of distributing the power to govern the colony to the men who
are qualified for the "very important and great mission" in
which the women could only be "aggregates."

The women of the PNP are not progressive; they are a
tragic example of how reactionary forces use women against
the progress of the people. These women have the degrad-
ing role of participating in election campaigns in support of
the party, which, when it wins the election, rewards them
with the "mop and the broom," thanks them, and greets
them again in another four years.

The leftist parties in Puerto Rico, the Puerto Rican
Independence Party (PIP) and the Puerto Rican Socialist
Party (PSP), believe in the integration of women at all
levels of the revolutionary struggle and their postulates are
feminist. They support the elimination of the total juridical
and economic structure which oppresses women and the
consciousness-raising of women, as well as men in the
struggle to eradicate not only de facto discrimination, but
also the male chauvinist attitudes that permeate our society.
The PIP reactivated its Feminist Front to carry on certain
tasks prior to the 1976 election. Previously, in 1972,
before the division of the party, the Feminist Front carried
on an effective task of consciousness-raising within its
membership, and a group of women prepared feminist publications of a real progressive character. Most of the women
of this group who distinguished themselves as feminists
have now left the PIP. The PSP does not have a women's
organization (when it was known as the Movimiento Pro
Independencia it did have a Secretaría de Acción Femenina),
because, according to one of its leaders, "we do not believe
that the Party should be divided based on sex, although we
understand that the women's struggle is a particular one.
Therefore, we have a body of women in charge of discuss-
ing the feminist issues and submitting plans for the recruitment, integration and promotion of women within the Party
as a result of the Second Congress celebrated in 1975."

In spite of the more or less clear theoretical postulates contained in the platforms of both parties, the practical reality still leaves much to be desired for women. Many militant socialists still believe that the struggle for women's emancipation is something isolated from the struggle of the working class and see the feminist movement as a divisive factor with a particular struggle. Individuals who share such opinions are the ones who are separating the women's struggle from its logical integration to the emancipating struggles of all people. The chauvinist attitudes that permeate our society also have their expression within the Puerto Rican left, even by those who could be considered as well-intentioned socialists. Nevertheless, anyone who excuses the exploitation of women cannot be considered as a true and honest socialist. For this reason, those individuals who have a clear position with respect to the women's issue keep alive the struggle for women's emancipation within the parties. There is an increasing interest and a genuine concern and commitment by some socialist women and men to incorporate into their daily lives the struggle to eradicate prejudice and improve the status of women.

NOTES

1. The author of this chapter has been in contact with almost all of these organizations through her work as a journalist.
2. The official political parties in Puerto Rico are the Popular Democratic party (PPD), the New Progressive party (PNP), the Puerto Rican Independence party (PIP), and the Puerto Rican Socialist party (PSP). In the political spectrum we can place the PPD at the right-center, the PNP at the right, the PIP at the left-center, and the PSP at the left.
3. Sila Nazario de Ferrer occupied a senate seat in the Puerto Rican Legislature for eight years. During the June 1976 primaries she was a PNP candidate for mayor of San Juan and lost to Hernán Padilla.

REFERENCES

Brau, Salvador. 1972. "La campesina"; "Las clases jornaleras." In Ensayos: Disquisiciones Sociológicas. Río Piedras, P.R.: Editorial Edil. First published in 1882 and 1886.
Comisión de Derechos Civiles, Estado Libre Asociado de

Puerto Rico. 1973. La igualdad de derechos y oportunidades de la mujer puertorriqueña. San Juan: La Comisión.

Combas Guerra, Eliseo. 1963. "Prudencio Rivera Martínez." El Mundo, 12 de octubre, p. 2.

Cruz Monclova, Lidio. 1974. "El movimiento de las ideas en el Puerto Rico del siglo XX." Boletín de la Academia Puertorriqueña de la Lengua Española, Segundo y Tercer Trimestre.

Federación de Mujeres Puertorriqueñas. 1975. Estatutos. Mimeograph.

Federación Libre de Trabajadores. 1920a. "Documentos Legales de la FLT." Justicia, 6 de septiembre.

—————. 1920b. "La Asociación Feminista Popular de Puerto Rico." Justicia, 3 de enero.

Ferrer, Gabriel. 1881. La mujer en Puerto Rico. Imprenta El Agente.

Justicia, September 6, 1920; June 14, 1920; January 3, 1920.

Mujer Intégrate Ahora. Objetivos, Propósitos, Reglamento, Posiciones. Mimeograph.

Negrón Muñoz, Angela. 1935. Mujeres de Puerto Rico: desde el primer siglo de la colonización hasta el primer tercio del siglo XX. San Juan: Imprenta Venezuela.

—————. 1931. "Conversando con las principales feministas del país." El Mundo, 22 de marzo, p. 14.

Rivera de Alvarado, Carmen. 1972. "La contribución de la mujer al desarrollo de la nacionalidad puertorriqueña." In La mujer en la lucha hoy, ed. Nancy Zayas and Juan A. Silén, pp. 37–48. Río Piedras, P.R.: Ediciones KIKIRIKI.

Toro, Hilda del. 1976. "La política, la mujer y el hombre." El Mundo, 11 de junio, p. 8A.

6

Female Employment and the Social Reproduction of the Puerto Rican Working Class

Helen I. Safa

By now, the role that women play in the social reproduction of working-class families through the maintenance and reproduction of the labor force is fairly well acknowledged. However, the contribution that they make in terms of paid employment still tends to be minimized. Women of working-class families still tend to be seen as supplementary wage earners, dependent on men as the primary breadwinners. This "supplementary" role has been used to justify the continued inequality in wages for men and women, as well as occupational segregation in low-paying, unskilled jobs in the manufacturing, clerical, and service sectors.

This chapter is an attempt to assess the contribution women make to the social reproduction of working-class families in Puerto Rico, a society that has undergone rapid industrialization and urbanization in the period since 1940. Certain features of the industrialization program in Puerto Rico, which will be detailed later, intensified the demand for female labor and women's role in social reproduction. However, since the Puerto Rican model of economic growth

A version of this essay was published in Women and Change in Latin America, ed. June Nash and Helen Safa (South Hadley, MA: Bergin and Garvey, 1986), pp. 84–105. Reprinted with permission of the author and publisher. © 1986 by Bergin and Garvey.

through export-based industrialization has been followed by so many developing countries, particularly the smaller economies of the Caribbean, the lessons from the Puerto Rican experience are certainly applicable elsewhere. This is particularly true now that the Caribbean Basin Initiative is advocating industrialization for the rest of the region.

Critics of export-based industrialization as a development model have tended to ignore the crucial role played by female labor in this process, both in Puerto Rico and elsewhere. With the initiation of Operation Bootstrap, as the Puerto Rican industrialization program is known, the rate of female employment increased from 22.1 percent in 1960 to 27.8 percent in 1980 (Departamento del Trabajo 1981:2). In part, this was due to an increased demand for female labor, not only in manufacturing, but in the service sector and government employment, which by 1980 constituted the primary source of employment for women (Departamento del Trabajo, 1981:4). More than half the new jobs created between 1960 and 1980 went to women (Departamento del Trabajo, 1981:2), while the labor force participation rate for Puerto Rican men declined sharply, from 80 percent in 1950 to 60 percent in 1975. Many of these men are disadvantaged workers, who withdrew from the labor force rather than continuing to seek employment. It was difficult for men to find jobs, due both to the decline in agriculture and to the industrialization program which made factory employment more available to women than to men. Heavy outmigration rates starting in 1950 often affected men more than women, particularly in certain regions (Monk, 1981).

The change from an agricultural to an urban, industrial economy displaced men from agricultural employment, but did not offer them a suitable alternative in factory employment, much of which favored women. This was particularly true of the garment industry, which has been the leading industrial employer on the island since the 1950s, employing over one-fourth the labor force. In the following pages, we shall pay special attention to the garment industry because of its key role in female employment and because it demonstrates many of the problems that the industrialization program in Puerto Rico is now encountering. We shall also examine the results of a study of a small sample of women garment workers in the western part of the island conducted by the author in 1980. By combining macro-level data with the micro-level results of our study, we shall attempt to demonstrate the role which women are playing in the social reproduction of Puerto Rican working class families.

MANUFACTURING AND THE APPAREL
INDUSTRY IN PUERTO RICO

The demand for female labor was critically affected by the growth and subsequent stagnation of the industrialization program in Puerto Rico, known as Operation Bootstrap. Started in the 1940s, Operation Bootstrap was an ambitious program designed by the Commonwealth government to alleviate high unemployment brought about primarily by the stagnation of the rural plantation economy heavily dependent on sugar cane, coffee, and other export crops. It offered foreign investors, 90 percent of whom came from the United States (U.S. Department of Commerce, 1979: vol. 1,21), tax holidays of ten years and more, infrastructure such as plants, roads, running water and electricity and, above all, an abundant supply of cheap labor.

Women provided much of this labor, though this fact has largely been ignored in the extensive research on the Puerto Rican economy. Many of the earlier industries were labor-intensive, such as apparel, textiles, and food, all of which employ a high percentage of women. In the 1960s, there was a concerted effort on the part of the Commonwealth government to encourage more capital-intensive plants to the islands, such as petrochemicals, pharmaceuticals, electrical machinery, and instruments in an attempt to avoid the high instability and low wages associated with labor-intensive employment. While this effort was partially successful, the garment industry remains by far the largest industrial source of employment on the island. In 1957, with nearly 20,000 employees, it represented 25.6 percent of total manufacturing employment in Puerto Rico; in 1977, with 36,200 employees, it still stood at 25.1 percent. "The employment provided in 1977 was 2.7 times that of electrical machinery, 3 times that of instruments, and almost 4 times that of pharmaceuticals notwithstanding the rapid growth in employment in those industries after 1967" (U.S. Department of Commerce, 1979: vol. 2, 31).

Industrialization transformed Puerto Rico from an agrarian to an urban manufacturing economy. In 1940, manufacturing contributed 12 percent of total net income and agriculture 31 percent; in 1980, the shares were 47.1 percent and 4.4 percent. In 1940, agriculture provided employment to 44.7 percent of the labor force and manufacturing to 10.9 percent; in 1980, agriculture had declined to 5.2 percent while manufacturing had risen to 19 percent (Dietz, 1982:5).

While growth in manufacturing increased nearly threefold from 1950 to 1977, it still could not offset the enormous employment declines in agriculture over this period. Even during the 1950s and 1960s, with rapid industrialization and heavy outmigration, unemployment remained at 10 to 12 percent of the labor force. Industry in Puerto Rico was severely hit by the 1973–75 recession in the United States and has not fully recovered. As a result, after the recession, unemployment in Puerto Rico reached about 20 percent, with the sharpest drops occurring in construction and manufacturing (U.S. Department of Commerce, 1979: vol. 1, 40).

Unemployment rates for men have risen more rapidly than for women, and in 1980 stood at 19.6 percent and 12.3 percent respectively. This largely reflects the fact, noted previously, that the industrialization process and other changes in the occupational structure of Puerto Rico have tended to favor women over men. In 1980, their participation in the manufacturing sector was nearly equal (Departamento del Trabajo, 1981:3) and even some of the newer capital-intensive industries such as pharmaceuticals employ large numbers of women. Jobs have opened up for women in service and white collar jobs, particularly in the burgeoning government bureaucracy, where women represent over half the labor force (Departamento de Trabajo, 1981:4). At the same time, men have suffered from the sharp decline in agriculture and later in construction, traditional sectors of male employment. Here we see how macro-level changes in the economy affect the demand for female and male labor.

Women have not been totally exempt from the effects of growing unemployment in Puerto Rico, but they have been less affected than men due to their concentration in sex-typed "female" occupations. As in the United States during the Great Depression (cf. Milkman, 1976:76), these "female" occupations in clerical, service, and certain manufacturing jobs have suffered less contraction than male blue-collar jobs in the same period. Nevertheless, employment has declined in the garment industry, the leading industrial employer of women on the island since the 1950s. The garment industry never fully recovered from the recession of 1973, when employment fell from 40,300 workers in 1973 to 33,900 workers in 1980 (Departamento del Trabajo, 1981: Table 1).

Part of this is due to competition from cheaper wage areas in Asia (for example, Hong Kong, Korea, Singapore) as well as in Latin America and other areas of the Caribbean (Safa, 1981). With an average hourly wage of $3.39 an hour in 1980, Puerto Rico has lost its competitive advantage vis-à-vis these other developing countries. If President Reagan's proposed Caribbean Basin Initiative succeeds, this movement of production abroad is likely to be accelerated, since much of the program is based on incentives to export processing industrialization. There is also some evidence of a twin plant syndrome developing between Puerto Rico and other Caribbean islands like the Dominican Republic, with the cheaper, less skilled operations being performed in free trade zones like La Romana in the Dominican Republic, to be shipped to Puerto Rico for final processing. Such a twin plant syndrome has proved eminently successful along the Mexican border (Fernandez Kelly, 1980).

Though wages in the garment industry in Puerto Rico are much higher than in these other areas, they are still considerably lower than in the United States. In 1977, the wage differential was $1.07 an hour, or 69 percent of the U.S. average hourly wage (U.S. Department of Commerce, 1979: vol. 2, 257). The goal of the Fair Labor Standards Act was to bring all industries in Puerto Rico up to the U.S. minimum wage by January 1981, whereas previously they were set specifically for each industry. Like in the United States, the garment industry is the lowest paid industry on the island, with an average annual salary per worker in 1977 of $4,885 (U.S. Department of Commerce, 1979: vol. 2, 46). Given the living costs in Puerto Rico, this is scarcely enough to support a single person, no less a family. Thus, we shall find that many garment workers in Puerto Rico have to depend on additional workers or other sources of income to sustain an adequate standard of living.

Growing unemployment has led to increasing reliance on federal transfer payments to sustain the Puerto Rican economy. With the collapse of Operation Bootstrap, Puerto Rico has become a prime example of an advanced welfare state, with heavy reliance on social security, veterans benefits, unemployment insurance, food stamps, etc. In 1976, the net injection into Puerto Rico reached $2,182.9 million, or about $900 per Puerto Rican resident (Dietz, 1979:28). Because of low wages, even the working poor are eligible for food stamps, and it is estimated that almost 70 percent of the population now receives some benefits under this program, which in 1977 cost the federal government $802.1 million (Dietz, 1979:29). Though seen as a subsidy to the poor, food stamps and other income transfer payments may also be seen as a subsidy to low wage industries like apparel which otherwise would leave the island. Federal transfer payments to the island accelerated rapidly after 1970, and had grown to 28 percent of personal income by 1977 (Dietz, 1979:69).

Clearly, the Puerto Rican economy is in deep trouble. While industrialization provided a partial alternative to the decline in agriculture during the fifties and sixties, it has slowed down considerably to competition from other areas, high wages (compared to these areas), high fuel and energy costs, etc. The Commonwealth government attempted to combat this problem by shifting into more capital-intensive industries yielding higher profits and greater productivity. These capital-intensive industries generally employ more men. However, these industries also do not employ as many workers, resulting in continuing declines in male labor force participation rates and rises in unemployment. The government also attempted to counter the negative effect of rising unemployment and low wages by offering workers a variety of subsidies, such as food stamps, unemployment insurance, public assistance, and programs in health, education, and human development services. While the federal government provides the major source of funding for these subsidies, the public debt of the Commonwealth government has also grown enormously, and reached 80 percent of GNP in 1976 (Dietz, 1979:29).

The crisis of the Puerto Rican economy has placed an even greater burden on women. The high rate of male unemployment and male outmigration left many families without a primary breadwinner, and women were often forced to assume this role. We shall look at the impact of female wage earnings on the household economy in the next section.

WOMEN GARMENT WORKERS AND THE
HOUSEHOLD ECONOMY

While garment workers cannot be considered representative of the female labor force in Puerto Rico, the apparel industry presents us with a unique opportunity for examining the long-term effects of female industrial employment on women and working-class families on the island. Both in the United States and Puerto Rico, the garment industry employs mostly women (90 percent according to a recent islandwide sample of workers in the International Ladies Garment Workers Union). Many of these women have been employed since the earliest plants opened in the early 1950s.

The data presented here were collected in 1980 on a sample of 157 women working in three different branches of the same garment firm in Puerto Rico. This firm was chosen because a study had already been conducted among women in the oldest plant and headquarters of this firm in New Jersey, and therefore offered interesting possibilities of comparison. However, our analysis here will focus on the Puerto Rican sample, with a brief comparison with New Jersey in the conclusion.

Because of our initial interest in long-term employment, the sample was chosen on the basis of length of time employed. Approximately, one-third of the 157 women interviewed were long-term employees, who had been working for the company ten years or more, starting between 1950 and 1969. The remainder of the sample were short-term employees, who had worked for the company ten years or less, being employed since 1970 (see Table 6.1). It was felt that ten years was a sufficient time for the effects of long-term employment to be evident.

TABLE 6.1 Total Number of Employees and Interview Sample Sizes by Length of Employment in Three Puerto Rican Garment Plants

Factory		No. employed more than 10 yrs.	No. employed under 10 yrs.	Total
Factory 1				
	Total	90	38	128
	Sample	23	8	31
Factory 2				
	Total	66	218	284
	Sample	18	43	61
Factory 3				
	Total	44	271	315
	Sample	11	54	65
	Total Sample	52	107	157

Source: Compiled by author.

However, upon analysis it appeared that length of employment did not appear to be a crucial determinant of any crucial variables in this sample of working women. In fact, length of employment is highly correlated with other demographic factors such as age, marital status, and rural-urban residence, which appear to be far stronger determinants of differences in this sample than length of employment. Thus, short-term employees tend to be predominantly young, single rural women, while long-term employees tend to be predominantly older, urban married or formerly married women (see Table 6.2). If we break the sample into three age groups, under 30, 30–44, and 45 and over, we can see that we are dealing with a full developmental cycle, from single girls still living with their parent(s), to middle-aged women married and living with their husbands and children, to older women, 65 percent of whom are still married and 35 percent of whom are formerly married. These stages of the life cycle appear to be a major determinant of the role women play in the social reproduction of these working-class households.

TABLE 6.2 Length of Employment by Rural/Urban Residence, Age, and Marital Status

| | Length of Employment | | | |
| | Over 10 Yrs. | | Under 10 Yrs. | |
	No.	%	No.	%
Age:				
Under 30 yrs.	1	1.9	68	64.8
Aged 30-44	22	42.3	29	27.6
Over 45	29	55.8	8	7.6
Total	52	100.0	105	100.0
Rural/Urban Residence:				
Residing in rural setting	17	32.7	70	67.3
Residing in urban setting	35	66.7	35	33.3
Total	52	100.0	105	100.0
Marital Status:				
Married	38	73.1	67	63.8
Formerly married	13	25.0	12	12.0
Single	1	1.9	26	24.7
Total	52	100.0	105	100.0

Source: Compiled by author.

Life cycle affects women's role in social reproduction at two levels. First, life cycle is a major factor in labor recruitment policies and thus strongly affects who is hired for particular jobs. Second, it also affects the way in which women regard their earnings and the contributions they make toward the household economy. The importance of their contribution must be measured against the contributions of other household members as well as other sources of income such as transfer payments, which also vary over the life cycle. We shall begin with labor recruitment policies and then look at the differences between younger and older women workers.

It is clear that labor recruitment policies in the apparel industry have favored younger workers in recent years. Thus, in our analysis of the islandwide sample of ILGWU workers, almost 90 percent of the workers under 30 were recruited in the last five years (see Table 6.3). This is also evident by examining demographic differences in the three plants in which this study was conducted (see Table 6.4). The oldest employees are concentrated in the oldest plant (Factory 1) that opened in 1952 in Mayagüez, a major city on the west coast of Puerto Rico. As might be expected, most of the women working in this plant are urban residents, and only one in the sample is single. In the newer plants (Factory 2 and 3), however, there is a much higher percentage of young, single workers, especially in Factory 3. Though opened at about the same time (in 1964 and 1965 respectively), the higher percentage of middle-aged married women in Factory 2 is due primarily to transfers from Factory 1, because of a slowdown in production in the latter plant. Since these plants are located in rural towns a few miles from the city, we might expect that their

TABLE 6.3 Age by Length of Employment for International Ladies Garment Workers Union

	Length of Employment									
	Under 5 Yrs.		5-10 Yrs.		10-15 Yrs.		15-20 Yrs.		Over 20 Yrs.	
Age	No.	%	No.	%	No.	%	No.	%	No.	%
Under 30	186	40.9	22	19.6	0	0.0	0	0.0	1	50
30-44	215	47.3	62	55.4	12	75.0	1	33.3	0	0
45 and over	54	11.9	28	25.0	4	25.0	2	66.7	1	50
Total	455	100	112	100	16	100	3	100	2	100

Source: Compiled by author.

TABLE 6.4 Demographic Characteristics of Interview Samples in Three Puerto Rican Plants

Demographic Characteristic	Factory					
	1		2		3	
	No.	%	No.	%	No.	%
Age:						
Under 30 yrs.	4	12.9	25	41.0	40	61.5
Aged 30-44	11	35.5	24	39.3	16	24.6
Over 45	16	51.6	12	19.7	9	13.8
Total	31	100.0	61	100.0	65	100.0
Marital Status:						
Married	20	64.5	44	72.1	41	63.1
Formerly married	10	32.3	8	13.1	7	10.8
Single	1	3.2	9	14.8	17	26.2
Total	31	100.0	61	100.0	65	100.0
Rural/Urban Residence						
Residing in rural setting	2	6.5	35	57.4	50	76.9
Residing in urban setting	29	93.5	26	42.6	15	23.1
Total	31	100.0	61	100.0	65	100.0

(Total Number = 157)

Source: Compiled by author.

employees are primarily rural. Many of these women garment workers come from outlying rural areas, rather than from the rural towns.

Why does management seem to prefer these young, single, rural workers? Facile explanations of more nimble fingers or greater visual acuity are clearly inadequate. Management says that older women complain more and are not as productive as younger women. It has often been noted that younger women constitute a more docile labor force. Why should this be so? What helps account for the difference in attitude, if any, between younger and older women workers? Can this partly be explained by their role in social reproduction?

The contrast will be primarily between young women under 30, who constitute 43.9 percent of the sample, and older women 45 and over, who constitute 23.6 percent. A comparison of these two groups may help us explain why management has such a distinct preference for young, single women in labor-intensive industrial employment, not only in Puerto Rico, but in many parts of the Third World.

Young, Single Women

The single women in this sample tend to be members of large rural households, consisting of over four and in 40 percent of the cases, over seven persons (see Table 6.5). As a result, there are often three to five persons working in each household, usually also in factory employment. The effects of this multiple wage-earning strategy can be seen in the relatively high family incomes among these single women, where over 40 percent of the households have annual incomes over $14,000 (see Table 6.6). On a per capital basis, however, incomes are considerably lower. Thus, in households where the daughter lives with her parents and siblings and contributes to the family income, per capita income never runs over $6,500 annually. Still, this is easier than supporting even a small household on this income, as we shall see many older, formerly married women do.

TABLE 6.5 Marital Status by Number of Persons in Residence

No. of Persons in Residence	Marital Status					
	Married		Formerly Married		Single	
	No.	%	No.	%	No.	%
1, 2, or 3 persons	38	36.2	13	52.0	5	18.5
4, 5, or 6 persons	63	60.0	11	44.0	11	40.7
7 or more persons	4	3.8	1	4.0	11	40.7
Total	105	100.0	25	100.0	27	100.0

(Total Number = 157)

Source: Compiled by author.

The decline in agricultural employment is clearly evident in the case of these rural households. Ninety percent of

our sample say it is easier for a woman to find a job than
for a man. Their fathers often worked as agricultural
laborers in sugar cane or coffee cultivation, before the

TABLE 6.6 Marital Status by Total Annual Family Income

Annual Family Income	Married No.	%	Formerly Married No.	%	Single No.	%
$5,000 to $7,999	8	7.6	13	52.0	4	14.8
$8,000 to $9,999	11	10.5	4	16.0	6	22.2
$10,000 to $11,999	27	25.7	1	4.0	4	14.8
$12,000 to $13,999	33	31.4	4	16.0	2	7.4
$14,000 and over	26	24.8	3	12.0	11	40.7
Total	105	100.0	25	100.0	27	100.0

(Total Number = 157)

Source: Compiled by author.

decline in this activity brought about by low wages (compared to other sectors), low profits, hurricanes, etc. Some
continue to rent houses or land, but few families cultivate
land, even for subsistence purposes. Most of these men
are too old to work, and live off their children's earnings
and social security, food stamps, and other supplementary
sources of income. In our sample, the households of
young, single women receive a larger share of nonwage
sources of income than older married or formerly married
women (see Table 6.7). This may be due to the larger size
of these rural families, the older age of the head of household, and other factors. However, it should be noted that
only about 20 percent of our sample receive supplementary
sources of income, chiefly food stamps.

The western region has also experienced heavy outmigration, starting in the 1950s, due largely to the decline
in male agricultural employment. In our entire sample, over
60 percent of the women have siblings and husbands who
have migrated to the United States. In a study conducted
in this area in 1977, outmigration is directly related to lack
of employment opportunities, which affected men more than
women (Monk, 1981). Work opportunities for high-school-
educated women are better than for men, particularly in
factory employment, and result in a lower rate of female

TABLE 6.7   Other Sources of Income by Age

Other Source	Age					
	Under 30		30-44		Over 45	
of Income	No.	%	No.	%	No.	%
None	32	46.4	35	68.6	27	73.0
Social Security	6	8.7	5	9.8	5	13.5
Food Stamps	18	26.1	9	17.6	2	5.4
Other	13	18.8	2	3.9	3	8.1
Total	69	100	51	100	37	100

Source: Compiled by author.

outmigration and a lower rate of female unemployment (Monk, 1981:41).

These rural peasant households are still strongly patriarchal, despite the man's loss of earning potential. As they marry, rural women transfer patriarchal authority to their husbands, who are still considered the boss in most households. Husbands often pay the bills and the wife may turn her paycheck over to her husband. Nevertheless, husbands tend to help out around the house and share important decisions with their wives.

Female employment is critical to the family's survival. As in most working-class families, women see work as a way of contributing to the family income, rather than as a way of establishing their own independence. Newly married couples commonly start out in the parental home until they have money to buy or build a home of their own, often on parental land. Although they may keep part of their salary for their own expenses and savings, women's earnings in this sample never constitute less than 40 percent of the total family income, and in a fourth of the households where the daughter is working, she is the sole support of her parents and siblings (see Table 6.8). Older women bear an even heavier financial responsibility in the household. Among female-headed households, all of the women living alone, and over half of the women living only with their children are the sole source of support for their families. Most married women contribute 50 to 60 percent of the total family income. No wonder most of these women say their families could not afford to have them stop working.

In these large, rural households, tasks are shared among all the members, following a strict sexual division of

TABLE 6.8 Women's Earnings as Percentage of Family Income by Family Type*

Type of Family	Percentage of Family Income													
	40-50		50-60		60-70		70-80		80-90		100		Total	
	No.	%	No.	%	No.	%	No.	%	No.	%	No.	%	No.	%
Nuclear:														
Woman alone	0	0.0	0	0.0	0	0.0	0	0.0	0	0.0	5	100.0	5	100
Woman and her husband	7	41.3	6	35.4	1	5.9	1	5.9	1	5.9	1	5.9	17	100
Woman, husband, and children	29	46.4	21	32.8	5	7.8	5	7.8	1	1.6	3	4.7	64	100
Woman and children alone	1	9.1	1	9.1	1	9.1	2	18.2	0	0.0	6	54.6	11	100
Extended														
Woman, husband, children, parents, and other relatives	2	18.2	1	9.1	1	9.1	4	36.4	0	0.0	3	27.3	11	100
Woman, head, children, and other relatives	4	80.0	0	0.0	0	0.0	0	0.0	0	0.0	1	20.0	5	100
Daughter, parents, and siblings	4	25.2	4	25.2	1	6.3	3	18.8	0	0.0	4	25.2	16	100
Daughter, parents, siblings, and other relatives	0	0.0	0	0.0	0	0.0	1	100.0	0	0.0	0	0.0	1	100

*These figures represent a comparison of women's earnings with total family income and may not represent the actual contribution made by these women.

Source: Compiled by the author.

labor. Young working girls, however, are often relieved of major housework responsibilities by their mother, who does the cooking, cleaning, etc. Such help is not available to older, married women, who often also have young children to care for.

Where children are working, parents generally pay the household expenses out of their pooled income. Judging by their possessions, these families are not poor. Most families have cars (now a necessity in the rural area), washing machines, televisions, and even stereos. Many of these consumer goods are purchased on installment plans, and over 80 percent of our respondents have debts ranging from under $100 to over $200 per month. Very few families have savings.

These rural households are part of tightly knit networks of kin and neighbors, who help each other out in many ways, including child care, house building, shopping, etc. Nearly all (96 percent) women under 30 have relatives living nearby, owing to a kin-based settlement pattern in the rural areas. Relatives frequently travel to work together in the same car, sharing expenses, and over 60 percent of the women working in Factory 2 and 3 have relatives working in the same factory. The first hired usually tries to secure employment for her relatives, but management has recently tried to discourage this policy, ostensibly because it contributes to greater absenteeism.

Most of these young women were hired in the past five years, and this is often their first job. Most started working between the ages of 18 and 20, after completing all or most of high school. They are very satisfied with their jobs and with their salaries, which averages between $120–129 weekly. (There is no salary increase with length of employment, but some earn considerably more, depending on piece work.) They have a strong work ethic, and do not complain about production cutbacks, problems with the union or management, etc.

If they lost this job, most of these young women would look for another job rather than stay home, because they need the money. Many of the younger, married women are now renting and are working to help buy or build their own home (still a tradition in rural areas, with one room added at a time). Although 71 percent of these young women consider themselves working class (see Table 6.9), they hope their children will be middle class and do not want their children, especially their daughters to work in factories. They generally think it has been easier for them to advance than for their parents, and think it will be easier still for their children.

TABLE 6.9 Class Identification by Age

| | Age | | | | | |
| | Under 30 | | 30-44 | | Over 45 | |
Class	No.	%	No.	%	No.	%
Middle	12	17.4	20	39.2	19	51.4
Working	49	71.0	26	51.0	15	40.5
Poor	8	11.6	5	9.8	3	8.1
Total	69	100.0	51	100.0	37	100.0

(Total Number = 157)

Source: Compiled by author.

Older Married and Formerly Married Women

Older married and formerly married women tend to be far less cheerful and optimistic. Many of them are employed in the old Factory 1, which experienced severe curtailments in production and employment in the 1970s and finally closed. In January of 1981, there were only 36 operators working, compared to 128 in 1980 when we chose the sample, and over 300 when the plant was at its peak. Management blames the curtailment on the unpopularity of styles in the plant and the lack of training of the women to produce other styles. However, the fact that women workers from this plant are offered the possibility of transferring to one of the newer plants where these new styles are producted tends to belie this argument. Despite a rather extensive building rehabilitation program three years earlier, supported by the Puerto Rican government, management also complains about the poor conditions of the plant, which has been subjected to floods, robberies, etc. Management gradually eliminated production from this plant entirely, retaining the building for offices and a storehouse, and moving all employees to the newer plants which still enjoy several years of tax exemption.

Women workers in Factory 1 are not happy about having to travel several miles to a nearby town to work, but many are forced to, because they are not eligible for unemployment or retirement if they stop working now. Such a move is considered reorganization, rather than a plant closing, which would entitle them to unemployment compensation.

Most of these women feel they are now too old to find another job, especially outside the garment industry, in which some of them have worked for nearly 30 years. They are very worried about job stability and security, and dissatisfied with the promises that management and the union have made them. Most of them feel conditions in Factory 1 have worsened in recent years, and are unlikely to get better. They complain strongly about production cutbacks, the union's medical plan, and other problems.

Older women are also in a more precarious economic situation, particularly if they are no longer married. Most formerly married women are divorced or separated from their husbands, and over half live in small households of one to three persons (see Table 6.5), either alone, with their children or other relatives. This limits the number of wage earners per family and, as we have seen, many of the formerly married women depend entirely on their own salary for a living (see Table 6.8). Since family income is highly dependent on the number of persons working per family (see Table 6.10), over half of these formerly married women have the lowest incomes of $5,000 to $8,000 annually (see Table 6.6).

However, older women who are married and whose husbands also contribute to the family often enjoy incomes as high as $12,000 to over $14,000 annually (see Table 6.6). Many of these men make over $175 a week and may be employed as managers or lower level professionals.

Most of these older women live in the city and are clearly more isolated than their younger, rural counterparts. Not only do they live in smaller households, but they have fewer kin living nearby, and tend not to socialize as frequently with neighbors or fellow workers than rural women. They often do all the household chores themselves, including paying the bills, and are very worried about inflation, which is eating up their meager incomes. In terms of savings, debts, and households possessions, these older women are no worse off than the younger women, except for some of the formerly married. In fact, a higher percentage of older women identify as middle class (see Table 6.7), but these are generally the married women noted above with higher incomes.

Nearly 80 percent of these older women have only a primary school education, which they admit has limited their possibilities of advancement. Although they believe strongly in education and have encouraged their children to finish high school and even go on to college, many say it is getting harder for their children to advance, due to inflation and unemployment. Many of the older women think

TABLE 6.10 Total Annual Family Income by Number of Persons Working

Number of Persons Working	Annual Family Income									
	$5,000-7,999		$8,000-9,999		$10,000-11,999		$12,000-13,999		$14,000/over	
	No.	%	No.	%	No.	%	No.	%	No.	%
Only 1	15	60.0	6	28.6	4	12.5	1	2.6	3	7.5
2 persons	6	24.0	13	61.9	25	78.1	31	79.5	27	67.5
3 or more persons	4	16.0	2	9.5	3	9.4	7	17.9	10	25.0
Total	25	100.0	21	100.0	32	100.0	39	100.0	40	100.0

(Total Number = 157)

Source: Compiled by author.

factory work is good for women but, like the younger women, they would not like to see their daughters work in factories.

CONCLUSIONS

From this brief comparison, it is easy to see why management might prefer young, single women as workers over the older, married and formerly married women. Young women are better educated, they work harder, and they complain less. As single women, they are not likely to be burdened with household or child-care responsibilities, which can lead to fatigue or even absenteeism on the job. Many come from strong patriarchal rural traditions, where they readily transfer the authority of their fathers or husbands to the company manager, whose word is seldom questioned. They are aware of problems in the plant such as production cutbacks, but they have not been as affected by this as the women in Factory 1, and they are more confident that they can find another job if they should be laid off, or given very little work. In fact, many of the younger women think they could obtain better paying factory jobs in electronics or a pharmaceutical company, while older women feel closed off from this possibility due to lack of education or experience. For younger women, their primary concern is not job stability but money. They need money for their parents, if they are still living at home, and for their future plans, which usually include a husband, children, and a new home.

In contrast, older women are more demanding. They have worked longer and have little opportunity of obtaining another job outside the garment industry. Therefore, they are very concerned with job stability and feel extremely threatened by production slowdowns and the closure of Factory 1. This could tend to make them more docile, but apparently among these older women, work has contributed to their sense of self-worth and independence, and to a breakdown of the patriarchal tradition still prevalent in the rural area. Thus, they are more likely to question management's authority and to argue for their rights than the younger, rural women.

Older women have more at stake in their jobs. In the case of formerly married women, often their entire livelihood depends upon their continued employment, since they are the sole source of income in the household. Married women at least share this responsibility with their husbands, and single women generally share it with a relatively large number of siblings. Thus, the contribution working women make to the social reproduction of Puerto Rican working-class households in most cases varies with their life cycle. Not only do older married women carry a heavier financial burden, but they assume a larger share of household responsibilities.

There are other distinct advantages to management in hiring young, single workers. They do not have to pay maternity benefits (which are quite generous through the I.L.G.W.U.) nor retirement benefits to women who are forced to retire before completing ten years on the job. The union benefits from this as well, since the larger the number of older workers, the greater the drain on the retirement fund. At the same time, by shifting production to the newer plants, management can take advantage of several more years of tax exemption, which has already expired at the older plant.

In contrast to Puerto Rico, in the New Jersey sample of this same firm, almost all the women were older, married, and urban residents. In part, this was due to the movement of production abroad, such as Puerto Rico, resulting in a sharp reduction in the number of women workers in the parent plant. Rather than firing workers, management followed a slow process of attrition, so that the workers remaining were usually the older, long-term workers, similar to the older workers in Factory 1 in Puerto Rico.

However, in the United States there are also more alternatives open to most working women, so that young women often shun the low-paying, unstable, jobs in the garment industry. Historically, the garment industry in the United States has attracted immigrant workers, such as Jews, Italians, or now Hispanics, who have fewer job alternatives due to their limited knowledge of English, lack of job experience, low educational levels, etc. Many of the older women in our New Jersey plant were second-generation white ethnics, who had started working in the garment industry as young girls.

Neither in Puerto Rico nor New Jersey do we find a high level of class consciousness among these working women, even the older women who have been employed 20 years and more. Most women in both areas still define themselves primarily in terms of their family roles as wives and mothers, rather than as workers. Paid work is still seen as a "male" sphere, despite the increasing contribution women are making to the household economy. In part, this stems from the nature of our sample, since the garment industry is a highly sex-segregated, female occupation, and much of the work routine in a garment plant tends to reinforce the paternalism of the patriarchal household. This patriarchal tradition is breaking down among older Puerto Rican women, but it appears to be due less to the length of employment per se than to the process of proletarianization accompanying the urbanization and industrialization process in Puerto Rico. While contributing to the breakdown of patriarchy, proletarianization also tends to isolate the family, break down the kin group, and increase the burden on individual women for the maintenance of the household economy.

It will be difficult for women to acknowledge their contribution to the household economy until their role is recognized by the larger society. Faced with an ideological contradiction between women's family and work roles, society has tended to emphasize the former since it still benefits from women's unpaid work in the home. This ideology also makes it easier to push women back into the home in times of economic contraction, or to use them as a cheap labor reserve. However, the increasing number of women in the paid labor force, both in Puerto Rico and the United States, is likely to accentuate this contradiction (Milkman, 1976) and eventually lead to increasing demands by women for equality in the work sphere and for recognition of the role they are playing in social reproduction.

REFERENCES

Departamento del Trabajo y Recursos Humanos, Estado Libre Asociado de Puerto Rico. 1981. La participación de la mujer en la fuerza laboral. San Juan: ELA. Informe Especial E–27.

Dietz, James L. 1982. "Delusions of Development: International Films in Puerto Rico." Pensamiento Crítico (Agosto/Septiembre).

—————. 1979. "Imperialism and Underdevelopment: A Theoretical Perspective and a Case Study of Puerto Rico." The Review of Radical Political Economics 11, no. 4:16–32.

Fernández Kelly, Patricia. 1980. "'Maquiladores' and Women in Ciudad Juárez: The Paradoxes of Industrialization under Global Capitalism." Mimeograph. Published in abridged version as "The 'Maquila' Women," NACLA Report on the Americas 14, no. 5(1980):14–19.

Milkman, Ruth. 1976. "Women's Work and Economic Crises: Some Lessions of the Great Depression." The Review of Radical Political Economies 8:73–97.

Monk, Janice. 1981. "Social Change and Sexual Differences in Puerto Rican Rural Migration." Papers in Latin American Geography in honor of Lucia G. Harrison. Muncie, IN: Conference of Latin American Geographers, vol. 1, pp. 28–43.

Safa, Helen I. 1981. "Runaway Shops and Female Employment: The Search for Cheap Labor." Signs 7, no. 2:418–33.

U.S. Department of Commerce. 1979. Economic Study of Puerto Rico, vols. 1 & 2. Washington, D.C.: U.S. Government Printing Office.

7

The Effects of Role Expectations on the Marital Status of Urban Puerto Rican Women

Marya Muñoz Vázquez

In Puerto Rico very little empirical research has been directed toward discovering and describing the impact of women's changing roles on the family structure. This fact plus the belief that this subject is of great importance for women's well-being, has led this writer to conduct some investigative work on the issue. Among the many possible options for research dealing with this topic, I decided to work on the conflict presented by the possible existence of a relationship between women's marital status and the expectations they hold concerning their role as wives. I hypothesized that women who are now divorced held, at the time of their marriage, a more egalitarian conception of their role as wives, and that they expected and expressed more demands for equality within their past marriage, than those women who have remained married. This hypothesis was based on the proposition that Puerto Rican women's expectations in their roles as wives had been changing in the direction of increased demands for a more egalitarian relationship with their partners, while the husbands' expectations still conformed more closely to a patriarchal pattern of marital relations. The two sets of different and contradictory expectations would, as a result, increase conflict in the marriage, leading to the resolution of the conflict through divorce.

The subjects in the study included 81 <u>divorced</u> Puerto Rican women and 81 <u>married</u> Puerto Rican women. The sample of divorced women was chosen randomly from a

universe of women living in the city of San Juan, who had
been married only once, had been married to Puerto Rican
men, and had at least one child, not older than nine years
of age. Married women were chosen from the same residential areas where divorced women lived. Fifty-one women
from each sample represented women from the lower class
sectors and 30 women from each sample represented women
from the middle-class sectors. Social class was defined in
the study by using residence as the indicator.

All women were interviewed with an instrument that was
developed by this writer to include four basic areas of the
marital relationship. They were defined as follows:
(1) preference—areas of marital interaction that have to do
with selecting, such as friends and recreational activities;
(2) tasks—areas of interaction that have to do with car-
rying out certain tasks such as cooking; (3) women's
personal growth—areas that reflect expanding personal
interests and freedom of choice; and (4) need for affection—areas of marital interaction that have to do with
giving and receiving affection. For each area of marital
interaction, the women interviewed were asked to answer
four questions which related to: (1) a particular situation
or event (behavior); (2) who made the decisions in the
particular situation; (3) whether or not the situation
produced conflict and the reasons for it; and (4) women's
preferred or ideal situation for each situation or event.
The interview contained a total of 24 areas of marital interaction, plus additional questions such as the one about the
reasons for the divorce.

The role expectation scores of divorced and married
women were compared. They ranged from an egalitarian
expectation (score of 3) to a patriarchal expectation (score
of 1) in their role as wives. A combined analysis of event
and decision questions was undertaken in order to obtain a
measure of the existing power structure in the marriage.
As the study was designed, the least power for women
(signified by a score of 0) meant that a patriarchal structure prevailed in the marriage; more power for women
(score of at least 3) meant that an egalitarian structure
prevailed in the marriage. Women's scores could reach a
high of 6 which meant that they had secured all the power
in their marriages.

The results obtained after interviewing the women
included in the sample did not confirm the proposed hypothesis. There was not an overall significant difference
between the wives' role expectation scores obtained from
divorced women and those obtained from married women, as
indicated by the analysis of variance undertaken.

Moreover, no significant difference was found in the wives' overall role expectation scores even when these results were analyzed in terms of social class.

The mean obtained by women, in answer to the questions included in the interview that yielded their role expectation score, was 2.3. Based on the instrument used in this study, it could be concluded that, on the average, the women interviewed held intermediate, leaning toward egalitarian, expectations in regard to their role in the marital relationship. Nevertheless, this average could conceal part of the present state of affairs regarding women's expectations in their role as wives. Other information gathered in the study might further clarify the interviewed women's ideas regarding that role.

Her subjective experience while interviewing the women led this writer to believe that at the present time, Puerto Rican women hold a variety of opinions and expectations of their role as wives. While some women expressed opinions favoring a patriarchal pattern of marital relations, others sustained beliefs that favored an egalitarian, or close to an egalitarian, way of relating to their husbands.

Some women whose beliefs mirrored those that can be associated with a patriarchal system would express opinions such as the following:

He won't let me go out, but it's O.K. with me, since it has to happen this way because he is the man.

He wants to help me with the cleaning of the house but I won't let him because people will say that he is "pato" (homosexual).

I don't let him take care of the baby because he doesn't know how and could let the baby fall down.

If a man goes out with another woman and when he comes home his wife starts fighting, he will leave again; if the wife greets him with affection, he probably will not go out again . . . then there would not be so many divorces.

Women who go out to work have complicated their lives . . . it is an obstacle to happiness and the best care of the children.

I believe that the best way to hold my marriage together is to withhold my sentiments and it is not difficult or hard to do so.

> There are women who want to be equal to men; women should be different from men.

> He restricts the way I dress but I please him because it is a way to show him that I love and respect him.

> It is men who need sexual relations.

Other women expressed opinions aligned with an egalitarian pattern of marital relations or in contradiction to a patriarchal pattern. Some of these were as follows:

> I believe that what makes my marriage a happy one is the independence I have gained through my work (my income is higher than my husband's); each of us knows that we are married because we want to and can decide otherwise; my attitude toward sex is very open and we had premarital relations before we got married; and I express openly those things that I do not like in the marriage.

> I would divorce him if I knew he was unfaithful.

> I hated the kitchen and understood that it was a responsibility to be shared by both; it became a symbol of repression and lack of liberty.

> If I got married, so did he, marriage is for both of us. Men and women have the same rights and values and there are men who forget that women are human beings like themselves.

> He would not listen to me, he wanted to be the judge, the prosecutor, everything, he was a tyrant, the "macho"; I like to talk in order to understand ourselves better.

> He said that bathing or changing the children is a woman's job; I believe that he can do the same things that I can do.

> I believe that if I work outside the home he should help equally with housework.

In summary, these beliefs and opinions expressed by

women throughout the interviews indicate that there coexists among the groups of women widely differing and contradictory views about the role wives should undertake in the marital relationship. These facts support one of the propositions Ramírez (1974) presents in an insightful analysis about the relationship between colonialism, culture, and the process of decolonization in Puerto Rico. Ramírez expounds on the idea that in Puerto Rico, cognitive, valuative, and ideological elements are found which maintain the stability of the colonial society. He includes among them an orientation toward authoritarian and sexual discrimination against women co-existing with other cultural elements that advance liberation—that is, a social order that promotes democratization of the sociopolitical institutions, economic equality, and solidarity in interpersonal relations. He also argues that sexual discrimination against women is being fought for the purpose of achieving a new way of relating between the sexes.

Ramírez further states that the cultural elements which promote liberation from our colonial modes should be studied thoroughly, as should the internal and external mechanisms of control of each individual, which do not allow the elements of liberation to emerge in our social and political behavior. This writer supports Ramírez's proposition and firmly believes that the study of the mechanisms which promote liberation, specifically the development of egalitarian relationships between the sexes must be considered a social priority.

In summarizing the data gathered from the interviews, it could not be concluded that a difference in women's expectations of their role as wives explains proneness to divorce. Nevertheless, the responses women gave to other questions that were included in these interviews led me to identify some clues about variables or factors that might lead marital couples to separation and divorce. One was identified as "power achieved within the marriage." The combination of events and decisions regarding those power-related events yielded a higher score for married women in all groups of events that were included in the interview. In other words, married women achieved more power in their marriages; they participated more in decision making; and they had achieved a division of tasks with the men which was more flexible than that obtained by divorced women while they were married.

The evidence gathered indicates: (1) that in some events of marital interaction, married women more often than divorced women (at the time of their marriage) receive help from their husbands in tasks such as those related to child care; (2) that married women's preferences regarding recreation, acquaintances, and so on were taken more into consideration than divorced women's preferences; (3) that married women's needs to communicate, plan the family together, and express affection were more satisfied than divorced women's needs; and, (4) that married women gained more freedom from restrictions within their marriage than divorced women had. Furthermore, married women claimed that they had more participation than divorced women in the decision-making process. Their participation was specifically in regard to recreation, budget, activities without the spouse, some areas of child care, family planning, communication, freedom from restrictions, and wife's self-improvement activities.

From these data it could be concluded that although there was no significant difference in the expectations about the role married and divorced Puerto Rican women hoped to achieve in their marriages, there was a difference between the women who remained married and those who had obtained a divorce. Married women had achieved more power; therefore, they had developed more egalitarian relationships with their partners, whereas in the previous marriages of divorced women, there was less equality between partners (although in both cases those marriages are far from real equality). Probably married women had achieved a congruence between their expectations in their role as wives and whatever goes on in their marriages. On the other hand, divorced women went through a process that could be described as an incongruence between their expectations and what actually happened in their marriages. In other words, they realized that their expectations were unattainable within their marriages, and opted for divorce.

What leads to this situation? How have those women who have remained married come to achieve more power within their marriages? The possible answer to this question is speculative, and further research has to be undertaken in this area. One hypothesis that might explain this reality is that sexual discrimination is currently being dealt with, not only by a sector of the female population but also by a group of men in our society. Men who have been inclined to change and put into practice behavior that helps them achieve a more egalitarian relationship are in accord with those women who expect to achieve more participation in their marriages. If this situation indicates a new trend, it is not often clearly evident to others. Men still have much to lose in terms of negative sanctions placed upon them when they openly express preferences for a more egalitarian relationship. For example, some men will clean the house or help out with their children as long as the windows are closed and neighbors are not able to find out about their behavior. If someone learned that the husband is helping his wife or catering to her wishes, he would be described as "sentado en el baúl" (the implication is that his wife dominates him).

This situation partially explains why some research data and other more subjective observations point to the fact that Puerto Rican men are still more traditionally inclined in terms of roles. After all, they have their "macho" image to protect. This may lead them to express themselves more conservatively even if simultaneously, behaviorally speaking, they come closer to conforming to their marital partner's demands for an egalitarian relationship. In the opinion of this author, this speculation poses an important question for further investigation regarding those elements that promote equality in men's expectations and behavior in their marriages.

The answers provided by women to the question inquiring about the reason for their divorce corroborate our conclusion as to the importance of the power variable in proneness to divorce; 41.9 percent of the respondents gave reasons to the effect that their husbands were too authoritarian or were unfaithful.

Another reason for their divorce frequently reported by women (23.4 percent of the respondents) was the fact that their husband would physically abuse them or frequently was drunk or used drugs. It seems that not only have divorced Puerto Rican women experienced the effects of subordination in the marital relationship, but they have also been the object of abuse and mistreatment from their ex-husbands. The latter was reported as a problem for married women in only 8.9 percent of the cases. The fact that divorced women gave this as a reason for their divorce, whereas married women reported that this did not occur frequently in their marriages, supports Safa's (1974) claim that women are no longer tolerating the abuse that women in earlier generations accepted from their husbands.

Deutch (1971) proposes that the most characteristic and important conflict of our time is the one that results between those groups that have considerable means of social and political influence and those groups that have little decision-making authority and little control over the conventional means of influence. The conflict arises from the increasing demands for more power and prosperity from those persons who have been largely excluded from the process of decision making, usually to their economic, social, psychological, and physical disadvantages. Deutch cites as examples the racial crisis in the United States, the revolutionary struggles in underdeveloped areas, and the student upheavals throughout the world. The data from my study point out that one of the reasons that marriages end in divorce is a struggle for power. It also suggests that we can look at this conflict within the context of that of those people who have been excluded or marginalized from the decision-making process but are nevertheless expressing what Deutch describes as "the growing recognition that social change is possible, that things do not have to remain as they are, that one can participate in the shaping of one's environment and improve one's lot" (p. 568).

This writer proposes that the facts presented here are in agreement with the notion that a group of women in Puerto Rico is trying to achieve a more powerful position within their marriages and are willing to enter into conflict and resolve it through divorce instead of remaining in a position of extreme subordination and powerlessness. Women stated, in 71.6 percent of the cases, that it was they who wanted the divorce; and only in 12.3 percent of the cases did both partners want and agree to it. Clearly it is women who are making the decision to divorce.

When it is stated that Puerto Rican women are trying to achieve more power and thus more equality, the question immediately arises as to what, specifically, is meant by more power and equality—that is, what will be used as a point of reference or comparison to determine the level of power and equality. It must be clearly stated that our conclusions are based strictly on a comparison of two samples taken of married women and divorced women in an urban area. This point must be emphasized because, taken as a whole, the data gathered in this study points out that women in Puerto Rico are still far from reaching an egalitarian relationship, and probably far from even wishing to have such a relationship as defined in this work (whereby the women would participate as much as the men in the marital decision-making process and household and child-care tasks, be able to determine the direction of their lives, and participate in activities of their own outside of the household circle).

The conclusion of this study which sustains that wives in Puerto Rico are still far from reaching an egalitarian relationship is based on the following facts:

1. Husbands, as compared with wives, make decisions much more frequently about the events in their marriage, with the notable exception of decisions about task events. This exception further supports our position, since doing tasks and deciding about chores has been traditionally an

area that pertains to women. On the other hand, decisions about preferences were on the average taken care of more frequently by husbands (40.1 percent of the cases) than by wives (8.0 percent of the cases). Decisions about the need for affection events were also, on the average, taken care of by husbands in 46.2 percent of the cases and in only 14.0 percent of the cases by the wives. Decisions regarding women's personal growth events were made by husbands in 30.2 percent of the cases and by wives in only 22.9 percent of the cases.

2. Household tasks such as cooking, doing dishes, and cleaning the house were carried out by wives in 90.8 percent of the cases.

3. Husbands, alone, never took care of the satisfaction of their children's physical needs, and in only 12.7 percent of the cases did both spouses take care of this task together.

4. Husbands initiated sexual relations in 81.5 percent of the cases.

5. Husbands in 73.0 percent of the cases were the ones who engaged in social activities on their own, much more frequently than their wives, who took the initiative in only 3.0 percent of the cases and both spouses, together in only 4.0 percent of the cases.

6. The mean score for the power achieved in the relationship by women is rather low for all women in the sample. The scale ran from 0 to 6, the latter being in the relationship by women. Subject's individual scores varied from a high score of 2.75 for need-for-affection events to a low score of 1.74 for women's personal growth events.

In addition we must consider that since it is the women's perceptions of the process that are being reported, there might be a gap between the power they perceive having secured in their marriage and the power they actually have achieved. In the case of women who are still married, they might view their marriage and their power position within it in better terms than divorced women viewed it.

A summary of the data supports the claim that some areas of marital relations are being handled in a more egalitarian fashion in some marriages but great advances still have to be made in order to achieve real equality within the marriage in Puerto Rico.

The conclusion that Puerto Rican women are still far from reaching complete equality, or even wishing it, indicates that a very important question is being left unanswered by data analyzed in this study, which certainly deserves to be considered. How important and to what extent is power a decisive element in the divorces that are taking place?

The evidence gathered throughout the interviews indicates that middle-class women have achieved slightly more power in their marriages than lower-class women have, although the difference is not as great for social class as it is for marital status. One hypothesis that might explain this fact is that men's expectations of their role as husbands might differ by social class, whereby lower-class men adhere most in their expectations to a patriarchal pattern of relations. Other structural variables might account for this difference, such as the economic disadvantages faced by lower-class women. In the sample a higher proportion of middle-class women were found to be gainfully employed, compared to lower class women. Research in this area which takes into account the socioeconomic variable, should be undertaken in order to answer some of the questions raised here in relation to the power variable. It is imperative, however, that any further research in this area consider the elements that may explain how women secure more power in marriage, which leads them to maintain a more egalitarian relationship and increases their likelihood of remaining married.

REFERENCES

Deutch, M. 1971. "Conflicts: Productive and Destructive." In Social Intervention: A Behavioral Science Approach, ed. H. Hornstein et al. New York: Free Press.

Ramírez, Rafael. 1974. "Cultura de liberación y liberación de la cultura." In Centro de Estudios Puertorriqueños: Taller de Cultura. New York: City University of New York.

Safa, H. I. 1974. The Urban Poor of Puerto Rico: A Study in Development and Inequality. New York: Holt, Rinehart and Winston.

Safilos-Rothschild, C. 1972. "Instead of a Discussion, Companionate Marriage and Sexual Inequality: Are They Compatible? In Toward a Sociology of Women, ed. C. Safilos-Rothschild. Lexington, MA: Xerox.

8

Ideology and Images of Women in Contemporary Puerto Rican Literature

Edna Acosta-Belén

The main objective of this study is to establish the relationship between the ideology of the group of Puerto Rican writers identified as the Generation of 1950 and the particular images of women reflected in their literary works. In order to establish this relationship, the historical experience that served as a framework for these writers' literary activity will be examined. Selected works by José L. González (b. 1926), René Marqués (1919–1979), Pedro J. Soto (b. 1928), and Emilio Díaz Valcárcel (b. 1929), who are the most representative members of the Generation of 1950, are analyzed individually and collectively to illustrate how the images of women found throughout their literary texts are an expression and an integral part of the ideological conceptions of a traditional patriarchal agrarian society.[1] Although the literary mistreatment and misrepresentation or stereotyping of women is commonplace in Western culture, and Puerto Rico is no exception, the work of the Generation of 1950 provides the opportunity to examine how women are fictionally represented within the constraints of a sexist ideology, during a period of rapid transformation and social change.

The first section of this study will provide a general overview of the theoretical foundations for the study of ideology in literature. Literature is seen as a translator of images that responds to existing social relationships within a particular historical context. The second section will examine the group of writers that is the focus of this study, their works, and their ideology. The last section will be devoted to a detailed examination of the images of women found in specific literary works of the Generation of 1950.

NOTES ON IDEOLOGY AND LITERATURE

The systematic treatment of the relationship among literature, society, and ideology is primarily a result of the emergence of Marxist philosophy during the second half of the nineteenth century and the application of its dialectical and materialistic principles of interpretation to cultural creation in general and to literary creation in particular. Through its overt adherents and its influence beyond its own circles, Marxist hermeneutics has proven to be an effective analytical method for the study of the individual, society, and cultural creations and institutions.

In the realm of literary criticism, Marxist criticism, or dialectical criticism, as it has been called, has gone much further than other conventional critical approaches to literature into the analysis of the relationship between the content of a work of art, and the world view or Weltanschauung of a given writer or generation of writers, and in understanding the artistic work as a potential expression of some concrete cultural, historical, socioeconomic, or political experience from which the work emerged as a vital response.[2] A dialectical-materialistic critical approach to the analysis of literary production, then, provides the opportunity for a systematic integrative study of the essential relations among literature, society, and ideology.

The possible functions of dialectical criticism are theoretically very broad and far-reaching, which makes it rather difficult to provide an analysis that comprises all the intricacies and complexities of the relationship among these elements. Hence, this analysis will concentrate on explaining only a portion of this relationship. Two main questions will be the focus of our discussion: (1) What are the principles underlying dialectical criticism that provide a method of interpreting cultural and artistic creation? (2) How can literature be ideological?

In all the fundamental writings of the founders of Marxist philosophy, Karl Marx and Friedrich Engels, the overall concern for the nature of art and artistic processes appears both in their most general philosophical categories and in specific references to art. Nevertheless, despite the scattered and often episodic nature of these texts, the fundamental ideas of Marx and Engels on these subjects emerge in a singularly clear, consistent, and coherent fashion.[3]

An adequate answer to the two questions that have been posed can be provided by extracting from the original Marxist texts, and from subsequent interpretations of Marxist aesthetics, explicit discussions about art and literature.

One of the central formulations of Marxist philosophy that will underlie future interpretations of artistic creation can be found in the preface to Marx and Engel's Critique of Political Economy:

> In the social production which men carry on they enter into definite relations that are indispensable and independent of their will; these relations of production correspond to a definite stage of development of the material powers of production. The sum total of these relations of production constitutes the economic structure of society—the real foundation, on which rise legal and political superstructures and to which correspond definite forms of social consciousness. The mode of production in material life determines the general character of the social, political and spiritual processes of life. It is not the consciousness of men that determines their existence, but, on the contrary, their social existence determines their consciousness (Ruiz, 1974:49).

This statement explains the essence of historical materialism and also illustrates that Marxism establishes a dynamic relationship between the economic base and the ideological superstructures of society, and considers all forms of social consciousness as conditioned and determined by the relations of production.

The dependence of all forms of consciousness upon social class relations and antagonisms is a fundamental tenet of this analysis. Since ideology is a form of social consciousness, it is inevitably shaped by class consciousness. Mikhail Lifshitz, who has summarized Marxist philosophy of art in his book The Philosophy of Art of Karl Marx, states: "No one is born an ideologist of a definite class; he becomes one . . . (1973:10). He also illustrates that all literature shows a class bias that is reflected in the work of art itself through different mediations and that can be independent of the primary intention of the artist. The artist will consciously or unconsciously express definite social attitudes and values that will directly or indirectly reflect the social relations and class struggles in his or her society at a given historical moment.

In a class society, the ideas that dominate any given historical period are the ideas of the dominant class. This, of course, does not imply that all the ideas emerge from the dominant class. Ideological changes from one historical period to another come as a result of changes in the socioeconomic structure of society as was discussed in Marx and Engel's The German Ideology:

> The ideas of the ruling class are in every epoch the ruling ideas, i.e., the class which is the ruling material force of society, is at the same time its ruling intellectual force. The class which has the means of material production at its disposal, has control at the same time over the means of mental production, so that thereby, generally speaking, the ideas of those who lack the means of mental production are subject to it. The ruling ideas are nothing more than the ideal expression of the dominant material relationships, the dominant material relationships grasped as ideas; hence, of the relationships which make the one class the ruling one, therefore, the ideas of its dominance. The individuals comprising the ruling class possess among other things consciousness, and therefore think. Insofar, therefore, as they rule as a class and determine the extent and compass of an epoch, it is self-evident that they do this in its whole range, hence among other things rule also as thinkers, as producers of ideas, and regulate the production and distribution of the ideas of their age: thus, their ideas are the ruling ideas of the epoch. For instance, in an age and in a country where royal power, aristocracy, and bourgeoisie are contending for mastery and where, therefore, mastery is shared, the doctrine of the separation of powers proves to be the dominant idea and is expressed as "an eternal law" (Freville, 1964:33).

The antagonism between old or decadent, and new or ascending classes plays an essential role in the propagation and prevalence of ideas during a particular historical period:

> For each new class which puts itself in the place of one ruling before it, is compelled, merely in order to carry through its aim, to represent its interest

as the common interest of all the members of society, that is, expressed in ideal form: it has to give
its ideas the form of universality, and represent
them as the only rational, universally valid ones
(Ruiz, 1974:72).

Changes in socioeconomic conditions do not necessarily
bring immediate changes in the ideas, values, or institutions of society. Neither does the social consciousness of
the diverse sectors of a society necessarily correspond to
the changes in social being, as explained by F. V. Konstantinov in Fundamentos de la filosofia marxista:

Old ideas and social theories, old concepts and
attitudes possess great vitality and are preserved
even a long time after the material conditions where
they emerged have radically changed. But their
vitality is not only explained by custom, but by the
interest of specific social forces which want them
preserved (1965:594).

This passage in Konstantinov is also essential for understanding the reasons why, in societies that have undergone
drastic changes in the economic base, the class that loses
its privileged position in society becomes the defender of
values and traditions which represent their interests and
embody its view of the world. Konstantinov further described how the spirit and values of a class are translated
into ideology:

Upon ideology and all its forms, the "spirit" that
dominates a class exerts a great influence. Ascending classes are characterized by their enthusi-
asm, their optimism and faith in the future. On
the contrary, the classes that abandon the historical scene are dominated by another spirit: pessimism, desperation, escape from reality, etc. We
can easily see how each of these spirits is reflected
in art (1965:589; emphasis added).

The influence of this class "spirit" as an element of
ideology explains the pessimistic or defeatist attitudes found
among decadent classes and how their ideological postulates
reveal themselves as incapable of including and accepting
new historical content. This explains their tendency toward
the mythification of history, their rejection of the present,
and idealization of the past.
The Italian critic Umberto Barbaro has described how

the social classes and their struggles are behind the ideo-logical forms and the possible conflicts within the super-structure during diverse periods of history. He establishes that various artistic ideas and manifestations consciously or unconsciously reflect this class character, and divides class character into two main thrusts: "the class in power, which serves, and tends to affirm and consolidate in the super-structure, the existing structure, and in art, to exalt it, liquidating the residue of past ideology and past struc-tures; and the opposition, which criticizes it, struggles against it, and tends to overturn it" (Lang and Williams, 1972:167). Barbaro also defines this ideological antagonism as being fundamentally a class antagonism: "The battles between various artistic currents, new styles against old, new forms against old, can in sum almost always be traced to this antagonism, which is not always conscious in its authors, but is always profound and substantial" (168). Thus, ideology serves to represent and affirm the values and traditions of a class and its respective view of the world or conception of reality.

THE WRITERS, THEIR WORKS, AND THEIR IDEAS

The group of writers that is the focus of this study was first identified as la generación del 40 by Concha Meléndez, the first critic to study their works.[4] Subsequently, other literary critics—Paul J. Cooke, Seymour Menton, Josefina Rivera de Alvarez—and one of the writers of the gen-eration, Emilio Díaz Valcárcel, would also refer to it in their writings as the Generation of 1940.

It was René Marqués who first referred to the members of his generation as la promoción del 40 in his essays. Subsequently, José Luis González and Pedro J. Soto, two other writers associated with this generation, chose to identify themselves as members of the Generation of 1950.[5] Soto, in attempting to clarify this generational confusion, explains why the name Generation of 1950 would be more accurate than that of Generation (or promoción) of 1940.

> The carelessness in the proofreading, or his own confusion regarding terminology has made René [Marqués] interchange the words "promotion and generation," and as a result, he often talks about a Promotion of 1940 and at other times, about a Generation of 1940. This group of writers was in its formative stage at the time in which the Popular Party came into power [1940], but they initiated

their artistic endeavors during the period of the
establishment of the Commonwealth [1952]. During
the 1940s, only books by Jose Luis González [1943,
1945, 1948] and Abelardo Díaz Alfaro [1948] were
published. The bulk of this group of writers
became known after 1950; first René, and they all
form part of a group of artists born during the
decade of the 1920s (Soto, 1973a:71; brackets
added).

Soto's considerations cannot be ignored, since he is
correct in pointing out the periods of artistic formation,
age, dates of publication, and the historical period that
would influence the writings of this group—all considered to
be essential factors in defining a generation of writers.

Robert Escarpit, in his Sociología de la literatura,
provides a general basis for the identification of a generation of writers that could very well be used in supporting Soto's argument as to the appropriateness of the name
Generation of 1950:

When we speak about a generation of writers, the
significant factor cannot be a birth date or the fact
of reaching twenty years of age. One is not born
a writer, one becomes one and that is not likely to
happen by the age of twenty. The notion of generation which attracts us may not be absolutely
clear. It would be better to substitute it with the
notion of a "team" which is more flexible and organic. A team is the group of writers of all ages
(although with a predominant age) who at a given
time and as a result of certain events, dominate the
literary scene and consciously or unconsciously
restrict access to it (1971:36–37).

Taking into consideration the historical forces and
events described by Soto that influenced the writers in
question, and Escarpit's generational framework, the term
Generation of 1950 seems the most appropriate to identify
them.[6] Many of the commonalities and coincidences among
this group have been extensively pointed out by the critics. In this chapter, we will only concentrate on those
areas related to the portrayal of women as literary characters.

The Generation of 1950 expanded upon some of the
themes that were elaborated upon by earlier generations of
writers, and also introduced new ones. However, the
particular social and political realities of Puerto Rico as a

colony of the United States continued to be the prevalent feature of the literature of this period. Just like the generation of writers that preceded them, the Generation of 1950 represents a continuity of a defensive cultural nationalism which has become the major intellectual weapon against the U.S. presence on the island. It has been a common approach for Puerto Rican writers, both in fiction and nonfiction, to view any internal social or ideological conflicts on the island in reference to the colonial situation and define lo puertorriqueño (that which is Puerto Rican) as a homogeneous and monolithic entity which embodies the traditions, ideas, and value systems prevalent in Puerto Rico before the U.S. took over the island.

The national culture has been traditionally defined from the perspective or Weltanschauung of the old hacendado bourgeoisie which was displaced from its hegemonic position in Puerto Rican society by the U.S. invader. This class views the world as one based on patriarchal and seignorial relations of deference.[7] Within this framework women occupy a clear subordinate position to men, are limited to their roles as mothers, wives, and daughters, and are valued or judged by their moral behavior according to standards imposed by men.

A literature that reflected anti-American sentiments started to develop in Puerto Rico a few years after the U.S. takeover. With the U.S. occupation of the island came the large sugar and tobacco corporations that gradually monopolized the island's economy. The creole hacendado class began to be affected by the U.S. control of the economy, a control that proved to be detrimental to the native hacienda economy (Quintero Rivera, 1976). The U.S. economic and political control of the island eventually led to the destruction of the hacienda economy during the first decades of the twentieth century and in later years with the processes of industrialization and urbanization, to the disappearance of the agrarian way of life.

Since industrialization completely changed the socio-economic base of Puerto Rican society during the late 1940s and 1950s, the structures of the old patriarchal and seignorial agrarian society began to be replaced. In their literary works, the writers of the Generation of 1950 have viewed these drastic changes as negative, and expressed the alienating effects of technological modernization and industrial capitalism, as well as the detrimental impact of U.S. domination on the cultural identity and life of the Puerto Rican people. The defense of traditional and patriarchal values associated with the agrarian world of the past, and rejection of U.S. values became the way of expressing the writers' ideological commitment to the national liberation of Puerto Rico from its colonial bond.

The writers' political concern with the political status of Puerto Rico is central to the literature of the period, although most of them had not had any active involvement or participation in the independence movement.[8] This was noted by René Marqués when he first published Cuentos puertorriqueños de hoy (1959; rpt. 1971), an anthology to introduce the writers of his generation:

> With the exception of José Luis González, an active Marxist for a good number of years, the short story writers represented here keep themselves more or less at the margin of party struggles. They are not obviously committed to any island faction. The majority put forth their ideals with agressive independence, without yielding to the rigid discipline of a party. The minority feel allergic to, or perhaps disgusted at, the mere mention of the word "politics" (1971:29).

Marqués himself, however, had defined the role of the Puerto Rican writer in political terms in his essay "The Role of the Puerto Rican Writer Today":

> Puerto Rico has been for centuries and still is a colony. The fundamental problem of a person in a colonial situation is freedom. The writer, a lover of freedom because of his very condition as a creator, and inhabitant of a colony, will naturally identify with every movement of political emancipation. This, in our case, is not a mere theory, or an unrealized desire, but historical fact (1966:220).

Although the writers of the Generation of 1950 were not involved in any sectarian political struggles they nevertheless defended the ideal of independence through their literary works. This ideological commitment was emphasized not only by Marqués but also by Manuel Maldonado Denis (1969), who has argued that Puerto Rican writers from various generations have carried on a struggle against U.S. colonial domination through their writings.

What gives the group of writers that constitute the Generation of 1950 its sense of being a "team" during this specific period in Puerto Rican history is the collective worldview that they share. Marqués must be credited with being the first one to recognize some of these commonalities. He emphasized the pessimistic and defeatist character of the literature of his generation—a fact that, as he saw it, did not mesh with the political and economic optimism prevalent on the island during the 1950s. In searching for the roots of the contradiction, he developed the concept of the collective docility and defeatism of the Puerto Rican personality. In doing so he often resorts to questionable, idealistic, and pseudoscientific reasons:

> On the one hand there was a heritage of fatalism from three groups: The Taino Indian (which has chronological priority but does not act as decisively as the others), the Spanish, and the African. On the other, were the four centuries of colonialism and hardship experienced by Puerto Rico in its uncomfortable insular setting (1966:64).

Among other general characteristics of the literature of his generation, Marqués also emphasized what he described as an unfavorable image of the Puerto Rican woman as a literary character. He recognized this tendency in his own work and that of his contemporaries.

In his essay "El cuento puertorriqueño en la promoción del 40," Marqués begins by pointing out the importance of women in the literature of his generation, in contrast with the absence of female characters in previous generations:

> There is a significant fact: the appearance of women as protagonists in the new literature. The dramatists and the prose fiction writers . . . seem able to create feminine characterizations of tragic intensity and psychological depth. Until then, the female character had been no more than a secondary figure in our literature (1966:89).

He continues to explain the more evident presence of women in the literature of his generation from the perspective of the changes that had taken place in Puerto Rican society:

> The Puerto Rican feminist movement had already obtained political equality, but it had not been able—nor had it actually asked or attempted—to destroy the established social and cultural structure. It was in the forties that Puerto Rican society made a rapid turn toward the Anglo-Saxon style matriarchy. The cultural and ethical patterns of a social structure based on the tradition of the pater familias rapidly deteriorated . . . (1966:89).

It is evident from these words that Marqués attributed to the feminist movement the destruction of what he defines as "the established social and cultural structure"—that is, those values associated with the agrarian patriarchal structure. He concludes that "this may explain why the female frequently has a prominent role in the literature of today and . . . why she does not always appear in a flattering light" (1966:89).

The political changes, material progress, and "modernization" of Puerto Rico during the 1950s was rejected by Marqués as well as the other writers of his generation. In opposition to what they saw as the infiltration of U.S. values and ways of life, they emphasized patriotism and nationalism, and either longed nostalgically for the world of the past, or depicted the tragedy, anguish, and alienation of Puerto Ricans in their new, adulterated world. The changes that occur in the traditional role of the Puerto Rican woman and her more visible role in society as a result of industrialization and modernization are simplistically viewed as a direct consequence of a harmful U.S. influence and adoption of an Anglo-Saxon-style matriarchy. This is translated into the prevalence of a stereotyped or negative image of the woman as a literary character, especially when she does not conform to or breaks away from her traditional role of subordination.

In summary, all of the changes that have occurred in modern Puerto Rico (changes that are irreversible) are seen primarily as products of Americanization. Writers frequently express impotence to stop these changes and assume a critical position toward this new reality. Their ideology, therefore, expresses a mythification of historical reality. Hence, the ideology of the Generation of 1950 rejects or is critical of the present, and idealizes the preservation of a past tradition and way of life as a way of reconciliation. It is not surprising to find then that pessimism, violence, and tragedy occupy a common place in the literature of this generation.

IMAGES OF WOMEN IN LITERATURE

The works of José Luis González established him as the initiator of the Generation of 1950 since they represented literary innovation, and would serve as models to be followed by his contemporaries. His books En la sombra (1945b), Cinco cuentos de sangre (1945a), El hombre en la calle (1948), Paisa (1950), and En este lado (1964) represent a transition from a narrative that focused on the life of the rural peasant to one centered on the life of the urban proletariat.

González's first two books, En la sombra and Cinco cuentos de sangre, deal with Puerto Rican rural life during those critical years when the agrarian society had succumbed to the domination of the U.S. sugar and tobacco corporations. The stories in general emphasize the poverty, ignorance, exploitation, and moral deterioration faced by the Puerto Rican peasant. As a Marxist, González's primary intention in these works is to denounce those conditions. In his first book of short stories the characterizations are generally weak, and literary types or flat characters and Manichean situations (poor vs. rich, Puerto Rican vs. American) are prevalent. Women characters play a secondary role and are often presented in very traditional situations: as subordinate to the man's authority or as the cause of the man's tragedy. Some of the best examples are to be found in stories such as "La mujer" and "Breve historia de un hacha" (1945a), in which the author portrays the peasant woman as one who violates the established moral values by giving in to man's lust, getting pregnant, and bringing dishonor to the family. In both instances the father figure in the story assumes the traditional role of defender of the family's honor and is the one who must resort to vengeance by killing the daughter's lover, in order to restore the family's dignity. Patriarchal values of honor and dignity are related to the man, while the woman disgraces herself and the family by losing her virginity outside the sanctity of marriage. In the case of "Breve historia" the woman is seduced by a U.S. soldier.

González's third book, El hombre en la calle (1948), shifts the setting from a rural to an urban environment, trying to capture a world that gradually becomes less rural and more urban. The social commitment of the author to portraying the life of the oppressed and underprivileged is prevalent, and the images of women are basically similar to those found in his first books. Stories such as "La esperanza" and "La hora mala" are again examples of man's disgrace brought upon him by a woman. In both stories the daughter of the family can no longer take the poverty of the country and leaves for the city, where she becomes a prostitute. The brother is forced to assume the role of the defender of the family's honor, which has been disgraced by his sister, and once again resorts to violence to vindicate the family's dignity. Other stories, such as "Un hombre" and "Encrucijada" (1964), deal with the same problem from the perspective of the marital relationship and the problem of infidelity. The woman is presented as the unfaithful one, while the man attempts to vindicate his honor, and finds violence and tragedy.

The stories "Despojo" and "La galería" (1964) present many aspects of the woman's uselessness in the lower and upper socioeconomic classes, respectively, in matters that affect the family, but occur outside the home, and for which the man has to assume the responsibility and burden. In "Despojo," for example, the wife, María, is unable to help her husband José when he is evicted from his land by the capitalist corporation that took over the cane fields. Her uselessness is described by González in the final scene: "María, his wife stood silently beside him like a docile domestic animal." In the story "La galería," Carmencita, the daughter of an hacendado, is presented as a flirtatious and insensitive woman.

Even in more recent short stories from the collection Mambrú se fue a la guerra (1972), we find stories like "La tercera llamada," in which a man abandons his wife after 20 years of marriage because he is finally fed up with her constant nagging.

It is in the works of René Marqués, however, that a negative image of woman is most evident, perhaps because women characters have played a pervading place in his writing. In spite of the multifaceted nature of his literary activity, certain prevalent types of women characters are found throughout his plays, as well as in the rest of his works. It is common to find in Marqués' work a relation-ship between his particular view of women and his concern with the political status of Puerto Rico.

The two works that exemplify Marqués' image of the modern Puerto Rican woman are the story "En la popa hay un cuerpo reclinado," included in the collection En una ciudad llamada San Juan (1960; rpt. 1970a), and the play Un niño azul para esa sombra (1959; rpt. 1970e).

In "En la popa hay un cuerpo reclinado" Marqués tries to present the feelings of a man who is unable to find any meaning in life because of what he considers his wife's usurpation of his role as a man. The wife is presented as an individual who makes unrealistic demands on her hus-band for material objects and belittles him for not being able to provide her with all the things she wants. She represents for Marqués a symbol of the new Puerto Rican middle-class consumer:

Nobody can live without television, darling, Nobody can.

Don't you have any shame or pride darling? Decent

people today live in the new housing developments, but we . . .

You know, darling, a real man gives his wife the things she doesn't have (1970a:142, 145, 149).

In addition to the obvious characteristics of the domineering or castrating female seen in these passages, another dimension of antifeminism is evident: that of the woman portrayed as a destroyer of traditional ideals and as an obstacle to man's existential fulfillment. The woman's obsession with material gains constitutes a burden for the man, who feels limited in his own search for meaning and fulfillment in life. He expresses his frustration against women for always trying to influence and pressure him and control his life. The man is rowing the boat as a symbol of the control he would like to have over his life and destiny. The woman lying dead in the stern of the boat has been poisoned by him, and he contemplates her, trying to reaffirm his male supremacy:

And all this so that you could be here quiet on the stern of the boat, as though you hear and feel nothing, as though you didn't know that I am here, steering the boat, I, for the first time, on the course that I choose without consulting anyone, not even you; or my mother; because she is dead; or the principal of that school where they say I am a teacher; or the woman senator who asks me to vote for her; or the mayoress, who asks me to keep her town clean . . . (1970a:140).

The culmination of what Marqués considers female usurpation of traditional male roles is symbolically presented through the grotesque self-castration of the protagonist at the end of the story:

With his left he seized the spongy material and separated it as far as he could from his body. He lifted the knife to the sun and with a tremendous incision, he cut flush with the black fuzz. His scream and bleeding remains landed against the motionless body which remained lying gently, almost elegantly on the stern of the boat (1970a:152).

The portrayal of the woman as a betrayer of high ideals can be found in Marqués' Un niño azul para esa sombra (1970e), one of his most successful plays in terms of character development. The work deals with a Puerto Rican middle-class family. The protagonist is a ten-year-old boy named Michelín, the son of a university professor named Michel, a nationalist sentenced to prison because of his revolutionary activities. After spending eight years as a political prisoner, Michel returns home, but finds it impossible to reconstruct his life without having to renounce his political ideals and moral values. In spite of the impossibility of finding a job, Michel's pride will not allow him to depend on his wealthy wife, Mercedes, who has been unfaithful to him during his absence.

As a result of these circumstances, Michel decides to leave home in order to maintain his heroic image as a revolutionary in the eyes of his son, whose life centers on keeping the past alive through his fantasies about his absent and victimized father. Michel, however, faces only adversity, is unable to reconstruct his life, and dies in abject poverty. This fact is kept from Michelín until the end of the play, when Mercedes tries to make him accept reality by telling him about his father's death. When Michelín learns the truth, he commits suicide.

The play revolves about the character of the child and how he is affected by the events happening around him as he becomes a victim of a materialistic society and a frivolous mother. Marqués attempted to symbolize in this work, through the character of Michelín, the tragedy of the destruction of innocence, ideals, and traditional values by a new materialistic society. The child's character embodies innocence: his father's, the sacrifice of those who fought against the American invader; and his mother's, the betrayal of the native traditions and morality of the past.

In order to escape the reality that surrounds him, Michelín constantly hides in his fantasies, which revolve around the figure of his father and a tree, described as árbol de quenepo macho, that had been planted by him near the terrace of his residence. His mother had ordered that the tree be cut down in order to enlarge the terrace. Michelín constantly hovers about the fence that replaced the tree, a symbol of his mother's abandonment of his father.

Marqués uses the quenepo tree to establish the symbolic bond between father and son. The tree represents the strong male image of his absent father. Michelín's resistance to accepting the reality, the destruction of the tree, and the knowledge of his father's death provoke his final act of suicide. The metaphor of the quenepo tree is, however, much more complex and will be seen more clearly in its totality in the character of Mercedes.

Mercedes' personality has been presented by Marqués as

that of a castrating woman, which he had developed previously in his short story "En la popa hay un cuerpo reclinado" (1970a). The ideas found in Marqués' essays concerning assimilation and changes of cultural patterns in Puerto Rican society as a result of the growing U.S. influence are concretely fictionalized through the character of Mercedes. Marqués appears to resent what he considers to be the rise of a "matriarchal" society, since within his sexist ideology, he considers women's liberation as something alien to the cultural heritage of his people and characteristic of U.S. society. We see this resentment portrayed in the character of Michel, as he appears unable to accept the reality that he encounters upon his return home:

Michel: In the financial aspect there is a reality which is very clear in this family: the money belongs to the woman. The husband carried the title and a salary. The title is still in hand but not the salary. . . . There is only one alternative for a man who believes in the obsolete concept of honor.

Mercedes: You had your ideals, Michel. I did not. I was not educated for that purpose. The tradition in my family has been the struggle for only one liberty; that granted by money and social position (1970e:68–69, 75).

Mercedes is characterized as a product of a new materialistic society that has no ideals. It must be emphasized that Mercedes had the tree cut down for practical reasons and destroyed her husband's manuscript because she considered his nationalist ideals to be dangerous.

Marqués' obsession with the downfall of the macho represented through his "castrated" male characters and "castrating" female characters is justified in his essays: "Apparently, the writers are the only ones in Puerto Rican society who have rebelled against the disappearance of the last cultural bulwark from which one could still combat the collective docility: machismo. . . ."[9]

In contrast with these female characters, one of the most compelling female characters found in Marqués' works is Doña Gabriela in the play La carreta (1951; rpt. 1970b). This drama relates the story of a Puerto Rican peasant family that migrates to the city of San Juan, and finally to New York, searching for work and fortune. Doña Gabriela is portrayed by Marques as the backbone of the family, a country woman whose roots are in the land and who represents the traditional values of the culture. She endures the family's misfortunes and the death of her eldest son, and survives to return to the island with her daughter. This is one of the few instances in which a female character plays a forceful, positive role. Doña Gabriela belongs to the agrarian world of the past, and is viewed by Marqués as a symbol of the strength and preservation of the national culture: "Doña Gabriela: 'Now I realize what has happened to all of us. The curse of the land! The land is sacred. The land must not be abandoned. We must return to what we left behind . . .' " (1970b:179).

Marqués has an idyllic view of the world of the past. This is evident in La carreta (1951; rpt. 1970b) and other works such as Los soles truncos (1959; rpt. 1970d), La víspera del hombre (1959; rpt. 1970c), and Mariana o el alba (1968). The image of the woman fighter and defender of ideals, and upholder of Puerto Rican values is presented only within the context of the traditional society and the world of the past.

Even in more recent works such as his last novel La mirada (1976), Marqués continued to create women characters as a domineering force in man's life. Once again we find in this novel the picture of the child as an innocent victim of maternal arbitrariness.

The extent to which Marqués' characterizations of women reflect his own life and experiences has never been explored and will probably never be known. Although he often comes close to misogynism in his works, I concur with María Sola (1979) that in spite of his antifeminism, Marqués' female characterizations have served to illustrate the patriarchal principles of authority that are the core of Puerto Rican culture.

Of all the members of the Generation of 1950, Pedro Juan Soto is the one who has best captured the essence of Puerto Rican immigrant life. His first book, Spiks (1957; rpt. 1973b), came about as a result of the author's own experience living in New York. The characterization of women in some of the stories included in Spiks illustrates some of the same negative aspects that are found in the works of other writers of his generation and which are also present in some of his novels.

One of the best examples is the short story "Garabatos," which deals with the abject poverty of a Puerto Rican family that has migrated to New York City. Graciela, the wife, is portrayed as a domineering woman who is frustrated by her consecutive pregnancies and by what she sees as her husband Rosendo's lack of motivation and success in finding a useful job:

My God! I'm useful only to have children just like
a dog and this man does not even worry about
finding a job since he prefers for the government
to support us by mail while he walks around looking
like a fool and saying that he wants to be a painter
(1973b:15).

Graciela reflects the pressures of societal demands when she
informs Rosendo that the next day is Christmas, and that
he has not bothered to get presents for the children. She
refers to his artistic talent and work by calling them
garabatos (scribbles) and making it appear that the
garabatos are the only important part of his life: "God!
What a father! You are only concerned about your
scribbles! The artist! A man of your age!" (1973b:15).

Graciela is presented as a simpleminded woman who
cannot understand or appreciate Rosendo's artistic talent
and whose only concern is her material deprivation. This
is clearly demonstrated when Rosendo decides to paint a
picture for her of a naked couple to illustrate their life
together in the midst of scarcity and frustrations, as well
as the good memories of their loving years back on the
island. Since the walls in the other rooms of the apartment
are in very bad condition, he has to paint the picture on
the bathroom walls. Upon completing the painting, he goes
out to buy presents and a tree for the children—which, of
course, pleases Graciela very much. While Rosendo is out,
Graciela finds the painting and, in anger, completely re-
moves it from the walls because she considers it to be
pornographic and unfit for her children's eyes: "You have
no shame . . . allowing your children to look at such filth
and indecencies . . . I erased them and that's it; I don't
want it to happen again" (1973b:20). Rosendo feels that by
having destroyed the painting his wife has destroyed all of
his dreams:

When he got up from the chair, he felt that the
whole world sank from under his feet. His whole
being had been squeezed out of him like a wet rag;
her hands had removed life from him.
He went to the bathroom. There was nothing
of his own left there. Only the twisted, rusty
nails back in their places. Only the spiders in
their webs. That wall was nothing more than an
empty and clear tombstone of his dreams
(1973b:21).

Although the writer's main intention was to emphasize

how the environment of poverty and deprivation of the city does not allow Graciela to see any beauty, the fact is ultimately that the woman is seen as a destroyer of man's dreams.

Soto's first novel, Usmail (1959; rpt. 1970b) (which he divided into three parts, each bearing as a title the name of one of the three women in the protagonist's life), presents women as a controlling and ambivalent influence in the development of Usmail as a child and as a man.

First we have Chefa, the black mother who dies while giving birth. She had fallen in love with an American sailor stationed at Vieques Naval Base who abandoned her while she was pregnant with Usmail. Second there is Nana Luisa, madre de crianza, who raised him and protects him in such a way that he feels lost when she dies. Finally there is Cisa, Usmail's lover, who is older than he and who in many ways becomes a substitute for Nana Luisa. But Cisa gradually becomes merely a sexual object and a burden to Usmail when he decides to leave Vieques and go to San Juan in search of a better life. Shame about his origin and racial identity makes Usmail flee Vieques. Nevertheless, in San Juan he once again finds the U.S. presence, which this time leads him to murder and prison. Usmail goes to a bar, gets into a fight and kills an American sailor who has taken away the prostitute he is courting. This represents the the ultimate violation of his machismo.

In Soto's novel, Temporada de duendes (1970a), the protagonist's girlfriend, Matilde, an aspiring actress, is unfaithful to him by having an affair with a filmmaker. This event serves as a catalyst to his suicide. Once again, the woman is portrayed as the cause of man's tragedy.

The literary production of Emilio Díaz Valcárcel, the youngest member of the Generation of 1950, started with short stories that reflected his personal experiences and impressions in the Korean War. In his second book, El asedio y otros cuentos (1958), he demonstrated his talent for characterizations of great dramatic intensity and psychological penetration. The internal world of conflict of individuals besieged by life in modern society is presented through a great number of characters, including women.

In Díaz Valcárcel's writings the female characterizations are more profound than in the works of other members of his generation. He has attempted to examine the feelings, frustrations, and reactions of women in different contexts; however, the traditional view of female characters often surfaces.

The story "El asedio" (1958) is a psychological study of

a lesbian and her resentment upon being stared at by men. "La última sombra" (1958) reflects the frustration of a woman abandoned by a man and led to commit suicide. Other stories gathered in the book Panorama (1971), such as "María" and "Teresa," are character studies of frustrated women. María is a young woman who lives with her family in a poor community. She has been seduced by a young man from the city who has been sent to prison because of his revolutionary activities. María hates her life in the barrio and impatiently looks forward to the return of the young man, even though she does not clearly understand his revolutionary ideas:

> He is a very strange man she thought pleasantly; he is always talking about liberty, patriotism and justice. . . .
>   She was consumed by the impatience to see him. She was too attached to his peculiar style of men (1971:240, 251).

Teresa is portrayed as a frivolous, sensuous woman who likes to flirt and who is obsessed with her appearance:

> She looked at herself in the mirror: clear, bright and young eyes; the perfect oval face, thick sensuous and juicy lips, the honey color curly hair. You're young and beautiful, she said to herself, while she serenely looked at her image, the image of a goddess. She touched her breasts with tenderness and then slid her hands along her sides, feeling with her fingers the firm contour of her hips and the elastic band of her delicate underwear (1971:251).

The irony is that while Teresa is desired by many men, she is ignored and rejected by her husband. Both María and Teresa are psychological studies of the sexual frustration and frivolity of women.

In the short story "La prueba," (1971) Díaz Valcárcel develops the conflict that arises in a marriage when the woman tries to be independent and starts doing things that are of no interest to her husband, thereby causing him to resent her assertiveness. Using interior monologue, the author tries to transmit the thoughts and feelings of María and Rafael, as their communication begins to break down, by alternating the first-person point of view. Rafael's reactions to María's constant community meetings with other women and her increasing detachment from her duties at home cause him internal conflict:

> I felt like leaving and not letting anybody see me.
> Because if a man is not respected in his own house,
> what could become of him? A man is a man and a
> woman is a woman. Of course, this does not mean
> that women don't have any rights; we do not live in
> ancient times. It is not that. I work to support
> us. She works all day at home. I know it's a
> hard job. But she shouldn't complain. We have
> television and radio. I take her to the annual
> festivities. I am a democratic man! She can't say
> that I control her (1971:180).

María begins to resent her husband's negative reaction
every time she wants to go out to visit her friends:

> When he has problems, he smokes and smokes. If
> we could exchange a word for each cigarette, we
> would get somewhere. I would like to talk to him
> but he is furious. He won't listen to anything I
> have to say. What an easy way of seeing things!
> He thinks I went to Luisa's house only to bother
> him, to get away with something. If he'd only let
> me show him just how wrong he is. I don't like to
> see him that way. He hurts me with that look. If
> he really believes in what he says, he shouldn't be
> bothered that his wife enjoys the right to express
> herself and meet with other women who suffer for
> the same reason (1971:86).

The author's technique of alternating the narration
between the two characters in the story provides the reader
with a psychological study of each individual. Rafael
expresses the pride and machismo of a man who feels that
his whole way of life has been altered and his role as head
of the household threatened:

> Next, she will want to wear the pants. She would
> corner me like an old piece of furniture. She
> wouldn't let me express an opinion. Me, the man,
> who knows what he is talking about! The neigh-
> bors would talk to her and not to me, the man of
> the house (1971:189).

On the other hand, María finds Rafael's reactions
unreasonable and doubts the sincerity of what he has said
many times about democracy and the right of everyone to

express opinions: "I don't want to believe, Rafael, that it has all been a game" (1971:190). She has reached a point of self-affirmation and realizes that she cannot go back to her previous limiting role as a woman: "Democracy means to straighten up and fight for justice! You had better understand that. . . . Understand it, Rafael. We face yet another test because the next meeting is on Friday and I want you to know that I won't miss it" (1971:190).

Among all the male-female situations presented by Díaz Valcárcel in his stories, the one presented in this story is one of the most progressive, since the author tried to consider the husband-wife conflict and changes in the traditional marriage from both male-female points of view.

In his first novel, <u>Figuraciones en el mes de marzo</u> (1972), which has been internationally acclaimed, Díaz Valcárcel portrays the protagonist Eddy Leiseca as a neurotic and alienated man who is unable to cope with his limitations as a writer and his lack of success in life. He resents being supported by his wife Yolanda, and his inability to become a successful writer makes him place the blame on those who surround him, including his wife. Once again, the wife is seen as a destroyer of dreams:

> Aside from feeling uncomfortable, I recognize Yolanda's admirable capacity to laugh frankly and jokingly even when she was consumed by a ferocious anger; her nerves totally relaxed; Yoli, tender, peroxide blonde in a bathing suit or melodramatic black underwear with the day of the week embroidered on the border of her panties, always ready to destroy my castles with one thunder-struck word (1972:161).

The examples of negative images of women among the works of the Generation of 1950 are far too common and it would therefore be too exhaustive to illustrate each specific example from a given work. The main objectives of this study are to present several examples of the most prevalent images of women in support of our generalizations, and to discuss the ideological assumptions that underlie these particular literary images.

It has not been the intention of this study to place value judgments on the traditional ideology of the Generation of 1950 that underlies the images of women found in their works, or to support the idea that the presence of a negative image of women is the result of a conscious effort. Their literary works reflect a world view and ideology, in which the Puerto Rican woman either conforms or does not conform to traditional or patriarchal patterns and values. When she does not conform, she usually represents some form of moral deterioration or betrayal to the national culture. Strong female images are prevalent only within a traditional context.

With the emerging new generation of writers during the 1970s and 1980s, the images of women in Puerto Rican literature are responding to the presence of more women writers and to the development of a feminist consciousness. In contrast to the absence of women prose fiction writers, and to the traditional male perspectives and images of women found in the prior generation of writers, the new literature finally attempts to re-create the diversities, complexities, and perspectives of women's reality.[10]

NOTES

1. Other writers such as Abelardo Díaz Alfaro (b. 1919), Edwin Figueroa (b. 1925), and José Luis Vivas (b. 1926) have also been associated with this generation. Díaz Alfaro represents a bridge between the Generation of 1930 and the Generation of 1950. His books Terrazo (1948) and Isla en mi memoria (1970) deal primarily with rural rather than urban life. The other two writers have a limited literary production. For these reasons they have been excluded from this study.

2. The term dialectical criticism has been used by contemporary scholars, particularly by Fredric Jameson in his book Marxism and Form (Princeton: Princeton University Press, 1971). Jameson is a renowned Marxist critic.

3. Some of Karl Marx and Friedrich Engels' original writings on aesthetics have been compiled in several anthologies: Jean Freville, ed., Sobre arte y cultura (Buenos Aires: Ediciones Revival, 1964); Berd Lang and F. Williams, eds., Marxism and Art (New York: David McKay, 1972); Maynard Solomon, ed., Marxism and Art (New York: Alfred A. Knopf, 1973); Carlos Ruiz, ed., Sobre arte y literatura (Bogotá: Ediciones Suramérica, 1974); Carlos Salimari, Cuestiones de arte y literatura (Barcelona: Ediciones Península, 1975); Marx and Engels, Textos sobre la producción artística, ed. Valeriano Bozal (Madrid: Ediciones Comunicación, 1976). All citations are taken from these editions.

4. Marqués himself has acknowledged Concha Meléndez's contributions and leading role as a critic of his generation. See his introduction to Cuentos puertorriqueños de hoy (Río Piedras, P.R.: Editorial Cultural, 1971).

5. See Pedro J. Soto, A solas con Pedro Juan Soto (Río Piedras, P.R.: Ediciones Puerto, 1973); and Arcadio Díaz Quinones, Conversación con José Luis González (Río Piedras, P.R.: Ediciones Huracán, 1976).

6. Edna Acosta-Belén, in her "Literature and Ideology in the Works of the Puerto Rican Generation of 1950" (Ph.D diss., Columbia University, 1977), further expands on the generational classifications in Puerto Rican literature. She identifies four major generations of writers after 1898: the Generation of 1898 or of "transition and trauma"; the Generation of 1930; the Generation of 1950; and the Generation of 1970. Other writers have subsequently used these classifications.

7. Valuable studies by Angel Quintero Rivera have analyzed the relationship among social classes, political conflicts, and ideology in the Puerto Rico of the nineteenth and twentieth centuries. See his Conflictos de clase y política en Puerto Rico (Río Piedras, P.R.: Ediciones Huracán, 1976).

8. Although González has always identified himself as a Marxist, he was isolated from the Puerto Rican political scene for more than two decades. In 1953 he established residence in Mexico and renounced his U.S. citizenship. He was not allowed to visit Puerto Rico until the 1970s. Marqués was, nevertheless, affiliated with the political group Movimiento Pro-Independencia (MPI) for a short period.

9. Efraín Barradas, in his essay "El machismo existencialista de René Marqués," Sin nombre 7, no. 3 (octubre-diciembre 1977):69–81, provides an excellent analysis of this generalized trend in Marqués' literary production. In the essay "René Marqués ¿escritor misógino?" Sin Nombre 10, no. 3 (octubre-noviembre 1977):83–97, María Solá argues that most of Marqués' female characters respond to the archetypical Western dichotomy that attributes to women the duality or ambiguity of human nature and portrays her with two faces: that of a Madonna (the sacred and nurturing woman) and of the Meretriz (the woman who gives pleasure and contributes to man's downfall).

10. The characterization of women in contemporary Puerto Rican literature has changed, nevertheless, as illustrated by writers of the present generation. The works of Luis Rafael Sánchez, who is considered a precursor of or link to the new generation, has emphasized the inner strength of female protagonists. The best example is Antígona in the play La pasión según Antígona Pérez. Gloria Feiman Waldman presented a paper entitled "Female Figures in the Plays of Luis Rafael Sánchez" at the

Symposium on the Hispanic-American Woman held at the State University of New York at Albany in 1976, where she emphasized this aspect. In addition, literary works by women writers such as Myrna Casas, Rosario Ferré, Magali García Ramis, Carmen Lugo Filippi, and Ana Lydia Vega, among others, present new facets of women as literary characters. After this essay was published in the first edition of The Puerto Rican Woman (New York: Praeger, 1979, pp. 85–109) other literary critics have studied women characters in Puerto Rican literature as well as literary works by women writers. See Susana Homar, "Inferioridad y cambio: los personajes femeninos en la literatura puertorriqueña," Revista de Ciencias Sociales 20, no. 3–4 (dic. 1978):387–304; María Arrillaga, "La narrativa de la mujer puertorriqueña en la década del setenta," Homines 8, no. 1 (enero-junio 1984):327–34; Margarite Fernández Olmo, "Desde una perspectiva femenina: la cuentística de Rosario Ferré y Ana Lydia Vega," Homines 8, no. 2 (junio 1984/enero 1985):303–11.

REFERENCES

Díaz Valcárcel, Emilio. 1972. Figuraciones en el mes de marzo. Barcelona: Seix Barral.
————. 1971. Panorama, San Juan: Editorial Cultural.
————. 1969. "Apuntes para el desarrollo histórico del cuento literario puertorriqueño y la generacion del 40." Revista del Instituto de Cultura Puertorriqueña 43:11–17.
————. 1958. El asedio y otros cuentos. México: Ediciones Arrecife.
Escarpit, Robert. 1971. Sociología de la literatura. Barcelona: Ediciones Oikos-Tan.
Freville, Jean, ed. 1964. Sobre arte y cultura. Buenos Aires: Ediciones Revival.
González, Jose Luis. 1980. El país de cuatro pisos. Río Piedras, P.R.: Ediciones Huracán.
————. 1973. En Nueva York y otras desgracias, México: Siglo XXI.
————. 1972. Mambrú se fue a la guerra. México: Joaquín Mortiz.
————. 1964. En este lado. México: Los Presentes.
————. 1950. Paisa. México: Fondo de Cultura Popular.
————. 1948. El hombre en la calle. Santurce, P.R.: Editorial Bohique.
————. 1945a. Cinco cuentos de sangre. San Juan:

Imprenta Venezuela.
—————. 1945b. En la sombra. Santurce, P.R.: Editorial Bohique.
Jameson, Fredric. 1972. "The Great American Hunter or Ideological Content in the Novel." College English 24, no. 2 (November):180–87.
Konstantinov, F. V. 1965. Fundamentos de la filosofía marxista. México: Editorial Grijalbo.
Lang, Berd, and F. Williams, eds. 1972. Marxism and Art. New York: David McKay.
Lifshitz, Mikhail. 1973. The Philosophy of Art of Karl Marx. New York: Pluto Press.
Maldonado Denis, Manuel. 1969. Puerto Rico: mito y realidad. Barcelona: Ediciones Península.
Marqués, René. 1976. La mirada. Río Piedras, P.R.: Editorial Antillana.
—————. 1971. Cuentos puertorriquenos de hoy. Río Piedras, P.R.: Editorial Cultural. (First edition 1959).
—————. 1970a. En una ciudad llamada San Juan. San Juan: Editorial Cultural. (First edition 1960).
—————. 1970b. La carreta. San Juan: Editorial Cultural. (First edition 1951).
—————. 1970c. La víspera del hombre. San Juan: Editorial Cultural. (First edition 1959).
—————. 1970d. Los soles truncos. San Juan: Editorial Cultural. (First edition 1959).
—————. 1970e. Un niño azul para esa sombra. San Juan: Editorial Cultural. (First edition 1959).
—————. 1968. Mariana o el alba. Río Piedras, P.R.: Editorial Antillana.
Meléndez, Concha. 1955. "El cuento en la edad de Asomante—1945–55. Asomante 9, no. 1:39–68.
Menton, Seymour. 1970. El cuento hispanoamericano: Antología crítico-histórica. México: Fondo de Cultura Económica.
Quintero Rivera, Angel. 1976. "Conflictos de clase y política en Puerto Rico." Río Piedras, P.R.: Ediciones Huracán.
Rivera de Alvarez, Josefina. 1970. Diccionario de literatura puertorriqueña. San Juan: Instituto de Cultura.
Ruiz, Carlos, ed. 1974. Sobre arte y literatura. Bogotá: Ediciones Suramérica.
Sánchez Vázquez, Adolfo. 1975. Estética y marxismo. 2 vols. México: Ediciones Era.
—————. 1972. Las ideas estéticas de Marx. México: Ediciones Era.
Sastre, Silvestro, ed. 1969. Estética y marxismo.

Barcelona: Ediciones Martínez Roca.

Solá, María. 1979. "René Marqués ¿escritor misógino?" Sin Nombre 10, no. 3 (octubre-noviembre):83–97.

Soto, Pedro Juan. 1973a. A solas con Pedro Juan Soto. Río Piedras, P.R.: Ediciones Puerto.

————. 1973b. Spiks. San Juan: Editorial Cultural. (First edition 1957).

————. 1970a. Temporada de duendes. México: Editorial Diógenes.

————. 1970b. Usmail. San Juan: Editorial Cultural. (First edition 1959).

9

Puerto Rican Women in the United States: An Overview

Christine E. Bose

The situation of Puerto Rican women residing in Puerto Rico and those living in the United States is not identical. Even a quick overview of the statistics shows this. For example, the labor force participation rate of women in Puerto Rico was 28 percent in 1980, but was 37 percent in the United States; the average education of women in Puerto Rico was 12.6 years in 1980, and was only 9.9 years in 1978 in the United States; and women earned 58 percent of men's average income in Puerto Rico, while earning 52 percent of Puerto Rican men's income in the United States.

What are the causes of these differences? Social scientists frequently want to blame any problems of Puerto Rican women in the United States on their relative youth (the median age is 22.4 years compared to 30.6 years for all women in the United States) and on their lower education. Certainly these conditions do present problems. But by focusing on these "supply-side" variables it becomes too easy to "blame the victim" and to ignore the "demand" factors, those factors that either draw people into the labor market or erect barriers to entry into certain jobs. It is the intent of this chapter to explore the situation of Puerto Rican women in the United States and to look for explanations of their position by using geographic and structural demand factors, as well as the individual supply ones.

We begin with the patterns of migration which determine both which women leave Puerto Rico and which labor market they enter. Following this discussion we will look at Puerto

147

Rican women's employment rates, jobs, income, and education. Then we turn to the family-related factors of household composition and marital status, fertility rates and
children, and sex role socialization.

MIGRATION AND REGION OF RESIDENCE

The largest migration of Puerto Rican women and men to the
United States occurred in the 1950s when 20 percent of the
island population immigrated. In 1940 there were only
70,000 Puerto Ricans in the United States, but in 1950
there were 300,000 and by 1960 there were 900,000 (Ford
Foundation, 1984). During the 1960s migration slowed, but
there was still a net movement from Puerto Rico such that
by 1970 1.4 million or 34 percent of all Puerto Ricans were
in the United States (Newman, 1978). From 1972 to 1977
there was a large return migration to Puerto Rico, but
since 1978 there has been net migration to the United States
again (Wagenheim, 1983). In 1980 there were about 2
million Puerto Ricans on the U.S. mainland. This historic
pattern is reflected in comparative statistics on Hispanic
immigration to the United States (see Table 9.1).

TABLE 9.1

Group	1950-59		1960-69		1970-79	
	Number	%	Number	%	Number	%
Mexican	293,000	30.7	431,000	33.2	567,000	40.8
Cuban	71,000	7.4	249,000	19.2	278,000	20.0
Puerto Rican	480,000	50.2	222,000	17.1	41,000	3.0
Other Hispanic	112,000	11.7	397,000	30.6	503,000	36.2
Total Percentage		100.0		100.0		100.0

Source: Davis, Haub, and Willette, 1983.

The net Puerto Rican migration has slowed for several
reasons. First, the total Puerto Rican population is not as
large as that in other originating countries. Second, the
U.S. government has increased its support for island
residents. Finally, the total statistics hide the fact that
there is actually much back and forth movement between
Puerto Rico and the United States. One effect of this
movement is that in 1976 an estimated 80 percent of the

Puerto Rican women living in the United States were born on the island. They had lived in the United States for a considerable time, with 59 percent in residence for 12 years or more (Tienda and Guhleman, 1982).

Different age and gender groups are involved in migration. In the 1970s, the net flow back to Puerto Rico was of people over 35 years old and of older children, age 5 to 19 (Davis, Haub, and Willette, 1983). The return migrants and the nonmigrants had the same occupational distribution, but those who stayed had lower unemployment rates (Newman, 1978). At the same time, the net influx into the United States was composed of young Puerto Ricans, aged 20 to 29 and children under five years old. Surprisingly, 73 percent of these were men while in the 1950s and 1960s only 54 percent and 56 percent, respectively, of the migrants were male (Davis, Haub, and Willette, 1983). These figures may reflect improved job opportunities for women in Puerto Rico or any of several other factors. They will surely have an impact on the Puerto Rican population in the United States, particularly if their migration is not evenly dispersed.

The distribution of the total Puerto Rican population in the United States has already been changing over the years. In 1940, 88 percent lived in New York City and 93 percent in the Northeast region; in 1950, 82.9 percent lived in New York and 88.7 percent in the region; by 1970, only 58.4 percent of the U.S. Puerto Rican population lived in New York and 81.2 percent were in the Northeast (Jaffe, Cullen, and Boswell, 1980). Today we find 43 percent of the total U.S. Puerto Rican population in New York City (Russell, 1983) and 73 percent in the Northeast region (U.S. Bureau of the Census, 1983). A further 11 percent live in the Northcentral area, 8 percent in the South, and 7 percent in the West of the United States (U.S. Bureau of the Census, 1983). Thus, Puerto Ricans have become less geographically concentrated. Nonetheless, the majority still live in the three states of New York, New Jersey, and Illinois.

Hispanics in general, and Puerto Ricans in particular, are urban people. While only 81 percent of blacks and 75 percent of the total U.S. population live in metropolitan areas, 88 percent of the Hispanic population does so (Davis, Haub, and Willette, 1983). Puerto Ricans are the most urban group with 74.7 percent living in central cities and a full 94.5 percent residing in standard metropolitan statistical areas (U.S. Bureau of the Census, 1981).

Population distribution has important impacts on Puerto Rican women's lives. First, whether or not one lives in an area with other Puerto Ricans affects cultural maintenance, the likelihood of in-group marriage, and the availability of relatives to aid in child care. Second, the labor market is different in various regions and even among various cities. We will indicate below that a decline in Puerto Rican women's labor force participation was largely caused by the contraction of the textile industry in New York City. Other research (Santana Cooney, 1979a) on 56 U.S. cities finds that industrial mix, numbers of (nondurable) operative jobs, the male unemployment rate, and average total female earnings in a city can greatly determine Puerto Rican women's labor force participation rate; the percentage of female household heads, married, and percentage of Puerto Rican residents are also influential. Interestingly, these variables help to explain both 86 percent of the decline in female employment in New York City and 39 percent of the increase in Chicago between 1960 and 1970. Thus, where Puerto Rican women live in the United States can have a tremendous impact on their family and work life.

EMPLOYMENT AND UNEMPLOYMENT RATES

Puerto Rican women's employment patterns in the U.S. labor force have captured the interest of social scientists because of two unique characteristics. First, Puerto Ricans are the only group of women to experience a decline in labor force participation rates, particularly in the period between 1950 and 1970. Second, Puerto Rican women are becoming female household heads at a faster rate than any other group. These trends are related: it is the female heads of households (and not wives or single women) who have decreased their rates of labor force participation, contrary to single mothers' patterns among other groups. However, this factor is not the only one to explain Puerto Rican women's labor force participation rates. Let us look at Table 9.2 for the trends in the last 35 years.

We can see that in 1980 women were much more likely to work than in 1950, with Mexican-American women increasing their labor force participation rate by as much as 28 percent. While Puerto Rican women began in 1950 with the highest rates of any group, during most of these decades their employment rates actually declined. This decline cannot be explained by Hispanic culture since other Hispanic women were increasingly likely to enter employment, and all Hispanic groups had higher rates of employment in the United States than in their country of origin. The decline is also not explained by education or fertility (Newman, 1978; Santana Cooney and Colon, 1980; Roth, 1983).

TABLE 9.2

Women	1980	1970	1960	1950
White	51.2%	38.9%	33.6%	28.1%
Black	53.2	44.5	42.2	37.4
Puerto Rican	37.2	29.8	36.3	38.9
Mexican[a]	49.1	33.8	28.8	21.9
Cuban	54.0	47.0	NA	NA

[a]Data for 1950-70 is for Spanish surname; data for 1980 is for Mexican-American women.

Sources: 1950-1970 data for non-Cuban women from Santana Cooney, 1979a; 1970 data for Cubans from Ferree, 1979; 1980 data from U.S. Department of Labor, Women's Bureau, 1983.

In fact, the decline is probably related to changes in the economy of New York City (Santana Cooney and Colón, 1980; Roth, 1983). Between 1969 and 1977, employment in New York fell by 12.6 percent, with three-fourths of the decline occurring in clerical and operative jobs (Roth, 1983). Over half of the working age Puerto Rican mainland residents were in New York then, with the majority of Puerto Rican women employed in precisely those operative jobs, particularly textiles, which were evaporating. In the 30 years between 1950 and 1980, New York City lost 59 percent of its apparel and textile industry jobs, and nationally Puerto Rican female employment changed from 72 percent operatives to 26 percent operatives (Ríos, 1985). Thus we can see that the decline in Puerto Rican women's employment has primarily been due to barriers in the labor market. Most individual factors, except the presence of children, do not statistically influence Puerto Rican women's employment (Tienda and Guhleman, 1982).

In U.S. government statistics, the labor force is defined to include both those who are employed and those who are unemployed. Since being in the labor force does not necessarily mean holding a job, it is important to also examine unemployment rates. Among all working women who were 16 years and older in 1981, a total of 7.9 percent were unemployed. Comparatively, 9.0 percent of Cuban women,

11.3 percent of Mexican-American women, and 12.6 percent of Puerto Rican women were unemployed (Roth, 1983). Thus, while Mexican-American women are much more likely to be employed than Puerto Ricans, both experience extremely high unemployment rates. This is particularly exacerbated for 16- to 19-year-old Puerto Rican women whose unemployment rate was 40.1 percent. Among Hispanics, Puerto Ricans have the longest periods of unemployment (Newman, 1978).

Compared to other groups of the unemployed, Puerto Rican and Mexican-American women are the most likely to be job market entrants (40.9 and 42.5 percent respectively) rather than job losers or job leavers (Roth, 1983). Thus their main reason for unemployment is re-entering the labor market after some period of absence. The cause of that absence is not revealed by the statistics: it could be time out for child care, discouragement over the loss of suitable operative jobs, or some mixture of these reasons.

OCCUPATIONAL SEGREGATION AND JOB STATUS

If Puerto Rican women are less likely to be employed in operative work than in previous years, where are they now employed? Table 9.3 shows the occupational distribution, in percentages, for three different groups of Hispanic women, and indicates that Puerto Rican women are now most likely (36.4 percent) to be employed in clerical work. Operative work is still the second most common employment (25.8 percent), followed by service work (13.1 percent) and professional and technical employment (11.6 percent). We also see that Puerto Rican women are more likely than either Mexican-American or Cuban women to be employed in the white-collar fields of professional/technical, managerial/administrative, or clerical work.

In spite of the large numbers of women in white-collar employment, Puerto Rican women are still occupationally segregated. In 1976, 78.9 percent of all Puerto Rican women would have had to change jobs in order to have the same occupational distribution as Anglo males and 48.3 percent would have had to change to have the same distribution as Anglo women (Alvirez, 1981).

Nonetheless, there has been a tremendous change in the employment patterns of Puerto Rican women over the last 30 years. In 1950, 71.7 percent of employed Puerto Rican women were operatives and only 15.3 percent were in white collar jobs (Ríos, 1985). By 1981, 57.1 percent were employed in white-collar jobs, and only 25.8 percent were employed in operative work. However, this impressive move into white-collar jobs came at some cost: many Puerto Rican women lost their operative jobs, and could not find other work, thus helping to lower the labor force participation rate of Puerto Rican women in the United States for about 20 years.

TABLE 9.3

Occupation in 1981	All Women (%)	Puerto Rican (%)	Mexican-American (%)	Cuban (%)
White Collar Workers				
Professional/Technical	17.0	11.6	8.0	9.9
Managers/Administrators	7.4	6.1	4.3	5.5
Sales Workers	6.8	3.0	5.2	4.9
Clerical Workers	34.7	36.4	32.4	31.9
Blue Collar Workers				
Craft & Kindred	1.9	2.5	2.5	2.2
Operatives, except Transport	9.7	25.8	21.6	29.7
Transport Operatives	0.7	0.5	0.5	NA
Nonfarm Labor	1.3	0.5	2.2	1.1
Service Workers	19.4	13.1	21.1	14.8
Farm Workers	1.1	0.5	2.5	NA
Total	100.0	100.0	100.0	100.0

NA = not available
Source: Roth, 1983; U.S. Department of Labor, 1983.

This shift in jobs also differentially affected island- and U.S.-born Puerto Rican women (Jaffe, Cullen, and Boswell, 1980). Among those women employed in 1970 for example, 57 percent of the U.S.-born and only 28.5 percent of Puerto Rican-born women were in clerical and sales jobs, while only 13.3 percent of U.S.-born and as many as 46.3 percent of island-born women still held operative jobs. As a result, island-born women held jobs with an average status of 54 out of 100 points, while U.S.-born women had an average status of 63 points.

There is some debate among researchers as to what helps Hispanic women get ahead in the U.S. labor force. Tienda and Guhleman (1982) find that there are two significant determinants of job status for Puerto Ricans. The first is employment in the periphery sector of the economy, which depresses job status. Fortunately, Puerto Rican women are less likely than other groups to be employed in these industries. However, the presence of large proportions of Hispanics in an area economy lowers the status rewards that Puerto Rican women gain from employment. This finding suggests that there is more discrimination in regions with high percentages of Hispanics than in those with lower ones, but the authors' data did not allow them to check this hypothesis. The second factor in getting ahead is education—and not English language proficiency or nativity (born in the United States or in Puerto Rico). Education is important in increasing status.

Research by Santana Cooney and Ortiz (1983) modifies these findings. They say that English language proficiency does increase the labor force participation of island-born Puerto Rican women, but has no impact on U.S.-born Puerto Rican women. Education is important for both groups, but has a greater influence on the employment of U.S.-born women. Jaffe, Cullen, and Boswell (1980), however, think that education is the main factor, and they point out that Puerto Rican women with the same education as non-Spanish whites held jobs (in 1970) with the same status (see Table 9.4).

TABLE 9.4

| | Average Status of Jobs Held By: | |
Years in School	Puerto Rican Women	Non-Spanish White Women
Total	56	63
Less than 12 years	50	52
High school graduation	62	64
Some college (13-15 years)	70	71
College or more education	84	85

Source: Jaffe, Cullen, and Boswell, 1980.

INCOME

Achieving higher status may be less important than achieving a higher income. The data for median family income in 1980 are shown in Table 9.5.

TABLE 9.5

Family	Median Income
Non-Spanish	$19,965
Puerto Rican	$ 9,855
Mexican-American	$15,171
Cuban	$17,538
Other Spanish	$15,470

Source: Wagenheim, 1983.

The figures do not improve much by 1982 (U.S. Bureau of the Census, 1983) when the median Puerto Rican family income increases to $11,256, Mexican-American income becomes $16,933, and other Spanish origin groups reach $17,914. At this point, 42.8 percent of all Puerto Rican families were classified as below the poverty level in comparison to 25.5 percent of Mexican-American families and 19.9 percent of other Hispanic groups. At the same time, 30.8 percent of black families were classified below the poverty level, thus making Puerto Rican families among the most poor in the United States.

Why should this be so and what does individual Puerto Rican women's income look like? Surprisingly, there is relatively little information on Puerto Rican women's income in comparison to men. Jaffe, Cullen, and Boswell (1980) indicate that in 1970, Puerto Rican women averaged $3,420 or 64 percent of Puerto Rican men's $5,340 income. Further, we do know that in 1978 the U.S. Commission on Civil Rights estimated that if earnings were adjusted for differences in age, education, occupational prestige, weeks worked, hours worked in the last week, and average income in the state, Puerto Rican women would still have earned 57 percent of the average Anglo male salary in 1975 while Puerto Rican men would reach 98 percent of Anglo male income (Alvirez, 1981).

The most recent data we have on Puerto Rican women's income is from the late 1970s. In 1979 (National Puerto Rican Forum, Inc., 1981) the median income of Puerto Rican men was $7,807. At the same time, the median income of Puerto Rican women was $4,050 or 52 percent of men's earnings. In fact in 1977, 62.2 percent of Puerto Rican women had incomes of less than $5,000, 92.8 percent earned less than $10,000, and almost all (99.1 percent) earned less than $15,000. Using slightly earlier information from the 1976 Survey on Income and Education, Guhleman and Tienda (1981) find that the median earnings among all workers were $3,137 for Mexican-American, $4,782 for Puerto Rican, $4,812 for Cuban, and $4,855 for non-Hispanic white women. The figures are somewhat higher for full-time year-round workers: $5,615 among Mexican-American, $6,913 among Puerto Rican, $6,816 among Cuban, and $7,965 among non-Hispanic white women with 38.3 percent, 41.5 percent, 57.4 percent, and 46.0 percent of each respective group of workers so employed. Thus, it is the full-time, full-year Puerto Rican women workers who are relatively disadvantaged compared to Anglo women.

Guhleman and Tienda (1981) also report income variations for Puerto Rican women by place of birth, primary language, and family status. Women born in Puerto Rico earn more ($4,902) on average than U.S.-born Puerto Rican women ($4,438). Language effects are more mixed. Workers who usually speak English earn $4,719 and those who usually speak Spanish earn a similar amount, $4,791, but among full-time, full-year workers those who usually speak English earn considerably more than those who usually speak Spanish ($9,171 vs. $6,184). Little difference in income is found among Puerto Rican women by family status, while there is considerable difference by family status among non-Hispanic whites (see Table 9.6). Non-Hispanic female household heads (including individuals) always earn more than married women, while Puerto Rican family heads do not.

TABLE 9.6

	Puerto Rican	Non-Hispanic White
All Workers		
Married, spouse-present	$4,982	$4,805
Head of family	$5,162	$7,021
Full-time, Full-year Workers		
Married, spouse-present	$6,986	$7,906
Head of family	$6,976	$8,899

Source: Guhleman and Tienda, 1981.

There seems to be considerable consensus that a major reason for the low Puerto Rican family income is the high number of Puerto Rican female household heads. First, occupational segregation means women earn less than men. Second, Puerto Rican female household heads are no more likely than wives to be employed, rather than more likely to work as among non-Hispanic women (Santana Cooney and Colón, 1980). Third, as indicated above, Puerto Rican female household heads who are employed earn the same as married women, but have no spouse to add to that low income. Finally, 44.7 percent of Puerto Rican families are headed by a female householder with no spouse present and 37.0 percent of the families are headed by female householders with children under 18 years old (U.S. Bureau of the Census, 1983). Thus, Puerto Rican median family income is greatly depressed by the poverty of the large number of female-headed households. Since the rate of increase in these families is greater among Puerto Ricans than among any other group (Santana Cooney and Colón, 1980), we can expect the income problem to grow if all other factors remain the same.

EDUCATION AND LANGUAGE

In 1976, the mean level of education for both Puerto Rican and Mexican-American women aged 18 to 64 (Tienda and Guhleman, 1982) was relatively low: 9.1 and 9.0 years, respectively. In comparison, Central and South American women had a mean of 11.0 years and non-Hispanic white women a mean of 12.3 years of education. These figures are slowly improving as young women are more likely to stay in school longer. In 1978 (National Puerto Rican Forum, Inc., 1981) the median school years completed by Puerto Rican women had increased to 9.9 years. By 1980 (U.S. Bureau of the Census, 1981) only 16.7 percent of Puerto Rican women age 25 or over had less than five years of education, 36.8 percent had four years of high school or more education, and 5.5 percent had a college degree or more education. At the same time (Davis, Haub, and Willette, 1983), 52.6 percent of all black women and 71.2 percent of all white women had completed high school or had more education. Thus, there is still a long way to go before educational parity is reached.

In fact, the Ford Foundation (1984) indicates that the Hispanic/non-Hispanic gap is greatest in the area of education, with segregation of Hispanic students being both high and increasing. Perhaps because of this, Hispanic student drop-out rates are higher than non-Hispanic ones. Nonetheless, there are differences among Hispanic students.

Those born in the United States attend school longer than their foreign or island-born parents, and parental education and high family income determine educational progress more than the use of Spanish per se (Davis, Haub, and Willette, 1983).

Some argue that education is the prime determinant of Puerto Rican women's status (Tienda and Guhleman, 1982), others argue that English language proficiency is most important (Ford Foundation, 1984), while the newest research is taking a compromise position. For example, Stolzenberg (1984) argues that both schooling and English language ability are significantly important, with much of the effect of schooling being determined by English ability. Meanwhile Santana Cooney and Ortiz (1983) indicate that education is important for both island- and U.S.-born Puerto Rican women, and English language proficiency is only important for island-born women. Thus, if there are large percentages of island-born women in the United States, it would appear that English language proficiency is more important than education. The recognition of the interactions of both education and language seems the best approach to understanding Puerto Rican women's achievement.

FAMILY COMPOSITION AND MARITAL STATUS

Whether we examine family composition or women's marital status, a similar picture of Puerto Rican households emerges. Table 9.7 illustrates the distribution of family types in 1982. We can immediately see that, among Hispanics in the United States, Puerto Ricans are the least likely to be living in a married couple and the most likely to be in a family with a female householder. A male householder is relatively uncommon among all groups.

There is an almost even split among Puerto Rican families with 51 percent being married couples and 45 percent female-headed. A female householder does not necessarily have children, but fully 37 percent of all Puerto Rican households are headed by women with children aged 18 or younger. Such households tend to have more children, as well: in 1979 female-headed households had an average of 1.91 children, while husband-wife households had an average of 1.52 children residing with them (Gurak, 1981). This may be because the largest increase in Puerto Rican female household heads has been among women who are aged 20 to 29—the women most likely to have resident young children (Hernández, 1983).

TABLE 9.7

All Families	Puerto Rican (%)	Mexican- American (%)	Other Hispanic (%)
Married Couple	50.8	78.2	73.7
(with own children under 18 years)	(36.0)	(57.6)	(43.0)
Female Householder	44.7	17.7	21.8
(with own children under 18 years)	(37.0)	(12.8)	(14.2)
Male Householder	4.5	4.1	4.5
(with own children under 18 years)	(2.3)	(1.0)	(1.7)
Total	100.0	100.0	100.0

Source: U.S. Bureau of the Census, 1983.

The implications of this household data for individual marital status are illustrated in Table 9.8. Again we find that greater proportions of Puerto Rican women are single and fewer are married than among other groups. In part, this reflects the general trend toward postponement of marriage (Gurak, 1981), but it is also because the Puerto Rican population in the United States is relatively young. The median age of all Puerto Ricans is 19.9 and that of Mexican-Americans is 21.1, while non-Hispanics average 30.4 years and Cubans are even older at 36.3 years (Gurak, 1981). The black population averages 25 years old. Interestingly, Puerto Rican women are an average of 4.4 years older than Puerto Rican men (Gurak, 1981).

The relative youth of the U.S. Puerto Rican population is not primarily due to high fertility, as stereotypes might lead us to believe. Rather, the major cause of the youthful population is migration from Puerto Rico (Gurak, 1981). Migrants who move for economic reasons are usually young, between 15 and 40 years of age, and at least 55 percent of Puerto Ricans are migrants from Puerto Rico, while only 18 percent of Mexican-Americans are migrants. Thus the youthfulness and singleness of the mainland population are not a surprise.

Once married, Puerto Ricans are among the most likely to marry persons of the same nationality. Gurak (1981) indicates that in 1975 only 29.5 percent of first- and second-generation Puerto Ricans married non-Puerto Ricans,

TABLE 9.8

Marital Status	Puerto Rican (%)	Mexican- American (%)	Cuban (%)	Central and S. American (%)
Women				
Single	33.2	27.6	20.1	26.8
Married	52.3	61.2	59.4	59.2
Widowed	6.4	5.5	11.4	5.3
Divorced	8.1	5.7	9.2	8.7
Total	100.0	100.0	100.1	100.0
Men				
Single	36.8	32.0	27.7	36.1
Married	60.0	62.9	68.1	59.3
Widowed	.7	1.6	.8	.9
Divorced	2.4	3.6	3.4	3.7
Total	99.9	100.1	100.0	100.0

Source: U.S. Bureau of the Census, 1981.

while 56.1 percent of Central Americans and 63.4 percent of Cubans married outside their group. Usually second generation members will be more likely to marry out-group members, but only 27.7 percent of Puerto Rican grooms and 30.2 percent of Puerto Rican brides did so in 1975. In fact, these rates have been dropping since 1959 rather than increasing. Those who marry non-Puerto Ricans frequently marry members of other Hispanic groups.

Why is there so much intramarriage? First, Puerto Ricans travel back and forth to Puerto Rico relatively often. This keeps up ethnic identity and discourages permanent settlement commitments in the United States (Gurak, 1981). Second, there is a high rate of residential segregation of Puerto Ricans in New York City, where the bulk of the U.S. Puerto Rican population was living at that time. In fact, the segregation of Spanish/non-Spanish language populations was higher in New York than in many other urban areas (Gurak, 1981). This segregation insures that there will be low rates of out-group contact and thus of out-group marriage. Higher occupational status is associated with higher out-group marriage rates, but economically better off Puerto Ricans have been likely to leave New York City or initially settle elsewhere. Such residential dispersion is usually associated with more inter-marriage.

Sometimes, neither inter- nor intra-group marriages survive. Has a rising divorce rate caused the rapid rate of increase in female-headed households among Puerto Ricans? In an interesting paper comparing two different methodologies, Santana Cooney (1979b) answers this question negatively. Among non-Hispanic whites she finds that changing living arrangements and population factors caused the rise from 1940 to 1970 in female household heads, but rising marital instability was important from 1960 through 1970. Thus, the major long-term problems were increasing numbers of married women who were eligible for divorce, and the increased likelihood that divorced women would live on their own instead of with their relatives. Santana Cooney concludes that over 60 percent of the increase between 1960 and 1970 in non-Hispanic white female-headed families was related to marital instability and living arrangements, but that such factors account for only 14 percent of the increase among Puerto Ricans. Different factors were important for black and Puerto Rican women. Population growth and increased likelihood that children were in the home when disruption occurred account for 53 to 55 percent of the growth in Puerto Rican and black female-headed households, but only 20 percent of the increase in female householders among non-Hispanic whites. Santana Cooney feels her findings indicate that the growth in Puerto Rican female-headed families is less voluntary than is that among non-Hispanic whites, who were choosing to change their living arrangements in order to be more independent. Elsewhere (Santana Cooney and Colón, 1980) she also postulates that these statistics mean that Puerto Rican family structure may be becoming more like that of blacks than of non-Hispanic whites.

One interesting feature of female-headed families is that they seem to vary by region of the country. Gurak (1981) has found that in 1970 the female head rates ranged from a high of 28 percent in New York, to 21 percent in New Jersey, 15 percent in California, and a low of 12 percent in Florida. It is hard to guess how the factors mentioned by Santana Cooney (population growth and increased likelihood that children were present) would vary with region. However, Jaffe, Cullen, and Boswell (1980) report that as a result of selective migration the ratio of Puerto Rican men to women was 84:100 in New York state, but 109:100 in other states as of 1970. Thus in New York there were fewer Puerto Rican men to marry, and a Puerto Rican woman frequently had to stay single or marry a non-Puerto

Rican. Given the low rates of out-group marriage, it seems that the prevailing choice was to be a female householder.

Other factors may be at play here as well. Santana Cooney and Ortiz (1983) have found that there is a positive relationship between female headship and labor force participation for U.S.-born Puerto Ricans, but an unusual negative relationship between these factors for island-born Puerto Rican women. Even taking into account the availability of low-skilled jobs and the attractiveness of welfare, a significant negative relationship between female-headship and employment remains for island-born women. This does not occur with foreign-born Cuban or Mexican-American women. While this analysis refers to the rates of employment, and not to the rates of female-headed households, it might be that rates of female-headed households vary with the regional mix of Puerto Rico- to U.S.-born women.

Households are not only composed of nuclear families. There are extended households which include non-nuclear members as well. Extended households are most common among minorities and those headed by women, and Puerto Rican households are 5 percent more likely to extend than non-Hispanic white ones (Angel and Tienda, 1982). Such households are formed for both economic and cultural reasons (Tienda and Angel, 1982). In general, black and Hispanic households have non-nuclear members who significantly contribute to total household income, while non-Hispanic white households have non-nuclear residents who do not generate income (Angel and Tienda, 1982). However, Puerto Ricans have a lower propensity to include economically active non-nuclear members than do non-Hispanic whites. Tienda and Angel (1982) suggest that this may be due to a reliance on public transfer systems among Puerto Ricans. Nonetheless, extended household composition can increase the labor force participation of single mothers (Tienda and Glass, 1983). If the non-nuclear member is a woman, a mother's employment is particularly likely to be facilitated. Presumably, this other woman is helpful in child care and allows the female household head to seek paid employment. This possibility brings us to a discussion of the role of children in the lives of Puerto Rican women.

FERTILITY RATES AND CHILDREN

It is popularly thought that Hispanics have more children than other groups. However, we are rarely clear as to what that means. One way is to look at family size. In

1978 the mean number of Puerto Rican persons per family was 3.78. However, 24 percent of Puerto Rican families contained 2 people; 22 percent had 3 people; 24 percent had 4 people; 17 percent had 5 people; and 12 percent had 6 persons or more. In contrast, 34 percent of all U.S. families had 2 people; 20 percent had 3 people; 18 percent had 4 people; 13 percent had 5 people; and 15 percent had 6 people or more (National Puerto Rican Forum, Inc., 1981). On the whole there are more two-person families and slightly fewer four- and five-person families among the general American population than are found among Puerto Ricans. The size of Puerto Rican households did decline between 1960 and 1970, but this was primarily due to fewer adults in the home or the increase in female-headed households (Frisbie et al., 1982).

A more typical measure of fertility is the number of births per 1,000 women who are in the childbirth years of 15 to 44. A 1980 study of fertility in 22 states found these rates, presented in increasing order in Table 9.9. We can see that Hispanic fertility rates vary from Cubans with the lowest rate to Mexican-Americans with the highest rate. The Puerto Rican rate is midway between these two, and is actually closer to the white female rate. In fact, Puerto Rican women average only one-third of a child more than white women, and if socioeconomic status, education, and age at marriage were the same, Puerto Rican and white women would have the same fertility (Gurak, 1981). Lower education and family income are factors associated with higher fertility among all U.S. groups, not only for Puerto Ricans.

TABLE 9.9

Women	Births per 1,000 Women, Age 15-44
Cuban	41.9
White	62.4
Other Hispanic	75.3
Puerto Rican	77.0
Black	90.7
Mexican-American	111.3

Source: Ford Foundation, 1984.

Less schooling is also related to the larger proportion of teenage mothers among Puerto Rican women. Fifteen percent of all mothers are teenagers, while 20 percent of Mexican and 23 percent of Puerto Rican mothers are under age 20 (Davis, Haub, and Willette, 1983). Age alone is not the determining feature; marital status is also important. Younger married Hispanic women are equally likely as non-Hispanics to use birth control, but never-married Hispanic women are half as likely to use contraception as Anglo women while both groups are equally sexually active (Davis, Haub, and Willette, 1983). Thus unmarried Puerto Rican teenagers who are sexually active are at higher risk of pregnancy than non-Hispanic teens.

Among married Puerto Rican women aged 20 to 34, fertility, or numbers of children, does reduce the likelihood of employment. It is recent fertility, or the presence of young children, rather than the total number of children that has the greatest inhibiting effect on employment. Further, fertility constrains work less among those of lower socioeconomic status than among high-income groups (Bean, Swicegood, and King, 1981). Said another way, those with high-family incomes prefer to stay home with young children, but those with little income cannot afford this choice.

If a Puerto Rican mother does work she must find some way to take care of her children during her absence. Hurst and Zambrana (1982) have studied the child care patterns of Puerto Rican women and they find some variation in methods used, according to the occupation of the mother (see Table 9.10).

TABLE 9.10

Mother's Occupation	Child Care Resources (%)			
	Self	Relatives	Nonrelatives	Total
Blue Collar	62	10	19	91
White Collar	21	68	11	100
Professional	21	38	41	100

Source: Hurst and Zambrana, 1982.

Blue-collar mothers perform much of the child care themselves, probably balancing work hours with children's school; white-collar mothers rely heavily on relatives; while professional mothers use relatives and nonrelatives almost equally.

Lower socioeconomic-status women felt the most conflict when not taking care of the children themselves, and all women felt the most preferable situation was for a grandmother to take care of the children, especially in their own home. In general, relatives were the preferred source of care until children were old enough for daycare or school.

As a result of these preferences, it is not marriage or childbearing per se that makes Puerto Rican women drop out of the labor force. The important question for them is availability of acceptable child care. The authors feel that family continuity of child care is the most important facilitator of women's employment. This may help to explain why there seems to be relatively little difference in the employment rates of married women and female household heads. It also means that there is a need for forms of public policy that facilitate child care by relatives. The authors suggest it would be helpful to find a way to pay relatives for child-care aid without jeopardizing any public assistance payments they might be receiving.

SEX ROLE ATTITUDES AND SOCIALIZATION

Social scientists who stress supply-side or individual variables often want to explain women's relative poverty using attitudinal variables. And, indeed, much of the literature on Puerto Rican culture does discuss the influence of machismo. To what extent do these attitudes actually affect Puerto Rican women's roles?

One recent article (Russell, 1983) highlights a survey which indicated that Puerto Rican attitudes about sex roles are more conservative than those of other Hispanics. While 55 percent of all Hispanics felt that masculinity was defined by being a good provider for a wife and children, two-thirds of Puerto Ricans agreed with this idea. Another survey (Ortiz and Santana Cooney, 1982) found that first-generation Hispanic women were more likely to hold traditional attitudes in comparison to second- and third-generation Hispanic women and to non-Hispanic white women.

However, in this same survey, Ortiz and Santana Cooney found that most of the differences between Hispanic and non-Hispanic white women's labor force participation rates are due to differences in educational attainment. Traditional sex role attitudes did not have a stronger impact on the labor force choices of young Hispanic women than on non-Hispanic women, once other demographic factors were controlled. Thus, while conservative sex role values are found among Puerto Rican women, it is not these attitudes that handicap them in the labor market. Their problems are based in their age, marital status, child bearing, and lower education which can place them in a disadvantaged position in the labor market.

DISCUSSION

This overview of the status of Puerto Rican women in the United States has examined both the problems and the gains that have been made. On the positive side, Puerto Rican women in the United States have a higher labor force participation rate than those on the island; they have a higher rate of employment in professional and technical jobs than other Hispanic groups in the United States; they have been able to make a tremendous switch from a concentration in operative jobs to one in white-collar roles; and they are increasing their average education levels. The Puerto Rican population has also become more geographically dispersed into better labor markets. On the other hand, Puerto Rican household income remains low. This is primarily due to the increasing numbers of female-headed households, whose low income brings down the median salary.

There are many factors that can explain such patterns. Some of the factors are individual ones. For example, level of education and presence of young children certainly influence employment. On the other hand, our review of the facts leads us to agree with Ríos (1985) that the major determining factors are structural and demand-side ones. First, region of residence can have a major impact on Puerto Rican women. This determines the types of jobs available; and, in the case of the New York City labor market, led to a great decline in employment when the garment industry contracted. Second, residential segregation, such as that in New York, increases the likelihood of marrying another Puerto Rican as well as the amount of social support received for cultural maintenance. Third, migration pools have important impacts on women by affecting the ratio of men to women and of U.S.- to Puerto Rico-born people in different parts of the country. This is correlated with rates of female headship and with the need for female employment. Fourth, government policies can affect women. The ability to move freely between the United States mainland and Puerto Rico both enhances cultural maintenance and allows families to move when ever job opportunities become poor in one place. And, of course, Puerto Rican women also labor under the burden of their double discrimination, by ethnicity and gender (Miranda King, 1979). These are the structural realities that Puerto Rican women collectively confront.

REFERENCES

Alvirez, David. 1981. "Socioeconomic Patterns and Diversity Among Hispanics." Research Bulletin of the Hispanic Research Center, Fordham University 4, nos. 2–3 (April–July): 11–14.

Angel, Ronald, and Marta Tienda. 1982. "Determinants of Extended Household Structure: Cultural Pattern or Economic Need?" American Journal of Sociology 87, no. 6: 1, 360–83.

Bean, Frank D., Gray Swicegood, and Allan G. King. 1981. "Fertility and Labor Supply Among Hispanic American Women." Austin, Texas: University of Texas Population Research Center Papers, No. 3.017.

Davis, Cary, Carl Haub, and JoAnne Willette. 1983. "U.S. Hispanics: Changing the Face of America." Population Bulletin 38, no. 3. Washington, D.C.: Population Reference Bureau, Inc.

Ferree, Myra Marx. 1979. "Employment Without Liberation: Cuban Women in the United States." Social Science Quarterly 60, no. 1 (June): 35–50.

Ford Foundation. 1984. "Hispanics: Challenges and Opportunities." Working paper no. 435. New York: Ford Foundation Office of Reports (June).

Frisbie, W. Parker, Jan Mutchler, Dudley L. Poston, Jr., William Kelly, Harley Browning, Lauren Krivo, and Frank Bean. 1982. "Household-Family Structure and Socioeconomic Differentials: A Comparison of Hispanics, Blacks, and Anglos." Austin, Texas: Texas Population Research Center, Paper No. 4.009.

Guhleman, Patricia, and Marta Tienda. 1981. "A Socioeconomic Profile of Hispanic-American Female Workers: Perspectives on Labor Force Participation and Earnings." Madison, Wisconsin: Center for Demography and Ecology, Working Paper 81–7 (March).

Gurak, Douglas T. 1981. "Family Structural Diversity of Hispanic Ethnic Groups." Research Bulletin of the Hispanic Research Center, Fordham University 4, nos. 2–3 (April–July): 6–10.

Hernández, José. 1983. Puerto Rican Youth Employment. New Jersey: Waterfront Press.

Hurst, Marsha, and Ruth E. Zambrana. 1982. "Child Care and Working Mothers in Puerto Rican Families." Annals, AAPSS 461 (May): 113–24.

Jaffe, A. J., Ruth M. Cullen, and Thomas D. Boswell. 1980. The Changing Demography of Spanish Americans. New York: Academic Press.

Miranda King, Lourdes. 1979. "Puertorriqueñas in the United States: The Impact of Double Discrimination." In The Puerto Rican Woman, ed. Edna Acosta-Belén, pp. 124–33. New York: Praeger.

National Puerto Rican Forum, Inc. 1981. The Next Step Toward Equality: A Comprehensive Study of Puerto Ricans in the United States Mainland. New York: National Puerto Rican Forum.

Newman, Morris J. 1978. "A Profile of Hispanics in the U.S. Workforce." Monthly Labor Review 101, no. 12 (December): 3–14.

Ortiz, Vilma, and Rosemary Santana Cooney. 1982. "Sex-Role Attitudes and Labor Force Participation: A Comparative Study of Hispanic Females and Non-Hispanic White Females." Paper presented at the annual meetings of the American Sociological Association, San Francisco.

Ríos, Palmira N. 1985. "Puerto Rican Women in the United States Labor Market." Paper presented at the conference on "The Changing Hispanic Community in the U.S.," State University of New York at Albany, March.

Roth, Dennis M. 1983. "Hispanics in the U.S. Labor Force: A Brief Examination." In Congressional Research Service, The Hispanic Population of the United States: An Overview. Report prepared for the House Subcommittee on Census and Population of the Committee on Post Office and Civil Service. Washington, D.C.: U.S. Government Printing Office.

Russell, Cheryl. 1983. "The News About Hispanics." American Demographics 5, no. 3 (March): 15–25.

Santana Cooney, Rosemary. 1979a. "Intercity Variations in Puerto Rican Female Participation." The Journal of Human Resources 4, no. 2: 222–35.

—————. 1979b. "Demographic Components of Growth in White, Black, and Puerto Rican Female-Headed Families: Comparison of the Cutright and Ross/Sawhill Methodologies." Social Science Research 8: 144–58.

Santana Cooney, Rosemary, and Alice E. Colón Warren. 1980. "Work and Family: The Recent Struggle of Puerto Rican Females." In The Puerto Rican Struggle: Essays on Survival in the U.S., ed. Clara E. Rodríguez, Virginia Sánchez Korrol, and José Oscar Alers, pp. 58–73. New York: Puerto Rican Migration Research Consortium, Inc.

————. 1979. "Declining Female Participation among Puerto Rican New Yorkers: A Comparison with Native White NonSpanish New Yorkers." Ethnicity 6, no. 3 (September): 281–97.

Santana Cooney, Rosemary, and Vilma Ortiz. 1983. "Nativity, National Origin, and Hispanic Female Participation in the Labor Force." Social Science Quarterly 64, no. 3 (September): 510–23.

Stolzenberg, Ross. 1984. "Occupational Achievement of U.S. Hispanic Women." Paper presented at the annual meeting of the Population Association of America, Minneapolis, May.

Tienda, Marta, and Ronald Angel. 1982. "Headship and Household Composition Among Blacks, Hispanics, and Other Whites." Social Forces 61, no. 2 (December): 508–30.

Tienda, Marta, and Jennifer Glass. 1983. "Extended Household Composition and Female Labor Force Participation." Madison, Wisconsin: University of Wisconsin Center for Demography and Ecology, Working Paper 83–27, June.

Tienda, Marta, and Patricia Guhleman. 1982. "The Occupational Position of Employed Hispanic Women." Madison, Wisconsin: Institute for Research on Poverty, Discussion Papers # 708–82, September.

U.S. Bureau of the Census. 1983. Statistical Abstract of the U.S.: 1984. Washington, D.C.: U.S. Government Printing Office.

————. 1981. Statistical Abstract of the U.S.: 1981. Washington, D.C.: U.S. Government Printing Office.

U.S. Department of Labor, Women's Bureau. 1983. Time of Change: 1983 Handbook on Women Workers. Bulletin 298. Washington, D.C.: U.S. Government Printing Office.

Wagenheim, Kal. 1975. A Survey of Puerto Ricans on the U.S. Mainland in the 1970's. New York: Praeger.

Wagenheim, Kal, with the assistance of Leslie Dunbar. 1983. "Puerto Ricans in the U.S." New York: Minority Rights Group, Report no. 58, January.

10

The Forgotten Migrant: Educated Puerto Rican Women in New York City, 1920-1940

Virginia Sánchez Korrol

Throughout the decades before the Second World War, thousands of working- and middle-class Puerto Rican women lived and labored in the early migrant settlements of New York City. Faced with the economic realities of the over-whelmingly poor communities, many found ways to combine a traditional home life with gainful employment. Others worked outside the home in factories, as seamstresses, domestics, laundresses, or as unskilled workers.[1] While the majority of the female migrant population fit into these categories, a handful, usually skilled, bilingual, or formerly educated women, wrested a foothold in other directions. Recognized and respected for their achievements in Puerto Rico, they proceeded to initiate enterprises and activities in New York City based on past experiences as well as current needs of the migrant settlements. Some sought clerical or white-collar jobs upon arriving in the city, contributing to the development of the community by virtue of their class and subsequent involvement. Others channeled middle-class goals and aspirations into volunteer organizational work. And others pursued artistic and creative talents writing poetry and essays, publishing the journals or newsletters of the community in much the same way they had done in Puerto Rico. All played pivotal roles in shaping and developing the dynamic Puerto Rican New York community of the interwar years.

A diverse community welcomed the migrants of that period. By the mid-twenties, the colonia hispana straddled the East River with barrios in the boroughs of Brooklyn and Manhattan. Their emigration engineered and conditioned by the particular political relationship between the island and the United States, Puerto Ricans predominated among a Spanish-speaking population of roughly 100,000 individuals. Theirs was a tightly-knit, introspective community where local, small business people enjoyed a degree of leadership among less privileged neighbors; where community organizations boasted substantial audiences of one or two hundred persons at any given function; and where Spanish-language newspapers and magazines found an eagerly supportive reading public. La Prensa, for example, was founded by 1913, and became a daily by 1918. Magazines like Gráfico, El Heraldo, and Revista de Artes y Letras enjoyed long literary lives. By the mid-thirties Puerto Ricans resided in all five boroughs, not only creating new neighborhoods, but re-creating individual roles and behavioral patterns based on island experience, redesigned to meet the needs of the New York community.[2]

How did the small group of educated women fit into this community and what directions did they take? A closer look into individual case histories underscores the connections between the earlier experiences of migrant women, their subsequent activities in the New York colonias and, in most cases, their conscious efforts to forge and maintain links between both geographic points. One case in point was Josefina Silva de Cintrón. She began her career as an elementary school teacher in Caguas, Puerto Rico. Distinguished before long as a community leader in Rio Piedras, Silva de Cintrón was also credited with establishing the first post office in Hato Rey, working with the Red Cross and with the Corte de Lourdes. In the field of journalism she collaborated with feminist Mercedes Solá in the publication of La mujer en el siglo XX, a journal which promoted suffrage and the rights of women. Moreover, Silva de Cintrón also wrote for the journals of her time using the pen name, Lidia.[3]

Successful enterprises followed in New York where she pursued similar intellectual and political inclinations. An active participant in numerous social, political, cultural, and professional organizations, Silva de Cintrón assumed leadership in several. These included the Unión de mujeres americanas and the League of Spanish-speaking Democrats. Among her many roles and contributions in the New York colonias, perhaps her most impressive was the creation of a monthly journal, Revista de Artes y Letras. Flourishing in the city from 1933 until 1945, the journal performed several functions. First, it deliberately promoted the preservation of the Spanish language, culture, and literary traditions. Second, it created awareness regarding the many social-cultural events and activities taking place among the Puerto Ricans and other Spanish-speaking groups in the city. Third, the journal assumed an international dimension by reporting significant cultural, social, and political events taking place throughout the Spanish-speaking world. Fourth, Artes y Letras highlighted the achievements and contributions of Latin women in the Americas. Finally, the journal presented a middle-class point of view which more often than not, rested on tacit acceptance of the colonial relationship between Puerto Rico and the United States.[4]

The journal featured articles on family and child welfare, while editorials abounded with relevant community issues and other concerns of the colonia. Its literary pages presented the writings of the feminist Julia de Burgos or lesser known poets such as Carmen Alicia Cadilla. Essays and short stories shared space with news of community groups, activities, and events. And the society pages divulged the private lives of community leaders, reporting their comings and goings in exaggerated fashion. In short, Artes y Letras reported the social-cultural interaction of the city's Spanish-speaking.

The unique structure of the journal's editorial board insured female input. The board consisted of eleven members, six of whom were women and each represented a different Latin American country. The majority of these women were well-educated and accomplished individuals who related somewhat to their peers in the United States and continued to maintain connections with others of similar class, ideology, and backgrounds in their home countries.

One issue recorded the 1938 Conference of Pan American Women whose theme on that occasion was the union of the "feminine element of the Western Hemisphere through culture." Another issue focused on the presentation of awards to outstanding women in community service and the proceedings of the International Sunshine Society—an association of women journalists. The column Valores Femeninos highlighted the careers of prominent women, holding them as proper models of behavior.[5]

Finally, Josefina Silva de Cintrón used Artes y Letras to convey an organizational network and social elite to the Hispanic community of New York. In the society columns privileged families frequently traveled between San Juan and New York, to Madrid and other European capitals. Students graduated with honors from good universities and exuberant newlyweds read of their elaborate celebrations in the journal's pages. Condolences were appropriately extended and congratulations expressed for a constellation of personal achievements.

When Silva de Cintrón committed her talents and energies to the betterment of the colonia hispana, she was, in a sense, following a familiar path. Others who had appeared at the helm of social, political, or educational group activities in Puerto Rico also claimed a New York interlude. Luisa Capetillo, for example, was employed for a time as a reader in the tobacco factories. She undertook organizational work as well as a quest for social reform in politics and in the factories. An avowed feminist and socialist, Capetillo brought vast experiences to the New York community.[6] Lola Rodríguez de Tío (1843–1924), poet and revolutionary, played a vital role in the island's independence movements but also interacted in the organizational life of the early settlements. Along with compatriots, Arturo Schomberg, José Martí, and Luis Muñoz Rivera, she was a welcomed speaker at numerous functions staged by the community, and frequently linked the political or cultural agendas of the colonia with island interests.[7] Yet another example in later years was provided by Julia de Burgos (1914–1953). The oldest child of a poor campesino family, she grew up in a working-class environment and struggled to obtain an education. As a teacher, her strong identification with the Nationalist movement led her to active political participation in Puerto Rico and later on in New York. Forced by circumstances to work in the city's factories, she was intimately acquainted with a working-class existence and the difficulties in adapting to a harsh and alien environment. These experiences provided themes for her poetry and insight into the urgent needs of the New York barrios.[8]

Like Julia de Burgos, others attempted to alleviate the plight of the working class through a variety of methods. One who did was writer and folklorist, Pura Belpré.[9] Intensely active in community organizational work during the period under consideration, Pura Belpré was considered the first Puerto Rican librarian in the city's public library system. Born in Cidra, Puerto Rico, in 1902, her earliest memories of life in the island were conditioned by hard times, frequent family upheavals, and a series of internal migrations which eventually led to New York. Arriving as a child, the major part of her education was undertaken in the city and by 1921, Belpré began library work at the 135th Street branch. She soon graduated to more responsibility as chief children's librarian and was transferred to the 115th Street branch in Southwest Harlem, a predominantly Puerto Rican neighborhood.

Articulating vivid recollections of life in the Puerto Rican colonia, Belpré observed two trends among the women. First, an emphasis on traditional family values and second, a remarkable interest in Puerto Rican culture and heritage. According to Belpré, women often struggled to keep family life intact. During critical economic periods, women sold their needlework and handicrafts from door to door in an effort to supplement their meager incomes. Grandmothers, charged with the obligation of caring for the young, frequently visited the library searching for books in Spanish to teach their grandchildren their native language. These observations inspired Belpré's contributions in this direction.[10]

She began telling stories focusing on Puerto Rican themes, values, and folkways, but soon graduated to translating the latter into English, writing her own children's stories, and designing programs for specific occasions. Part of these programs entailed convincing notable Hispanic visitors in New York to visit the library in the colonia hispana as well. Thus, a renowned poetess like Gabriela Mistral or the Puerto Rican tenor Antonio Paoli would include a special library presentation as part of their itinerary. Under Belpré's direction, the library could sponsor cultural events on Latin themes, confident of the participation of experts such as Dr. Federico de Onís, director of the Instituto de Las Españas, community leaders like Claudia Arán, or perhaps the well-known dance team of Pérez y Martínez or Lola Bravo. By 1937 the Aguilar branch was also presenting special programs commemorating important religious and cultural feast days like Three Kings Day, Columbus Day, or St. John's Festival. The crowning jewel of Belpré's professional activities was the South Bronx Project—the creation of a bilingual program within the New York City library system.[11]

Belpré's activities, while undoubtedly demanding, were not solely confined to the library, however. Like others in the colonia hispana Doña Pura extended her services throughout the community. She created cultural children's programs for the Educational Alliance, the Union Settlement House, Madison House, and Casita María, where her audiences consisted of mostly Irish students preparing to work with Puerto Rican youth. Similar programs were initiated at the YWCA between 5th and Lenox Avenues where she began an informal equivalent of the present-day head-start program. Finally, Belpré maintained an active membership in several community groups; among them, Puerto Rico Literario, and Asociación de Escritores y Periodistas Puertorriqueños, and supported the work of others such as the Liga

Puertorriqueña or the Alianza Obrera.[12]

Others like Belpré concentrated their efforts on improving their immediate surroundings, choosing to work with the everyday problems facing the migrants. Sister Carmelita Bonilla, a case in point, represented Puerto Ricans within the religious orders. She arrived in the city as a teenager en route to Georgia where she took her vows as a Trinitarian nun. Subsequently assigned to a convent in Brooklyn, her new responsibilities required involvement in social welfare, housing, educational and vocational counseling, public health, and religious education. Her recollections evoked memories of a poor working-class community where she was frequently called upon as a translator and as an intermediary between the Spanish-speaking residents and the non-Hispanics. The barrio's children were her greatest concern. She set up afterschool programs in arts and crafts and established tutorial services. Many youngsters of that period credited Sister Carmelita for encouraging their academic growth and aspirations. Her own education included earning a bachelor's and a master's degree. As one of the founders of the settlement house, Casita María, she continued to direct and influence the social, cultural, educational, and economic welfare of the pre-World War II colonia.[13]

Doctora Eloisa García Rivera, on the other hand, made her mark in politics and education. A university graduate upon her arrival in the city, Doña Eloisa completed graduate work in Spanish literature and devoted her attention to community service. Firmly believing that a woman's place was beside her husband's, García Rivera immersed herself in his political career. At the height of her political involvement, she directed her husband's campaign for the New York State Legislature. Speaking on his behalf, she also directed voter registration drives and provided a rudimentary daycare system so that mothers could vote. In addition to community politics, Doctora García Rivera taught courses in Spanish literature at the college level, maintained an active membership in numerous community organizations, and was among the founders of the Puerto Rican Forum.

Yet another perspective appeared in the case of Honorina Irizarry, who came to live in her brother's comfortable Brooklyn home during the decade of the twenties. An accomplished secretary in Puerto Rico, Irizarry had studied and perfected her clerical skills before undertaking the move. Once in the Brooklyn barrio, determined to work and use her mind and skills, she sought employment in spite of her family's objections. They considered working "unladylike."[14]

An exceptional woman for her times, Irizarry embarked on a successful career as a bilingual secretary and studied at Erasmus Hall High School at night. In time she mastered five languages fluently and earned a degree in liberal arts. Her community contribution was mainly in the political area. She also participated actively on campaigns and fund raisers for the Puerto Rican Democratic clubs and her position within the community afforded her a degree of leadership as well.

Finally, the experiences of Raquel Rivera Hernández provided yet another dimension of community involvement. Doña Raquel came to New York in 1938 en route to college in Pennsylvania. After graduation she returned to New York where her first job consisted of intercepting coded materials—letters, newspapers, and magazines—destined for Spain, Latin America, or the Spanish Caribbean. It was 1942, and the onset of the Second World War motivated the hiring of over 1,000 Puerto Rican postal workers to fill essential positions as censors in that unit's division. Many of these individuals, including Doña Raquel, held university or advanced degrees. Others were college professors, writers, or artists. All were required to demonstrate their language and academic proficiency by passing the civil service examination.[15]

Recalling that period in her life, Doña Raquel often marveled at the many talented, well-educated Puerto Ricans who through unforeseen circumstances found themselves working together in the wartime post office. Had the Puerto Rican community harnessed the leadership potential and abilities displayed within this setting, it would have made a tremendous impact at a critical point in the community's development. She also believed that her work and that of the others was was crucial to the war effort. In addition to performing her work tasks carefully and efficiently, Doña Raquel also participated in numerous work-oriented activities. These included membership in postal worker's organizations and programming cultural and social events. The earliest associations of Spanish-speaking postal workers emerged at this time. One such group sponsored recreational programs, fund raisers for group projects or worthy causes, cultural affairs, the publication of a newsletter, and the staging of various musical extravaganzas. The latter featured the talents of the employee-members themselves.

The task of recovering and defining the Puerto Rican experience during the inter-war years is clearly underway. The issue of women at work in and outside of the home has already formed the basis of several studies, while their involvement in the formation of the ILGWU and in New York City's educational system is under investigation.[16] We have identified a small group of migrant women who early in the settlement process assumed the reins of leadership, embraced demanding volunteer projects, or engaged in securing professional, creative, or clerical outlets following in the wake of aborted island careers.

Without doubt, the majority within this group opted to civilize rather than liberate their working-class sisters who stubbornly clung to the sanctity of their domestic, subordinate roles. This attitude, inherent also among the community activists and educated women, inhibited the spread of anything other than the most basic feminist consciousness. As products of a patriarchal society, they neither expected nor demanded profound changes, concentrating instead on influencing the transfer of a bourgeois Puerto Rican family model to the new environment. Many mystified the home and family, writing and lecturing on domestic economy, health, hygiene, and morality within a North American capitalist orbit.[17] Others exhibited an overriding preoccupation with maintaining culture and traditions at a time when both faced eradication and colonial policies. Fewer radically confronted the migrant condition head-on, laying its causes on the political, colonial doorstep.

On the other hand, their actions aided in the stabilization of the infant community at a significant historical juncture. From the decade of the twenties to just after the Second World War, Puerto Ricans in New York struggled to lay the foundations for a distinctive community with formal and informal coping institutions, internal leadership, businesses, professionals, common cultural interests, and modes of behavior. The population movements alone, punctuated by the unique circular nature of the Puerto Rican situation, evidenced repeated ruptures and renewals of ties, dismantlings and reconstructions of familial, individual, and communal networks. Through group work and involvement, women like Belpré or García Rivera were frequently in the public eye; their actions reported in community presses intended to saturate the pioneer settlements. As fund raisers, sponsors of cultural affairs, sentinels of culture and tradition, others, like Silva de Cintrón, occupied somewhat exalted niches in the community—las damas, senoras y senoritas of a bygone island era. As writers and journalists, they re-enacted a multifaceted role—they created and articulated the community's innermost concerns; maintained active bonds with their peers and class across the ocean; and shaped feminine ideology.

While their numbers remained inconsequential in

comparison to the overall population, they were trailblazers during a transitional period. We have yet to evaluate their actual influence in terms of community and individual conformations—indeed, we have just begun to discover them! Yet in traditional Latin, class-conscious style, the actions of the more privileged would set the tone for others to emulate. Although the actual circulation of a publication like Artes y Letras is unknown, it is clear that someone was buying the high-quality journal over a long period of time. Similarly, the contributions and subsequent influence exerted by community activists, writers, artists, white-collar workers, and professionals cannot be overlooked.

NOTES

1. See Virginia Sánchez Korrol, "Settlement Patterns and Community Development Among Puerto Ricans in New York, 1917–1948," (Ph.D. diss., SUNY at Stony Brook, 1981), pp. 152–207. Also "On the Other Side of the Ocean: Work Experiences of Early Puerto Rican Migrant Women in New York," Carribbean Review, 7, no. 1 (January-March 1979): 22–28.
2. See Virginia Sánchez Korrol, From Colonia to Community: History of Puerto Ricans in New York City, 1917–1948 (Westport, CT: Greenwood Press, 1983), chap. 2, pp. 11–50.
3. Pedro Caballero, "Doña Josefina Silva de Cintrón ante los hispanos," Revista de Artes y Letras, June 1935, p. 3. Also telephone interview with J. Silva Cintrón, New York City, 1977.
4. Sánchez Korrol, From Colonia to Community, pp. 74–75.
5. Pedro Caballero, "Del Madrid literario," Revista de Artes y Letras, October 1938, p. 9.
6. Isabel Picó de Hernández, "The History of Women's Struggle for Equality in Puerto Rico," and Norma Valle Ferrer, "Feminism and its Influence on Women's Organizations in Puerto Rico," in The Puerto Rican Woman, ed. Edna Acosta-Belén (New York: Praeger, 1979), pp. 25–37 and pp. 38–50.
7. César Andreu Iglesias, Memorias de Bernardo Vega (Río Piedras, P.R.: Ediciones Huracán, 1977), pp. 106–7.
8. Margarite Fernández Olmos, "From the Metropolis: Puerto Rican Women Poets and the Immigration Experience," Third Woman 1, no. 2 (1982): 40–51.
9. Interview with Pura Belpré, Brooklyn College, Spring 1979. See also Lillian López, "Interview with Pura

Belpré," Columbia University Oral History Project.

10. Ibid.

11. Ibid.

12. Andreu Iglesias, Memorias de Bernardo Vega. See also Sánchez Korrol, From Colonia to Community, Appendixes 1 and 2, pp. 213–22, for a listing of members and organizations of that period.

13. Interview with Sister Carmelita Bonilla, Puerto Rican Oral History Project, Long Island Historical Society, Brooklyn, New York. See also Anthony Stevens-Arroyo, "Puerto Rican Struggles in the Catholic Church," in The Puerto Rican Struggle: Essays on Survival in the U.S., ed. Clara E. Rodríguez, Virginia Sánchez Korrol, and Oscar Alers (New York: Puerto Rican Migration Research Consortium, 1980), pp. 129–39.

14. Interview with Eloisa García Rivera, New York City, 1977. Oscar García Rivera was the first Puerto Rican to serve in the New York Legislature in 1937. Interview with Honorina Weber Irizarry, Puerto Rican Oral History Project, Long Island Historical Society.

15. Interviews with Raquel and Antonio Rivera Hernández, Río Piedras, Puerto Rico, August 1977. Also Certificates of Incorporation for (1) Puerto Rican Employees Association, File No. 68070–36C, 1936; and (2) Puerto Rican Veterans Welfare Postal Workers Association, File No. 5440–70-3, 1951, in the County Clerk's Office, New York City.

16. See Sánchez Korrol, "On the Other Side of the Ocean; Altagracia Ortiz, "Puerto Rican Women in the ILGWU, 1940–1950," paper presented at Women's Studies Conference, Brooklyn College, April 1984; Acosta-Belén, The Puerto Rican Woman.

17. Revista de Artes y Letras is a good example.

11

The Black Puerto Rican Woman in Contemporary American Society

Angela Jorge

In searching, in trying to capture, that which the Puerto Rican woman can, and does bring to the feminist movement in the United States, this writer has been struck by the rather low profile of the black Hispanic woman in the struggle for women's rights. Her apparent reticence to join, and her apparent low visibility in the movement are based, perhaps, on the belief that for her there is another struggle that if not won will cause her immolation, her genocide. Admittedly, this is a strong statement. However, my own personal and professional experiences, coupled with the many informal gatherings with other black Puerto Rican women in which we have invariably discussed not only our role within (or feelings about) the feminist movement, but also our role in general within the Puerto Rican community, give validity to the quality of the statement.

From these gatherings, personal observations, and experiences, some not-too-evident truths have emerged which need to be analyzed. First, there is a difference between the black Puerto Rican woman raised in Puerto Rico with its covert racism, often overshadowed by the issue of social class differences and colonial status, and the woman

---

This paper was originally presented at the <u>Symposium on the Hispanic-American Woman</u> held at the State University of New York at Albany in 1976.

raised in the United States, an openly racist society. In addition, since Puerto Ricans express racial differences according to gradations of color (Seda Bonilla, 1970), each classification represents a gradation of color among black Puerto Rican women which is accompanied by different attitudes and perceptions about color. The terms mulata, jabá, trigueña, prieta, negra, and grifa are all defined according to color gradations and traits.[1] Finally, differences also exist between the first, second, and third generations of black Puerto Rican women in contemporary American society which are the result of their ability or inability to cope with the racism that confronts them. Each of the differences cited warrants a detailed analysis that is long overdue, and almost nonexistent in the literature found today about the Puerto Rican experience on the mainland. In the absence of such research, this writer has decided to limit her remarks to personal observations about the black Puerto Rican woman in our present-day society. Although many of these personal observations and conversations have taken place in New York, what will be recounted here is something that I suspect black Puerto Rican women in other areas of the United States can readily identify with.

For many, the title of this chapter will be unacceptable, since it will be perceived of as divisive precisely at a time when the Puerto Rican people need to be united. However, it seems to me that nothing can be more obviously divisive than the exclusion of this topic in particular and of the question of color in general from the debate on Puerto Rican identity on the mainland. The uniqueness of the problems faced by the black Puerto Rican woman in American society must be discussed openly. Furthermore, these problems must not be ignored by the feminist movement which is seeking the emancipation and liberation of the Hispanic woman. The fact of being considered three minorities in one: Black, Puerto Rican, and woman, is, in and of itself, a tremendous psychological burden which must be understood.

The black Puerto Rican woman's blackness is attacked from two fronts. First, American society constantly reaffirms through schooling, employment, housing, social interactions, and institutions the inferior status of black people in this country. Second, the continued denial of the existence of racism among Puerto Ricans because of the racial mixture of its population creates a sense of ambiguity in personal relationships with family and friends. The one overriding feeling generated by the ambiguity of the Puerto Rican community about color is that of guilt at having disgraced first the family and then the community by simply being black or darker than other members of the family. The popular dictum adelantar la raza tends only to reinforce this feeling of guilt.[2]

The imperative of the above dictum and the accompanying societal commitment, whether conscious or unconscious, so rules our lives that the Puerto Rican people are progressively "whitening" themselves. This whitening process is aided by the myth of color blindness that is perpetuated by several U.S. writers. For instance, according to Clarence Senior "the 1950 U.S. Census classified the people of Puerto Rico as 79.9 percent white and 20.3 percent non-white. The proportion of non-whites has been dropping steadily since the 38.6 percent found in the first United States Census taken in the island in 1899" (1965:46). He also says that "there are no . . . major differences in life chances associated with skin color in Puerto Rico and supposedly on the mainland as are reflected in differential birth, death, and morbidity rates in the States" (p. 45). Senior underscores his point by quoting a statement made before the New York City Board of Education by a representative of the Puerto Rican Forum that ". . . the Puerto Rican looks at himself as being wholly integrated racially" (pp. 46–47). The mutual contradiction between the concept of whitening, or adelantar la raza, and the supposed "wholly integrated racially" character of the Puerto Rican community is too obvious to warrant further comment. At least it is obvious to any black Puerto Rican woman who wishes to develop and maintain an integrated black identity devoid of guilt and, at the same time, maintain her Puerto Rican identity.

If the Puerto Rican is so integrated, and if miscegenation had solved all the problems associated with identity crisis, then Eduardo Seda Bonilla (1970) would not have found that the black Puerto Rican in the United States tends to adapt and progressively assimilate into society as a black. For many, the assimilation is so complete as to affect their speech in English to such an extent that they, according to Seda Bonilla, speak English with a Southern accent (p. 93). (This writer would venture to say that what he calls a Southern accent may well be black English.) Obviously, by the next generation—if not by the present one—the black Puerto Rican who has assimilated will no longer identify—or be identified—socially and emotionally with the Puerto Rican community.[3] The black Puerto Rican in this situation gives birth to non-Puerto Ricans. Because of the proximity of the black American community to our own, the racial attitudes of the Puerto Rican community on the mainland have been challenged to a degree that they have never been on the island. According to a Puerto Rican Forum document, although to the Puerto Rican ". . . his racial heritage is neither a subject of shame nor of particular pride simply a fact," it is ". . . an important social fact that whereas the census allows a percentage of Puerto Ricans to classify themselves as White, the great majority of non-Puerto Ricans in the United States do not classify the great majority of Puerto Ricans as White (1964: 19). Thus, while "10 percent of Puerto Ricans are Negro, another 50–60 percent are non-White by social classification" (Rodríguez, 1974: 92–93). The mainland Puerto Rican community can continue to turn away from this challenge or it can choose to analyze it and use it as a catalyst to the undertaking of an in-depth study of the entire question of racism, within the already established issue of the Puerto Rican identity crisis.

Certainly more background information can be given to reinforce what has already been stated. First of all, this writer is defining as black, that Puerto Rican woman who would be described as negra or prieta by the Puerto Rican community. This delimitation is necessary because although the trigueña, mulata, jabá, and grifa are considered black by American racial definitions (and periodically they do experience the impact of the descendant rule that dictates that a Negro is anyone having one drop of Negro blood), each can opt to delude herself in ways not available to black—definitely Negroid—Puerto Rican women. She can choose to emphasize her Indian and European heritage, rather than the black. It is the prieta, the negra who is perceived beyond any doubt as black by both the American and Puerto Rican communities. There is no ambiguity about her. Her Negritude in terms of hair texture, features, and finally color is undeniable. Therefore, the black Puerto Rican woman in contemporary society is in a unique position since her oppression is threefold. She is oppressed because of her sex, cultural identity, and color. One would think that this three-sided oppression is sufficient; however, she is further oppressed by the act of omission or absence of literature addressing her needs. She is an endangered species which has attracted little attention or outcry from a concerned Puerto Rican professional community.

As the black Puerto Rican woman goes through the various stages of life—childhood, adolescence, and adulthood—the blackness of her skin and the clearly Negroid physical characteristics make her experiences within each stage different from those of her lighter-skinned sister in the struggle for emancipation and liberation. The traumatization of the black Puerto Rican woman during childhood and adolescence is generally subtle, since she is somewhat insulated by her community (the barrio). Although she is a minority within a minority, identity as a Puerto Rican during the early stages of her life is fairly strong. Her early school years are spent in the neighborhood and with a Spanish-surname she will definitely be identified as Hispanic. Furthermore, the negative feelings that are generated by non-Puerto Ricans in this social setting are directed against Puerto Ricans as a group and not specifically against the individual. With the barrio, she will also be identified as Hispanic, because the neighborhoods tend to have strict demarcations that separate the black Americans from the Puerto Rican neighborhood, although both live in the same ghetto.

Generally, at this early stage, the feelings of inadequacy and guilt are developed within the immediate family. The young black Puerto Rican woman begins to sense that everything about her—her short kinky hair, her thick lips, and most of all her color are things to be resented. Never has a kind word been said about her hair; consequently, the day she can comb her own hair is a day of jubilation. No longer is someone pulling on it and muttering invectives such as, ¡Maldito sea este pelo! (Damn this hair!) or making the following statement in a martyred tone: ¡Dios mio! ¡Este pelo! (Dear Lord, this hair! the tone is usually of one who feels that this is their cross to bear in their lifetime.) This is a particularly painful experience, both physically and psychologically.

The black Puerto Rican woman must, furthermore, always be sure to keep her lips together so that the lower lip is never found hanging down. Whenever she forgets, a family member will dutifully tell her ¡Cierra la bemba! (Close your mouth! Demanding that you avoid leaving your lower lip, generally the thicker lip, hanging.) These remarks are said emphatically, and never cease to bewilder. At first, it is difficult to understand why her hair and lips can bring proof that the family failed to contribute meaningfully to the dictum adelantar la raza. She also becomes the living proof of the guilt the family feels, and finally, the receiver of the family's effort to transfer that guilty feeling to her.

As if growing up in this hostile environment were not enough, when the black Puerto Rican woman begins to develop peer-level relationships beyond the boundaries of her barrio, the traumatization becomes truly dramatic.

When she begins to seek companionship with others who look like her (that is, black Americans), with those who will not reject her, she will hear ¡Con esa no juegues! (Literally, "Don't play with that one!" but it conveys a meaning of not getting involved with a particular individual because of a potential threat.) Nothing more is said. However, a strong and racist statement has been implicitly made which is that one should associate with certain people and that there is something inherently wrong with seeking out certain relationships. Now this young woman is made to believe that in addition to not being pretty, her color has the potential of also making her unacceptable.

When she begins attempting to establish meaningful relationships with the opposite sex, her blackness presents still other unique problems for her. The Puerto Rican obsession with adelantar la raza makes it impossible for her to make a choice independent of the consideration of color. Whether the phrase has been said seriously or en forma de broma (jokingly) the family has reaffirmed the inferiority of her blackness and the need for her to change that situation by marrying someone very light, if not white. With such a marriage, the black Puerto Rican woman experiences the embrace of a loving family. Conversely, the rejection of a dark-skinned, or a darker-skinned, potential suitor is explicit in the dictum. In fact, it is so explicit that the black Puerto Rican woman is forced automatically to do so. She quickly understands that any intimacy with a black American male is absolutely taboo, and that to engage in such a relationship is to be forced to assimilate socially into that group, essentially giving up her identity as a Puerto Rican.

With a widening of the social circle to include social activities, either at college or the place of employment, the young black Puerto Rican woman begins to hear statements like, "I didn't know you were Puerto Rican," or "You don't look Puerto Rican." This obviously becomes still another reaffirmation of her blackness, since essentially what the speaker is admitting is that her blackness takes precedence over every other consideration. For her, there is no middle ground. Even the simple daily experience of walking on the streets becomes a major trauma. In her neighborhood someone invariably would echarle flores (make a complimentary remark to a woman). However, now that she has left the confines of her barrio and the protection of her neighborhood, she becomes one more black woman among many others. A black woman is not admired, or even glanced at, by most Latin men, since they too are operating under the dictum of adelantar la raza. An excellent example is given in a Brookings Institution study about a Puerto Rican automobile mechanic, residing in an upstate city in New York, who inserted an advertisement in an island paper for a wife, who, among other qualifications, had to be either white or mulatto (1930:8). The white man too, will not look at the black Puerto Rican woman (unless he thinks she is a prostitute), since to establish a friendship which may lead to marriage, is to invite the wrath of the dominant society. The black man, on the other hand, will venture forward, but will fail to understand why his friendly overtures are rebuffed. For the black Puerto Rican woman knows that to accept his offer of friendship, of intimacy, is to invite the wrath of her family and, to some degree, of her community.

Since the outer society, the white-dominant American society perceives the black Puerto Rican woman in terms of black vs. white, she is under constant pressure to make choices within these limits only. Admittedly, she has the option of avoiding this conflict by staying exclusively within the confines of her barrio. Never venturing out of the barrio, however, does not help her to integrate the parts of herself—black, Puerto Rican, and woman—into a meaningful whole anymore than does the larger racist American society, or even her assimilation into black American society. Without that integration, she is susceptible to all types of psychological pressures that force her to play an active role in her own genocide, eventually leading to the total disappearance of people like her from the Puerto Rican group. As I mentioned earlier, the role of the black Puerto Rican woman in the Hispanic woman's effort for emancipation and liberation cannot be isolated from her need to integrate within herself the three minorities that she represents.

These observations on the black Puerto Rican woman in contemporary American society have not offered solutions, primarily because none will be forthcoming until such time that the Puerto Rican community is able to recognize overtly its racism and deal with it within the context of the search for a meaningful Puerto Rican identity. While some individuals may achieve, through reflection and discussion, psychological and moral liberation from the consequences of racism, the Puerto Rican community as a whole still needs to address the wider social questions of injustice, inequality, and prejudice which are the heart of racism in the society at large.

NOTES

1. Jabá refers to someone who is light-skinned, but has features or hair texture which indicate African ancestry. Trigueña is an olive-skinned, dark-complexioned brunette. It is also an expression used to describe a non-white person when wishing not to use the words negra or prieta, which are generally considered offensive. Prieta is defined as dark, swarthy; tight, compact; stingy, niggardly. Grifa is a term that is interchangeable with jabá and both are used to describe someone who is light-skinned and has Caucasian features but frizzled hair.

2. Adelantar la raza means literally to improve the race; to go through a whitening process by marrying someone light-skinned, if not white.

3. A classic example of an instance in which a black Puerto Rican who moves into the black American community and is lost to the Puerto Rican community is Arturo Alfonso Shomburgh. By the turn of the century he had moved into the black community (although he continued to identify with the Puerto Rican community and was one of its most ardent defenders), in order to continue his research into the history of the black man. Today, the Shomburgh Collection on Black History is located in Central Harlem, a predominantly black community. Shomburgh's rightful place as an outstanding Puerto Rican has not been claimed by the Puerto Rican community and, consequently, many Puerto Ricans—particularly Puerto Rican blacks—are not even aware of his contribution.

REFERENCES

Brookings Institution. 1930. Porto Rico and Its Problems. Washington, D.C.: Brookings Institution.
Puerto Rican Forum, Inc. 1964. The Puerto Rican Community Development Project: A Proposal for a Self-Help Project to Develop the Community by Strengthening the Family, Opening Opportunities for Youth and Making Full Use of Education. New York: Puerto Rican Forum.
Rodriguez, Clara. 1974. "Puerto Ricans and the Melting Pot," Journal of Ethnic Studies 1 (Winter): 92–93.
Seda, Bonilla, Eduardo. 1970. Requiem por una cultura. Río Piedras, P.R.: Editorial Edil.
Senior, Clarence. 1965. The Puerto Ricans: Strangers, then Neighbors. Chicago, IL: Quadrangle Books.

Bibliography

Acín, María N. Información estadístíca sobre la mujer puertorriqueña. San Juan, P.R.: Mimeograph, 1980.
————. "Perfil estadístico de la mujer puertorriqueña." San Juan, P.R.: Comisión para el Mejoramiento de los Derechos de la Mujer, 1979.
Acosta-Belén, Edna, ed. La mujer en la sociedad puertorriqueña. Río Piedras, P.R.: Ediciones Huracán, 1980.
————. "Women in Twentieth Century Puerto Rico." In The Puerto Ricans: Their History, Culture, and Society, edited by Adalberto López, pp. 273–82. Cambridge, MA: Schenkman, 1980.
Acosta-Belén, Edna, and Barbara R. Sjostrom. "The Educational and Professional Status of Puerto Rican Women." In The Puerto Rican Woman, edited by Edna Acosta-Belén, pp. 64–74. New York: Praeger, 1979.
Alamo Salgado, Carmen J. "Formulación de política pública: el caso de la mujer puertorriqueña." Master's thesis, University of Puerto Rico, 1975.
Albert Robatto, Matilde. "Feminismo y escritura femenina en Puerto Rico." Educación 51–52 (enero 1983): 188–97.
Albizu Campos, Pedro. "La mujer libertadora." In La mujer en la lucha hoy, edited by Nancy Zayas and Juan A. Silén, pp. 101–2. Río Piedras, P.R.: Ediciones KIKIRIKI, 1972. Also in El Mundo, 12 de mayo de 1930.
Alegría Ortega, Idsa E. "La representación de la mujer trabajadora en la televisión de Puerto Rico." Pensamiento Crítico 7, no. 44 (mayo/junio 1985): 2–5.
Alvarado, Mercedes R. "El hostigamiento sexual en el empleo." Homines 7, no. 1–2 (feb./dic. 1983): 259–63.
————. "Violación y virginidad." San Juan, P.R.: Comisión para el Mejoramiento de los Derechos de la Mujer, 1978.
Alvarado, Mercedes R., and María M. López Garriga. "La mujer y la experiencia amorosa a través de las canciones de Sylvia Rexach." In Documentos de la Conferencia Puertorriqueña de la Mujer, edited by Isabel Picó, pp. 80–85. San Juan, P.R.: n.p., 1977.
Andrade, Sally. "Family Roles of Hispanic Women: Stereo-

types, Empirical Findings, and Implications for Research." In Work, Family and Health: Latina Women in Transition, edited by Ruth E. Zambrana, pp. 95–106. New York: Hispanic Research Center, 1982.

Andreu de Aguilar, Isabel. "Reseña histórica del movimiento feminista en Puerto Rico." Revista Puerto Rico 1, no. 3 (junio 1935): 255–61.

Angelis, María Luisa de. Mujeres puertorriqueñas que se han distinguido en el cultivo de las ciencias, las letras y las artes desde el siglo XVII hasta nuestros días. San Juan, P.R.: Tipografía del Boletín Mercantil, 1908.

Angueira, Katherine. "Hacia una descripción del problema de la violación: características de la clientela del Centro de Ayuda a Víctimas de la Violación." Master's thesis, University of Puerto Rico, 1981.

Aponte Raffaele, Nilda. "Integración femenina y liberación nacional." In La mujer en la lucha hoy, edited by Nancy Zayas and Juan A. Silén, pp. 77–80. Río Piedras, P.R.: Ediciones KIKIRIKI, 1972.

Arocho Velázquez, Sylvia. "La mujer y el acceso al poder en Puerto Rico." Homines 7, no. 1 (enero/junio 1984): 345–49.

——————. "Participación de la mujer puertorriqueña en el gobierno y la lucha política." Homines 8, no. 2 (junio 1984/enero 1985): 270–77.

Arrillaga, María. "La narrativa de la mujer puertorriqueña en la década del setenta." Homines 7, no. 1 (enero/junio 1984): 327–34.

Asenjo, Conrado. "Feminismo a mi modo." Puerto Rico Ilustrado 12, no. 584 (mayo 1921).

Asociación de Damas para la Instrucción de la Mujer. Reglamento. San Juan: Imprenta del Boletín Mercantil, 1886.

Ayende-Sánchez, Lydia. "Attitudes of Puerto Rican University Students Toward Female Roles and Recommendations for Improvement." Ph.D. diss, Nova University, 1976.

Azize, Yamila. Luchas de la mujer en Puerto Rico: 1898–1919. San Juan, P.R.: Graficor, 1979.

Barreto, Marien. "La imagen de la mujer en las telenovelas." In La imagen de la mujer en los medios de comunicación, pp. 27–34. San Juan, P.R.: Comisión para el Mejoramiento de los Derechos de la Mujer, 1978. Also in La mujer en los medios de comunicación social, edited by Isabel Picó and Idsa E. Alegría, pp. 43–50. Río Piedras, P.R.: Universidad de Puerto Rico, Centro de Investigaciones Sociales, 1982.

Bean, Frank D., Gray Swicegood, and Allan G. King.

"Fertility and Labor Supply Among Hispanic American Women." Austin, TX: University of Texas Population Research Center Papers, #3.017, 1981.

Belcher, John C., and Kelly W. Crader. "Social class, style, life and fertility in Puerto Rico." Social Forces 52, no. 4 (1974): 488–95.

Benítez, Alejandrina. "Sobre la educación de las mujeres." Guirnalda Puertorriqueña 1, no. 14 (junio 1856): 1–3.

Benítez de Rexach, Celeste. "El Partido Popular Democrático y la lucha de la mujer puertorriqueña por su liberación." In La mujer en la lucha hoy, edited by Nancy Zayas and Juan A. Silén, pp. 59–63. Río Piedras, P.R.: Ediciones KIKIRIKI, 1972.

Benítez de Rodríguez, Celeste. "The Puerto Rican Woman in the International Women's Year." In Puerto Rican Women in the United States: Organizing for Change, pp. 71–78. Washington, D.C.: NACOPRW, 1977.

Benítez, Jaime. "La mujer universitaria en la vida puertorriqueña." Torre 14 (1966): 11–18.

Bobé, Lourdes. "La mujer frente al proceso de envejecimiento." San Juan, P.R.: Comisión para el Mejoramiento de los Derechos de la Mujer, 1978.

Bodarky, Clifford, J. "Chaperonage and the Puerto Rican Middle-Class." Journal of Marriage and the Family 26, no. 3 (1964): 347–52.

Bouvier, Leon F., and John J. Maciso. "Education of Husband and Wife and Fertility in Puerto Rico." Social and Economic Studies 17, no. 1 (1968): 49–59.

Brau, Salvador. "La campesina." In his Ensayos: Disquisiciones Sociológicas, pp. 92–122. Río Piedras, P.R.: Editorial Edil, 1972.

Burgos, Nilsa M. "A Preliminary Historical Analysis of Women and Work in Puerto Rico: 1899–1975." In Work, Family and Health: Latina Women in Transition, edited by Ruth E. Zambrana, pp. 75–86. New York: Hispanic Research Center, 1982.

——————. Análisis histórico preliminar sobre la mujer y el trabajo en Puerto Rico: 1899–1975." Homines 7, no. 1 (enero/junio 1984): 303–17.

Burgos Sasser, Ruth, ed. La mujer marginada por la historia. San Juan, P.R.: Editorial Edil, 1978.

Cadilla de Martínez, María. "La campesina de Puerto Rico." Revista de agricultura de Puerto Rico, 28 (1937): 423–35.

Calero, Elsie. "El acceso de la mujer a las estructuras de poder en los medios de comunicación masiva." In La mujer en los medios de comunicación social, edited by Isabel Picó and Idsa E. Alegría, pp. 32–35. Río

Piedras, P.R.: Universidad de Puerto Rico, Centro de Investigaciones Sociales, 1982.

Candelas, Laura. "La propaganda publicitaria y la mujer en la sociedad de consumo." In La imagen de la mujer en los medios de comunicación, pp. 21–26. San Juan, P.R.: Comisión para el Mejoramiento de los Derechos de la Mujer, 1978. Also in La mujer en los medios de comunicación social, edited by Isabel Picó and Idsa E. Alegría, pp. 37–42. Río Piedras, P.R.: Universidad de Puerto Rico, Centro de Investigaciones Sociales, 1982.

Cangiano, José E. "Actitudes de las madres hacia la disciplina en el hogar: comparación de la percepción de sus hijos adolescentes." Master's thesis, University of Puerto Rico, 1969.

Capetillo, Glorisa. "Transactional Family Patterns: A Preliminary Exploration of Puerto Rican Female Adolescents." In Work, Family and Health: Latina Women in Transition, pp. 25–36. New York: Hispanic Research Center, 1982.

Capetillo, Luisa. Ensayos libertarios. Arecibo, P.R.: Imprenta Unión Obrera, 1904–1907.

——. Influencia de las ideas modernas. San Juan, P.R.: Tipografía Negrón Flores, 1916.

——. La humanidad en el futuro. San Juan, P.R.: Tipografia Real Hermanos, 1910.

——. Mi opinión sobre las libertades, derechos y deberes de la mujer. San Juan, P.R.: The Times Publishing Co., 1911.

Caraballo, Carlos. "Exploración sobre la percepción de los roles conyugales en las finanzas familiares en un ámbito universitario." Master's thesis, University of Puerto Rico, 1976.

Carreras, Carlos N. Hombres y mujeres de Puerto Rico. México: Editorial Orión, 1957.

Castro, Héctor de. "La mujer y sus derechos políticos." Revista de Legislación y Jurisprudencia 4, no. 4 (julio y agosto 1917): 256.

Christensen, Edward. "The Puerto Rican Woman: A Profile." In The Puerto Rican Woman, edited by Edna Acosta-Belén, pp. 51–63. New York: Praeger, 1979.

——. "The Puerto Rican Woman: The Challenge of a Changing Society." Character Potential 7, no. 3 (March 1975): 89–96.

Cintrón de Crespo, Patria. "Puerto Rican Women Teachers in New York: Self-perception, and Work Adjustment as Perceived as Themselves and by Others." Master's thesis, University of Puerto Rico, 1965.

Collazo-Collazo, Genaro. "Participación de la mujer en la

fase educativa de la vida puertorriqueña." Educación 22, no. 27 (diciembre 1979): 41–53.

Colón, Alice. "La participación laboral de las mujeres en Puerto Rico: Empleo o sub-utilización." Pensamiento Crítico 7, no. 44 (mayo/junio 1985): 25–30.

Colón, Ana Isabel. "La noción del rol sexual en mujeres y hombres puertorriqueños." Master's thesis, University of Puerto Rico, 1977.

Colón Santaell, Carmen L. "Interacciones madre-infante y terapista-infante durante la intervención terapéutica en niños con daño cerebral." Master's thesis, University of Puerto Rico, 1981.

Comas-Díaz, Lilian. "Mental Health Needs of Puerto Rican Women in the United States." In Work, Family and Health: Latina Women in Transition, edited by Ruth E. Zambrana, pp. 1–10. New York: Hispanic Research Center, 1982.

Combs, J. W., and Kingsley Davis. "The Pattern of Puerto Rican Fertility." Population Studies 4, no. 4 (1951): 364–79.

Comisión de Derechos Civiles. La igualdad de derechos y oportunidades de la mujer puertorriqueña. San Juan, P.R.: Estado Libre Asociado, 1973.

Comisión para el Mejoramiento de los Derechos de la Mujer. Igualdad de oportunidades de empleo para la mujer. San Juan, P.R.: La Comisión, 1978.

————. La imagen mujer en los medios de comunicación. San Juan, P.R.: La Comisión, 1978.

Comisión para los Asuntos de la Mujer. La mujer y su salud. San Juan, P.R.: La Comisión, 1981.

Commission for the Improvement of Women's Rights. Sexism in the Classroom. Final Report of the Commission of the Women's Educational Equity Act Program. San Juan, P.R.: The Commission, 1977.

Correa De Jésus, Nydza. "Proyecciones en torno al sistema de roles de la mujer trabajadora en Puerto Rico." Master's thesis, UNAM, 1979.

Cuchí Coll, Isabel. Dos poetisas de América: Clara Lair y Julia de Burgos. Barcelona: Gráfica Pareja-Montana, 1970.

————. La mujer. México: Talleres de la Editorial Cultural, 1937.

Cunningham, Ineke, José L. Vázquez Calzada, and Zoraida Morales del Valle. "Las disoluciones matrimoniales y su efecto sobre la fecundidad en Puerto Rico." Revista/Review Interamericana 12, no. 2 (Summer 1982): 317–25.

Cypess, Sandra Messinger. "Women Dramatists of Puerto

Rico." Revista/Review Interamericana 9, no. 1 (Spring 1979): 24–41.

Dávila, Rodolfo. "El voto electoral femenino." Puerto Rico Ilustrado 8, no. 396 (septiembre 1917): 3.

Delgado Votaw, Carmen. "Puerto Rican Women: Some Biographical Profiles." Washington, D.C.: NACOPRW, 1978.

_____. "Puerto Rican Women in Poverty." In Puerto Rican Women in the United States: Organizing for Change, pp. 70–71. Washington, D.C.: NACOPRW, 1977.

Departamento del Trabajo de Puerto Rico. Negociado de Estadísticas del Trabajo. La participación de la mujer en la fuerza laboral. San Juan, P.R.: ELA, 1983.

Díaz Hernández, Emma. "Comentarios en torno al problema de la violación." Río Piedras, P.R.: Centro de Ayuda a Víctimas de Violación, 1978. Mimeograph.

Enciclopedia de grandes mujeres de Puerto Rico. Hato Rey, P.R.: Ramallo Brothers, 1975.

Estado Libre Asociado de Puerto Rico. La mujer y sus derechos. San Juan, P.R.: Departamento de Instrucción Pública, 1957. Libros para el pueblo, No. 11.

Eulate Sanjurjo, Carmen. La mujer en la historia. Sevilla: F. Díaz and Cía., 1915.

_____. La mujer moderna. Barcelona: Casa Maucci, 1924.

Federación de Mujeres Puertorriqueñas. Palabra de Mujer 1 (enero 1977).

Feeny, Thomas. "Woman's Triumph Over Man in René Marqués Theater." Hispania 65, no. 2 (May 1982): 187–93.

Fernández Cintrón, Celia, and Marcia Rivera Quintero. "Bases de la sociedad sexista en Puerto Rico." Revista/Review Interamericana 4, no. 2 (Summer 1974): 239–45.

Fernández Méndez, Eugenio. "La familia puertorriqueña: cómo la ve un antropólogo social." Pedagogía 3, no. 2 (1955): 35–51.

Fernández Olmo, Margarite. "Desde una perspectiva femenina: La cuentística de Rosario Ferré y Ana Lydia Vega." Homines 8, no. 2 (junio 1985/enero 1986): 303–11.

Fernández Valledor, Roberto. "La mujer puertorriqueña y el quehacer literario del siglo XIX." Mi Ruta 2, no. 11 (febrero-marzo 1983): 21–25.

Ferré, Rosario. "La autenticidad de la mujer en el arte." In her Sitio a Eros, pp. 13–18. Mexico: Joaquín Mortiz, 1980.

_____. "La cocina de la escritura." In La sartén por

el mango, edited by Patricia Elena González and Eliana Ortega, pp. 136–54. Río Piedras, P.R.: Ediciones Huracán, 1984.

Ferrer, Gabriel. *La mujer en Puerto Rico*. San Juan, P.R.: Imprenta El Agente, 1881.

Fonfrías, Ernesto Juan. *La mujer en la política de Puerto Rico*. Hato Rey, P.R.: Master Typesetting and Word Processing, 1984.

Font de Calero, Marta. "La mujer y la política." *Homines* 7, no. 1–2 (feb./dic. 1983): 265–69.

García Ramis, Magali. "Los estereotipos de la mujer en la televisión." In *La mujer en los medios de comunicación social*, edited by Isabel Picó and Idsa E. Alegría, pp. 58–64. Río Piedras, P.R.: Universidad de Puerto Rico, Centro de Investigaciones Sociales, 1982.

García Ramis, Magali, Isabel Picó, Mariní Acín, and Carmen Eneida Molina. *Mujeres de Puerto Rico*. Río Piedras, P.R.: Universidad de Puerto Rico, Centro de Investigaciones Sociales, 1980.

García Ramis, Magali, Isabel Picó, and Mariní Acín. *Yo misma fui mi ruta*. Río Piedras, P.R.: Universidad de Puerto Rico, Centro de Investigaciones Sociales, 1983.

Garrison, Vivian. "Support Systems of Schizophrenic and Nonschizophrenic Puerto Rican Migrant Women in New York City." *Schizophrenia Bulletin* 4, no. 4 (1978): 561–96.

Gil, Rosa María. "Cultural Attitudes Toward Mental Illness Among Puerto Rican Migrant Women." In *Work, Family and Health: Latina Women in Transition*, pp. 37–45. New York: Hispanic Research Center, 1982.

González, Iris G. "Sexism in the Church: A Sociolinguistic-biblical Perspective." *Revista/Review Interamericana* 12, no. 2 (Summer 1982): 185–99.

González, María, and Peter Guarnaccia. "'La Operación': An Analysis of Sterilization in a Puerto Rican Community in Connecticut." In *Work, Family and Health: Latina Women in Transition*, edited by Ruth E. Zambrana, pp. 47–61. New York: Hispanic Research Center, 1982.

González del Valle, Ambrosio. "La mujer casada comerciante: problemas jurídicos que plantea esta situación." *Revista de Derecho Puertorriqueño* 7, no. 27 (enero–marzo 1967): 219–24.

Grovas, Teresita. "Maltrato físico a la mujer en Puerto Rico." *Homines* 7, no. 1–2 (feb./dic. 1983): 240–43.

Gruber, Ruth. *Felisa Rincón de Gautier: The Mayor of San Juan*. New York: Dell, 1972.

Guevara, Carlos I., and Myrna J. Sesman. *La madre y el*

aprendizaje del niño: La experiencia urbana puertorriqueña. Río Piedras, P.R.: Editorial Universitaria,
1978.

Gurak, Douglas. "Family Structural Diversity of Hispanic
Ethnic Groups." Research Bulletin of the Hispanic
Research Center 4, no. 2–3 (April–July 1981): 6–10.

Guzmán, Carmen. "La política de control poblacional y la
mujer puertorriqueña." Revista Puertorriqueña de
Derechos Humanos 2, no. 1 (Fall 1968).

Hatt, Paul. Backgrounds of Human Fertility in Puerto
Rico. Princeton, N.J.: Princeton University Press,
1952.

Hernández Alicea, Carmen. "El discrimen contra la mujer
en el Programa de Instrucción Vocacional y Técnica del
Departamento de Instrucción Pública de Puerto Rico."
Master's thesis, University of Puerto Rico, 1977.

Hernández Alvarez, Lilia de. Matrimonio en Puerto Rico.
Río Piedras, P.R.: Editorial Edil, 1971.

Herrera, Sylvia. "La mujer casada y la acción por daños y
perjuicios." Revista Jurídica de la UPR 34, no. 3
(1965): 397–422.

Hidalgo, Hilda, and Elia Hidalgo Christensen. "The Puerto
Rican Cultural Response to Female Homosexuality." In
The Puerto Rican Woman, edited by Edna Acosta-Belén,
pp. 110–23. New York: Praeger, 1979.

————. "Puerto Rican Women in the U.S.A." In Puerto
Rican Women in the United States: Organizing for
Change, pp. 57–58. Washington, D.C.: NACOPRW,
1977.

————. "Two Women: A Story of Success." In The
Puerto Rican Woman, edited by Edna Acosta-Belén, pp.
142–59. New York: Praeger, 1979.

Hill, Reuben. "Courtship in Puerto Rico: An Institution in
Transition." Journal of Marriage and the Family 17,
no. 1 (1955): 26–35.

Homar, Susana. "Inferioridad y cambio: Los personajes
femeninos en la literatura puertorriqueña." Revista de
Ciencias Sociales 20, no. 3–4 (diciembre 1978): 287–304.

Hostos, Eugenio María de. "La educación cientifica de la
mujer." In Páginas Escogidas, edited by José D.
Forgione, pp. 81–94. Buenos Aires: Estrada y Cía.,
1952.

Hurst, Marsha, and Ruth E. Zambrana. "Child Care and
Working Mothers in Puerto Rican Families." Annals
AAPSS, 461 (May 1982): 113–24.

————. "The Health Careers of Urban Women: A Study
in East Harlem." Signs: A Journal of Women in Culture
and Society 5, S (1980): 112–26.

Infante, Isa M. "Politicalization of Immigrant Women from Puerto Rico and the Dominican Republic." Ph.D. diss., University of California, Riverside, 1977.
Instituto de Cultura Puertorriqueña. Poemario de la mujer puertorriqueña. San Juan, P.R.: Instituto, 1976.
Irigoyen, Matilde, and Ruth Zambrana. "The Utilization of Pediatric Health Services by Hispanic Mothers." In Work, Family and Health: Latina Women in Transition, edited by Ruth E. Zambrana, pp. 63–73. New York: Hispanic Research Center, 1982.
Jiménez de Wagenheim, Olga. "The Puerto Rican Woman in the 19th Century." Revista/Review Interamericana 11, no. 2 (Summer 1981): 196–203.
King, Marguerite N. "Cultural Aspects of Birth Control in Puerto Rico." Human Biology 20, no. 1 (1948): 21–35.
Knudson, Doris G. "La asertividad: alternativa para la mujer." Homines 7, no. 1–2 (feb./dic. 1983): 244–47.
Labra, Rafael María de. Conferencias dominicales sobre la educación de la mujer. Madrid: Imprenta Rivadeneyra, 1869.
Laureano, Sandra M. "The Economic Crisis and the Puerto Rican Woman." Homines 9, no. 1–2 (feb./dic. 1985): 283–90.
Lee, Muna. "Puerto Rican Women Writers: The Record of One Hundred Years." Books Abroad 8, no. 1 (1934).
Lewis, Oscar. La Vida: A Puerto Rican Family in the Culture of Poverty. New York: Random House, 1966.
López, Iovanna, and Alba Nydia Rivera Ramos. "Factores asociados a la conducta delictiva de las confinadas en la cárcel de Vega Alta." In La mujer puertorriqueña: investigaciones psico-sociales, edited by Alba Nydia Rivera Ramos, pp. 73–83. Rio Piedras, P.R.: CEDEPP, 1985.
López-Garriga, María M. "Estrategias de auto-afirmación en mujeres puertorriqueñas." Revista de Ciencias Sociales 20, no. 3–4 (diciembre 1978): 257–85.
López, María M. "Reflexiones en torno al debate feminista en Puerto Rico." Homines 9, no. 1–2 (feb./dic. 1985): 307–11.
————. "Feminist Perspective on Pornography and Prostitution: A Rejoinder." San Juan, P.R.: Comisión para el Mejoramiento de los Derechos de la Mujer, 1978.
————. "Strategies of Self-Assertion: The Puerto Rican Woman." Ph.D. diss., The City University of New York, 1976.
López Landrón, Rafael. La mujer puertorriqueña ante el Bill Jones. San Juan, P.R.: Boletín Mercantil, 1916.
Lubrano, Andrea. "The struggle of Puerto Rican Women."

The Militant, March 12, 1976, pp. 19–20.

Malaret y Yordán, Augusto. "Condición jurídica de la mujer puertorriqueña." Nuestro Tiempo 8, no. 120 (diciembre 1908): 321.

Manning, Caroline. The Employment of Women in Puerto Rico. Washington, D.C.: Government Printing Office, 1934.

Marcano, Juan S. "Páginas Rojas. La mujer obrera." In Lucha Obrera, edited by Angel G. Quintero Rivera, pp. 66–67. Río Piedras, P.R.: CEREP, 1971.

Marqués Llompart, Mercedes. "Actitudes hacia la mujer trabajadora en la sociedad puertorriqueña." Master's thesis, University of Puerto Rico, 1972.

Marrero, Norma, Norma Tapia, Margarita Mergal, Annie Cuevas, and Isabel Picó. "La problemática de la mujer en Puerto Rico." In La mujer en la lucha hoy, edited by Nancy Zayas and Juan A. Silén, pp. 49–57. Río Piedras, P.R.: Editorial KIKIRIKI, 1972.

Martínez de Calderón, María H. "Conducta agresiva en niños como efecto de la ausencia o presencia de la madre en el hogar." Master's thesis, University of Puerto Rico, 1977.

Massara, Emily Bradley. "¡Que gordita! A Study of Weight Among Women in a Puerto Rican Community." Ph.D. diss., Bryn Mawr College, 1979.

Maymí, Carmen R. "Using Existing Individual and Collective Resources." In Puerto Rican Women in the United States: Organizing for Change, pp. 78–81. Washington, D.C.: NACOPRW, 1977.

McBride, Nina L. "Women Workers of Puerto Rico." International Socialist Review 17, no. 12 (June 1917): 717.

Meléndez Muñoz, Miguel. "El feminismo de la mujer en el siglo XX." Puerto Rico Ilustrado 8, no. 393 (septiembre 1917): 38.

Miller, Luz Elenia. "Implicaciones del movimiento de liberación femenina en la conducta individual de la mujer puertorriqueña que reside en la ciudad de Nueva York." Ph.D. diss., Instituto Caribeño, 1979.

Miranda King, Lourdes. "Aurora: A New Dawn of Awareness." In Puerto Rican Women in the United States, pp. 81–84. Washington, D.C.: NACOPRW, 1977.

——————. "Puertorriqueñas in the United States: The Impact of Double Discrimination." In The Puerto Rican Woman, edited by Edna Acosta-Belén, pp. 124–33. New York: Praeger, 1979. Also in Civil Rights Digest 6, no. 3 (1974): 20–27.

——————. "Puerto Rican Female Heads of Household." In Puerto Rican Women in the United States: Organizing for Change, pp. 53–56. Washington, D.C.: NACOPRW, 1977.

Molina, Carmen Eneida, and Magali García Ramis. Modulos de una serie para maestros de escuela elemental. San Juan, P.R.: Comisión para el Mejoramiento de los Derechos de la Mujer, 1977.

Morales del Valle Zoraida, José L. Vázquez Calzada, and Ineke Cunningham. "El tipo de matrimonio y su relación con la fecundidad en Puerto Rico." Revista/Review Interamericana 11, no. 4 (Winter 1981/82): 545–56.

National Conference of Puerto Rican Women. Puerto Rican Women in the United States: Organizing for Change. Washington, D.C.: NACOPRW, 1977.

Myers, George C., and Earl Walker Morris. "Migration and Fertility in Puerto Rico." Population Studies 20, no. 1 (1966): 85–96.

Nazario de Ferrer, Sila. "Más justicia para la mujer." In La mujer en la lucha hoy, edited by Nancy Zayas and Juan A. Silén, pp. 73–80. Río Piedras, P.R.: Ediciones KIKIRIKI, 1972.

Negrón Muñoz, Angela. "Figuras sobresalientes de nuestra filantropía: Josefina Bird de Barceló." Puerto Rico Ilustrado 20, no. 1010 (julio 1929): 36, 74.

————. Mujeres de Puerto Rico: desde el primer siglo de la colonización hasta el primer tercio del siglo XX. San Juan, P.R.: Imprenta Venezuela, 1935.

Nieves Falcón, Luis. "El niño puertorriqueño: bases empíricas para entender su comportamiento." In his Diagnóstico de Puerto Rico, pp. 41–89. Río Piedras, P.R.: Editorial Edil, 1972.

Ortiz, Ana C. "Características en el uso de bebidas alcohólicas entre mujeres y hombres puertorriqueños." Master's thesis, University of Puerto Rico, 1978.

Ortiz Chevere, Aida. "Comportamiento efectivo de madres puertorriqueñas." Ph.D. diss., Instituto Caribeño, 1980.

Ortiz de Hadjopoulos, Theresa. Antología de la poesía de la mujer puertorriqueña. New York: Peninsula Publishing Co., 1981.

Padilla de Sanz, Trinidad, et al. "La mujer puertorriqueña." In El libro de Puerto Rico, edited by E. Fernández García, pp. 812–45. San Juan, P.R.: n.p., 1921.

Pagán, Bolívar. El sufragio femenino. San Juan, P.R.: n.p., 1924.

Partido Popular Democrático. Informe del Comité de la Mujer y sus Derechos. Santurce, P.R.: n.p., 1972.

Mimeograph.

Peña Beltrán, Lydia. "Proceso de clasificación para mujeres ofensoras en Puerto Rico." Homines 8, no. 2 (junio 1984/enero 1985): 278–83.

Picó, Isabel. "Aportación de la mujer: su participación en las luchas políticas y sociales." In La mujer en la lucha hoy, edited by Nancy Zayas and Juan A. Silén, pp. 81–84. Río Piedras, P.R.: Ediciones KIKIRIKI, 1972.

————. "Apuntes preliminares para el estudio de la mujer puertorriqueña y su participación en las luchas sociales de principios del siglo XX." In La mujer en América Latina, edited by María del Carmen Elú de Lenero, Vol. 1, pp. 98–113. Mexico: Sepsetentas, 1975.

————, ed. Documentos de la Conferencia Puertorriqueña de la Mujer. San Juan, P.R.: Comité Coordinador, 1977.

————. "Estudio sobre el empleo de la mujer en Puerto Rico." Revista de Ciencias Sociales 19, no. 2 (June 1975): 141–65.

————. La mujer y la política puertorriqueña. Río Piedras, P.R.: Universidad de Puerto Rico, Centro de Investigaciones Sociales, 1983.

————. "La mujer puertorriqueña y su participación en la vida pública." In La mujer marginada por la historia, edited by Ruth Burgos Sasser, pp. 119–29. San Juan, P.R.: Editorial Edil, 1978.

————. Machismo y educación en Puerto Rico. San Juan, P.R.: Comisión para el Mejoramiento de los Derechos de la Mujer, 1979.

————. "The History of Women's Struggle for Equality in Puerto Rico." In Sex and Class in Latin America, edited by June Nash and Helen I. Safa, pp. 203–13. New York: Praeger, 1976; and in The Puerto Rican Woman, edited by Edna Acosta-Belén, pp. 25–37. New York: Praeger, 1979. Also reprinted in this volume.

————. "Women and Puerto Rican Politics Before Enfranchisement." Homines 9, no. 1–2 (feb./dic. 1985): 291–306.

Picó, Isabel, and Idsa Alegría. El texto libre de prejuicios sexuales y raciales. Río Piedras, P.R.: Universidad de Puerto Rico, Centro de Investigaciones Sociales, 1983.

————. La mujer en los medios de comunicación social. Río Piedras, P.R.: Universidad de Puerto Rico, Centro de Investigaciones Sociales, 1982.

Picó, Isabel, Idsa Alegría, and Marcia Rivera Quintero. "Datos básicos sobre la mujer en la fuerza trabajadora." San Juan, P.R.: Comisión para el Mejoramiento de los

Derechos de la Mujer, 1970. Also in La mujer en América Latina, edited by María del Carmen Elú de Lenero, vol. 2, pp. 114–20. Mexico: Sepsetentas, 1975.

Picó, Fernando. "Los trabajadores del tabaco en Utuado, Puerto Rico, según el censo de 1910." Homines 9, no. 1–2 (feb./dic. 1985): 269–82.

—————. "Mitos y realidades en la historia de la familia puertorriqueña en la zona cafetalera en el siglo 19." Homines 7, no. 1–2 (feb./dic. 1983): 223–26.

Picó de Silva, Teresita. "Memoria del Seminario 'La mujer en los medios de comunicación social.'" In La mujer en los medios de comunicación social, edited by Isabel Picó and Idsa E. Alegría, pp. 171–86. Río Piedras, P.R.: Universidad de Puerto Rico, Centro de Investigaciones Sociales, 1982.

Pineda, Magali, and Quintina Reyes. "Los estereotipos de la mujer en la televisión." In La mujer en los medios de comunicación social, edited by Isabel Picó and Idsa E. Alegría, pp. 51–57. Río Piedras, P.R.: Universidad de Puerto Rico, Centro de Investigaciones Sociales, 1982.

Piñeiro, Carmen Noelia, and Alba Nydia Rivera Ramos. "Efecto de la esterilización en el auto concepto de un sector de la mujer puertorriqueña." In La mujer puertotorriqueña: investigaciones psico-sociales, edited by Alba Nydia Rivera Ramos, pp. 117–30. Río Piedras, P.R.: CEDEPP, 1985.

Presser, H. B. "Puerto Rico: Recent Trends in Fertility and Sterilization." Family Planning Perspectives 12, no. 2 (1980): 102–6.

Quesada, Pura, and Alba Nydia Rivera Ramos. "La satisfacción de vida de la mujer envejeciente puertorriqueña blanca y negra en dos areas geográficas de Puerto Rico." In La mujer puertorriqueña: investigaciones psico-sociales, edited by Alba Nydia Rivera Ramos, pp. 117–30. Río Piedras, P.R.: CEDEPP, 1985.

Quiñones, María Isabel. "Rituales, encuentros y contextos entre mujeres puertorriqueñas: una investigación etnográfica." Master's thesis, University of Puerto Rico, 1981.

Quiñones-Rodríguez, Carmen F. "Families of Working Mothers in Puerto Rico." Ph.D. diss., Ohio State University, 1976.

Ramos de Sánchez, Jeanette. El delito de la violación en Puerto Rico. San Juan, P.R.: Comisión para el Mejoramiento de los Derechos de la Mujer, 1977.

—————. La mujer y la nueva legislacion sobre derecho de familia. San Juan, P.R.: Comisión para el Mejoramiento de los Derechos de la Mujer, 1977.

Reichard-Cancio, Haydeé E. "El personaje de la mujer en la literatura actual puertorriqueña." Mi Ruta 2, no. 11 (febrero-marzo 1983): 11–17.

—————. "Venciste mujer, venciste." Mi Ruta 2, no. 9 (diciembre 1982): 3–11.

Ribes Tovar, Federico. La mujer puertorriqueña. New York: Plus Ultra, 1972. Trans. by A. Rawlings. The Puerto Rican Woman. New York: Plus Ultra, 1972.

Rieckehoff-Naviera, Angelita. The Legal Status of Homemakers in Puerto Rico. San Juan: Comisión para el Mejoramiento de los Derechos de la Mujer and Liga de Mujeres Votantes, 1978.

Ríos de Betancourt, Ethel. "La influencia de los medios de comunicación, la educación, la literatura y el arte en la visión de la mujer." In La imagen de la mujer en los medios de comunicación, pp. 11–20. San Juan, P.R.: Comisión para el Mejoramiento de los Derechos de la Mujer, 1978. Also in La mujer en los medios de comunicación social, edited by Isabel Picó and Idsa E. Alegría, pp. 10–19. Río Piedras, P.R.: Universidad de Puerto Rico, Centro de Investigaciones Sociales, 1982.

Rivera, Miguel. "Salud mental en la mujer." Homines 7, no. 1–2 (feb./dic. 1983): 249–53.

Rivera, Flavia, and Blanca González. "Socialismo y feminismo." In La mujer en la lucha hoy, edited by Nancy Zayas and Juan A. Silén, pp. 89–92. Río Piedras, P.R.: Ediciones KIKIRIKI, 1972.

Rivera de Alvarado, Carmen. "La contribución de la mujer al desarrollo de la nacionalidad puertorriqueña." In La mujer en la lucha hoy, edited by Nancy Zayas and Juan A. Silén, pp. 37–47. Río Piedras, P.R.: Editorial KIKIRIKI, 1972.

Rivera de Ríos, Trina. "La familia puertorriqueña ante la criminalidad." Homines 7, no. 1–2 (feb./dic. 1983): 227–33.

Rivera Quintero, Marcia. "Condiciones del empleo doméstico asalariado en Puerto Rico." San Juan, P.R.: Comisión para el Mejoramiento de los Derechos de la Mujer, 1975.

—————. "Educational Policy and Female Labor, 1898–1930." In The Intellectual Roots of Independence, edited by Iris Zavala and Rafael Rodríguez, pp. 349–53. New York: Monthly Review Press, 1980.

—————. "Las adjudicaciones de custodia y patria potestad en los tribunales de familia de Puerto Rico." Revista del Colegio de Abogados de Puerto Rico 39, no. 2 (mayo 1978): 177–200.

—————. "Puerto Rican Women in the Economic and Social

Processes of the Twentieth Century." In The Intellectual Roots of Independence, edited by Iris Zavala and Rafael Rodríguez, pp. 335–43. New York: Monthly Review Press, 1980.

—————. "The Incorporation of Women into Wage Labor During the First Decades of the Twentieth Century." In The Intellectual Roots of Independence, edited by Iris Zavala and Rafael Rodríguez, pp. 344–48. New York: Monthly Review Press, 1980.

Rivera Ramos, Alba Nydia. La mujer puertorriqueña: investigaciones psico-sociales. Río Piedras, P.R.: CEDEPP, 1985.

—————. "Causas, efectos y consecuencias del estrés en la mujer trabajadora puertorriqueña." In La mujer puertorriqueña: investigaciones psico-sociales, edited by Alba Nydia Rivera Ramos, pp. 57–72. Río Piedras, P.R.: CEDEPP, 1985.

—————. "Efectos de modelos literarios en cambio de actitudes sexistas." In La mujer puertorriqueña: investigaciones psico-sociales, edited by Alba Nydia Rivera Ramos, pp. 34–47. Río Piedras, P.R.: CEDEPP, 1985.

—————. "Percepción de la productividad de la mujer puertorriqueña en el mundo del trabajo." In La mujer puertorriqueña: investigaciones psico-sociales, edited by Alba Nydia Rivera Ramos, pp. 48–56. Río Piedras, P.R.: CEDEPP, 1985.

—————. "La mujer y la política educativa." In La mujer puertorriqueña: investigaciones psico-sociales, edited by Alba Nydia Rivera Ramos, pp. 19–33. Río Piedras, P.R.: CEDEPP, 1985.

Rivera Ramos, Alba Nydia, and José Acevedo. "Actitudes y autopercepción de un sector de mujeres puertorriqueñas." In La mujer puertorriqueña: investigaciones psico-sociales, edited by Alba Nydia Rivera Ramos, pp. 3–18. Río Piedras, P.R.: CEDEPP, 1985.

Rivero, Eneida. "Educación sexual en Puerto Rico." Revista de Ciencias Sociales 19, no. 2 (junio 1975): 167–91.

—————. "El noviazgo en Puerto Rico." Atenea 9, no. 3–4 (sept.-dic. 1972): 97–107.

Rodríguez, A., and E. Lagares. "La mujer puertorriqueña en la lucha revolucionaria." Pensamiento Crítico 7, no. 44 (mayo/junio 1985): 31–33.

Rodríguez, Flor de María, Angelita Rieckehoff de Naveira, and Rosa Santiago-Marazzi. Mujer, conoce tus derechos. San Juan, P.R.: Comisión para el Mejoramiento de los Derechos de la Mujer, 1978.

Rodríguez, Vivianne. "Conductas indicativas de aceptación y control de las madres y el nivel de autoestima de sus hijos." Master's thesis, University of Puerto Rico, 1975.

Rosario, Charles. "Dos tipos de amor romántico: Estados Unidos y Puerto Rico." Revista de Ciencias Sociales 2, no. 3 (1958): 349–68.

Rosario, Lillian M. "The Self-Perception of Puerto Rican Women Toward their Societal Roles." In Work, Family and Health: Latina Women in Transition, edited by Ruth E. Zambrana, pp. 11–16. New York: Hispanic Research Center, 1982.

Safa, Helen I. "Class Consciousness Among Working-Class Women in Latin America: The Case of Puerto Rico." In Sex and Class in Latin America, edited by June Nash and Helen I. Safa, pp. 69–85. New York: Praeger, 1975.

——————. "Conciencia de clase entre las trabajadoras latinoamericanas: un estudio de casos en Puerto Rico." In La mujer en América Latina, edited by Carmen Elú de Leñero, vol. 1, pp. 166–90. México: Sepsetentas, 1975. Also in La mujer en la sociedad puertorriqueña, edited by Edna Acosta-Belén, pp. 157–82. Río Piedras, P.R.: Ediciones Huracán, 1980.

——————. "From Shantytown to Public Housing: A Comparison of Family Structures in Two Urban Neighborhoods in Puerto Rico." Caribbean Studies 4, no. 1 (1964): 3–12.

——————. "The Female-Based Household in Public Housing: A Case Study in Puerto Rico." Human Organizations 24, no. 2 (1965): 135–39.

Sánchez Hidalgo, Efraín. "El sentimiento de inferioridad en la mujer puertorriqueña." Revista de la Asociación de Maestros 11 (1962): 170–80.

——————. "Machismo versus Momism in Puerto Rico." In Emotional Disturbances in Puerto Rican Children. Río Piedras, P.R.: Colegio de Pedagogía, U.P.R., n.d.

——————. "Posibles efectos de la industrialización rápida sobre la familia puertorriqueña." Pedagogía 2, no. 1 (1954): 17–28.

Sánchez Korrol, Virginia. "On the Other Side of the Ocean: The Experience of Early Puerto Rican Migrant Workers." Caribbean Review 7, no. 1 (Jan.-March 1979): 22–28.

——————. "Survival of Puerto Rican Women in New York before World War II." In The Puerto Rican Struggle: Essays on Survival in the U.S., edited by Clara Rodríguez, Virginia Sánchez Korrol, and José O. Alers, pp. 47–57. New York: Puerto Rican Migration Research Consortium, 1980.

_____. "The Other Side of the Ocean." In From Colonia to Community: The History of Puerto Ricans in New York City 1917–1948, pp. 85–117. Westport, CT: Greenwood Press, 1983.

Santana Cooney, Rosemary. "Demographic Components of Growth in White, Black, and Puerto Rican Female-Headed Families: Comparison of the Cutright and Ross/Sawhill Methodologies." Social Science Research, 8 (1979): 144–58.

_____. "Intercity Variations in Puerto Rican Female Participation." The Journal of Human Resources 14, no. 2 (1979): 222–35.

Santana Cooney, Rosemary, and Alice Colón Warren. "Declining Female Participation among Puerto Rican New Yorkers." Ethnicity 6, no. 3 (September 1979): 281–97.

_____. "Work and Family: The Recent Struggle of Puerto Rican Women." In The Puerto Rican Struggle: Essays on Survival in the U.S., edited by Clara Rodríguez, Virginia Sánchez Korrol, and José O. Alers, pp. 58–73. New York: Puerto Rican Migration Research Consortium, 1980.

Santana Cooney, Rosemary, Alice Colón Warren, and Vilma Ortiz. "Nativity, National Origin, and Hispanic Female Participation in the Labor Force." Social Science Quarterly 64, no. 3 (September 1983): 510–23.

Santiago, Zoraida. "Los estereotipos sexuales en la selección de carrera." Homines 7, no. 1–2 (feb./dic. 1983): 255–57.

Santiago, Zoraida, and Alba Nydia Rivera Ramos. "Discrimen hacia la mujer en el proceso diagnóstico y psicoterapia entre estudiantes y profesionales de psicología." In La mujer puertorriqueña: investigaciones psico-sociales, edited by Alba Nydia Rivera Ramos, pp. 131–92. Río Piedras, P.R.: CEDEPP, 1985.

Santiago-Marazzi, Rosa. "Discrimen por razón de sexo en los Programas de Instrucción Vocacional y Técnica en Puerto Rico." San Juan, P.R.: Comisión para el Mejoramiento de los Derechos de la Mujer, 1977.

_____. "La inmigración de mujeres españolas a Puerto Rico en el periodo colonial español." Homines 7, no. 1 (enero/junio 1984): 291–302.

_____. "La mujer y su experiencia cultural en Puerto Rico." Homines 7, no. 1 (enero/junio 1984): 318–26.

Santos, Loreina, and José Berríos. Women in Higher Education in Puerto Rico. Mayagüez, P.R.: University of

Puerto Rico, Office of Scientific Research, 1982.

Serrano, Helga. "Las mujeres en la prensa de Puerto Rico." In La mujer en los medios de comunicación social, edited by Isabel Picó and Idsa E. Alegría, pp. 100–7. Río Piedras, P.R. Universidad de Puerto Rico, Centro de Investigaciones Sociales, 1982.

Silén, Juan A. "La mujer: la doble opresión." In La mujer en la lucha hoy, edited by Nancy Zayas and Juan A. Silén, pp. 105–8. Río Piedras, P.R.: Ediciones KIKIRIKI, 1972. Also in his Hacia una visión positiva del puertorriqueño, pp. 177–86. Río Piedras, P.R.: Editorial Edil, 1970.

Silva-Bonilla, Ruth. La televisión y la socialización infantil. Río Piedras, P.R.: Universidad de Puerto Rico, Instituto de Investigaciones de Problemas del Consumidor, 1977.

————. "La violencia contra la mujer trabajadora." Pensamiento Crítico 7, no. 44 (mayo/junio 1985): 6–10.

Silvestrini, Blanca G. "La mujer puertorriqueña y el movimiento obrero en la década de 1930." Cuadernos de la Facultad de Humanidades 3 (1979): 84–104.

————. "Women as Workers: The Experience of the Puerto Rican Woman in the 1930s." In Women Cross-Culturally: Change and Challenge, edited by Ruby Rohrlich-Leavitt, pp. 247–60. The Hague: Mouton, 1975. Also reprinted in this volume.

Solá, María. "Elevar la conciencia de la mujer." In La mujer en la lucha hoy, edited by Nancy Zayas and Juan A. Silén, pp. 85–86. Río Piedras, P.R.: Ediciones KIKIRIKI, 1972.

Solá, Mercedes. Feminismo. San Juan, P.R.: Cantero Fernandez y Cia., 1922.

Soto, Elaine. "Sex Role Traditionalism, Assertiveness, and Symptoms in First- and Second-Generation Puerto Rican Women Living in the United States." Journal of Community Psychology 11, no. 4 (October 1983): 346–54.

Soto, Elaine, and Phillip Shaver. "Sex Role Traditionalism, Assertiveness, and Symptoms of Puerto Rican Women Living in the United States." Hispanic Journal of the Behavioral Sciences 4, no. 1 (March 1982): 1–19.

Stycos, J. M. Family and Fertility in Puerto Rico. New York: Columbia University Press, 1951.

Sued Badillo, Jalil. La mujer indígena y su sociedad. Río Piedras, P.R.: Editorial El Gazir, 1975.

Sumaza, Irene. "The Effects of an Assertiveness Training Program for Puerto Rican College Women Planning to Emigrate to the United States." Homines 7, no. 1 (enero/junio 1984): 335–44.

Tapia y Rivera, Alejandro. "El aprecio de la mujer."
  Azucena 1, no. 2 (noviembre 1870): 9–10.
Thimmesch, Nick. "Puerto Rico and Birth Control."
  Journal of Marriage and the Family 30, no. 2 (1968):
  252–62.
Tienda, Marta, and Patricia Guhleman. "The Occupational
  Position of Employed Hispanic Women." Madison, Wis-
  consin: Institute for Research on Poverty Discussion
  papers # 708–82, September 1982.
Torres-Matrullo, C. "Acculturation and Psychopathology
  among Puerto Rican Women in Mainland United States."
  American Journal of Orthopsychiatry 46, 4 (1976):
  710–19.
U.S. Senate. Women's Suffrage in Porto Rico. Hearing
  before the Committee on Territories and Insular Pos-
  sessions. Washington, D.C.: Government Printing
  Office, 1928.
Universidad Interamericana de Puerto Rico. Igualdad de los
  sexos en la selección de carrera. Manual para coor-
  dinar un taller dirigido a profesionales de orientación.
  San Juan, P.R.: Universidad, 1981.
Valle, Norma. Luisa Capetillo. San Juan, P.R.: n.p.,
  1975.
Vázquez Nuttall, Ena. "The Support System and Coping
  Patterns of Female Puerto Rican Single Parents."
  Journal of Non-White Concerns 7 (1979): 128–37.
Vázquez, Eneida. "Union Organization of Women in the
  Puerto Rican Labor Force." In The Intellectual Roots
  of Independence, edited by Iris Zavala and Rafael
  Rodríguez, pp. 311–21. New York: Monthly Review
  Press, 1980.
Vázquez Calzada, José Luis. "Fertility Decline in Puerto
  Rico." Demography 5, no. 2 (1968): 855–65.
————. "La esterilización femenina en Puerto Rico."
  Revista de Ciencias Sociales 17, no. 3 (septiembre
  1973): 281–308.
Vásquez Calzada, José Luis, Ineke Cunningham, and
  Zoraida Morales del Valle. "Patrones de nupcialidad de
  la mujer puertorriqueña." Revista/Review Interameri-
  cana 11, no. 3 (Fall 1981): 418–37.
Vélez, Elizabeth. "Trends Among Puerto Rican Women."
  Political Affairs 15, no. 3 (1976).
Vera Irizarry, Jesús. "La mujer en los medios de comuni-
  cación. ¿Problemas de ellas o de todos?" Homines 8,
  no. 2 (junio 1984/enero 1985): 284–86.
Viverito, Elizabeth, Maggie Mendez, and Ana I. Rivera
  Lassén. La esterilización en Puerto Rico. San Juan,
  P.R.: MIA, 1976.

Vivó, Paquita. "Educational Status of Puerto Rican Women." In Puerto Rican Women in the United States: Organizing for Change, pp. 68–69. Washington, D.C.: NACOPRW, 1977.

————. "Puertorriqueñas in the '70s: The Challenges and Opportunities Before Us." In Puerto Rican Women in the United States: Organizing for Change, pp. 63–67. Washington, D.C.: NACOPRW, 1977.

Weller, Robert. "A Historical Analysis of Female Labour Force Participation in Puerto Rico." Social and Economic Studies 17, no. 1 (March 1968): 60–72.

Yordán Molini, Haydeé. "La influencia de los textos primarios de instrucción pública en la diferenciación de roles femeninos y masculinos en los niños." Master's thesis, University of Puerto Rico, 1974.

————. "La visión de la niña en cinco libros de lecturas escolares." San Juan, P.R.: Comisión para el Mejoramiento de los Derechos de la Mujer, 1976.

Young, Kate, and Marcia Rivera Quintero. Women and Social Production in the Caribbean. San Juan, P.R.: IDS/CEREP, 1982.

Zayas, Nancy. "La mujer en la lucha de hoy." In La mujer en la lucha hoy, edited by Nancy Zayas and Juan A. Silén, pp. 67–72. Río Piedras, P.R.: Ediciones KIKIRIKI, 1972.

Zayas, Nancy, and Juan A. Silén, eds. La mujer en la lucha hoy. Río Piedras, P.R.: Editorial KIKIRIKI, 1972.

Zambrana, Ruth E., ed. Work, Family and Health: Latina Women in Transition. New York: Hispanic Research Center, 1982. Monograph #7.

Index

Winship, Blanton, 69–71

women's employment, 20–21,
34–36, 50–52, 67, 94–96,
150–51; income, 20–21,
41, 48–49, 101, 105, 147,
155–57; occupations, 21,
34, 47, 49–52, 99–100,
153, 155–57; labor force
participation, 20, 23, 34,
43, 47–50, 147

women's liberation (see
feminist movement)

women's organizations:
advocacy, 23; civic,
80–82; feminist, 83;
political, 81–82;
professional, 23, 81;
research, 23; service,
80–81; suffragist, 7–8,
55

working-class women, 52–54,
61–62

Yupart, Tomasa, 63

Zequeira, Belén, 5

About the Editor and Contributors

EDNA ACOSTA-BELEN is an Associate Professor in the departments of Puerto Rican, Latin American, and Caribbean Studies, and Hispanic and Italian Studies at the State University of New York at Albany. She is editor of the books The Puerto Rican Woman (New York: Praeger, 1979) and La mujer en la sociedad puertorriqueña (Río Piedras, P.R.: Ediciones Huracán, 1980), and has published numerous articles on Latin American and U.S.-Hispanic literature and culture, and the women's experience in culture, history, and society. She received her Ph.D. from Columbia University and has been a postdoctoral fellow at Princeton and Yale universities. She is currently Chair of the Department of Puerto Rican, Latin American, and Caribbean Studies at SUNY-Albany.

CHRISTINE E. BOSE is an Associate Professor of Sociology at SUNY-Albany, where she also served as director of the Women's Studies Program from 1978–81. She is the author of Jobs and Gender: A Study of Occupational Prestige and has published in the areas of occupational prestige, gender, and status attainment, women's home and paid employment, the social impact of household technology, and Hispanic women in the United States. She received her Ph.D. from Johns Hopkins University.

ANGELA JORGE is an Associate Professor of Spanish and Hispanic literature and culture at SUNY College at Old Westbury. She has lectured and published on class, race, and sex issues and is presently working on a book on spiritism. She received her Ph.D. from New York University.

MARYA MUNOZ VAZQUEZ is a psychologist and a faculty member at the University of Puerto Rico. She has conducted research in the area of changing women's roles and the family in Puerto Rico. She received her Ph.D. from the University of Missouri.